new Great Dishes of the World

Robert Carrier

new Great

Photographs by Robert Carrier

Dishes of the World

SMITHMARK

This edition published in 1997 by SMITHMARK Publishers, a division of U.S. Media Holdings, Inc., 115 West 18th Street, New York, NY 10011.

SMITHMARK books are available for bulk purchase for sales promotion and premium use. For details write or call the manager of special sales, SMITHMARK Publishers, 115 West 18th Street, New York, NY 10011.

Produced by: Boxtree an imprint of Macmillan Publishers Ltd, 25 Eccleston Place, London SW1W 9NF

ISBN:0-7651-9127-X

Printed in Italy by New Interlitho S.P.A. - Milan

10 9 8 7 6 5 4 3 2 1

Designed by Hammond Hammond
Edited by Mari Roberts

Library of Congress CIP

Contents

Introduction

So much has changed since I wrote *Great Dishes of the World*, my first cookbook, a careful distillation of four years of articles in the *Sunday Times* and *Vogue*, and a loving record of the gastronomic discoveries of the many years I lived in France, Italy and Morocco before coming to Britain.

It was the 1960s and Britain was just discovering how to be exciting and extravagant and fun. *Great Dishes of the World* was a signal part of that new way of living. My enthusiastic culinary samplings found an immediate response: 20,000 copies sold in the first week; 70,000 by the end of the year, and eventually over 2 million copies worldwide in fourteen languages. *Great Dishes of the World* had found world favour.

Things were different then. Garlic was sold by only one company in London, zucchinis (as distinct from vegetable marrows) and green peppers were available in the summer months only and then only in the more sophisticated greengrocers, and I was told that if I wanted my food articles printed in the provinces I would be permitted to use a tablespoon or two of heavy cream or brandy only at Easter or Christmas.

Imagine! And so I, self-created Pied Piper of Gastronomy, happily tootled a bemused public into the glamorous by-ways of the greatest recipes in the world. My weekly articles permitted housewives and amateur cooks in Cardiff and Cheam to create glittering recipes from the great three-star restaurants of France as well as from the peasant kitchens of Spain and Italy and from the open Berber fires of the Moroccan Rif. I got a reputation for being outrageous. I was even pilloried by *Private Eye*. But the outrageous cooks of Britain followed me enthusiastically with quiches, soufflés, separate vegetable courses, open-fire grilled meats, slow-simmered ragouts and daubes and rich puddings laced with Calvados and cream.

Now foods once deemed exotic are commonplace. Oriental sesame oil, rice and balsamic vinegars, fresh basil, coriander and ginger, and four colours of peppers are all as ubiquitous as fresh pasta and sun-dried tomatoes. And my cooking today is about as different as it was when I first started writing about food in the newly created supplements and the glossy magazines.

Modern cooking is about taste, about flavour – whether robust or delicate, sweet or earthy,

pungent or aromatic. There is a new simplicity which we might almost call minimalist, a postmodern cooking style that does away with disguises, complex sauces and elaborate combinations of ingredients and lets the essential qualities of the food shine through. And, as a result, our cooking is lighter, fresher, more immediate, and healthier too.

Fish and meat are 'griddled' for minutes only and served – modern touch – with acidulated olive oil-based sauces sparked with the oils of fresh basil leaves, fresh parsley, reductions of choice wines and even the juice of pressed black olives or the occasional essence of a rare black truffle.

Rich sauces become a light *jus* made from the pan juices of quickly seared meats or fish or poultry, given flavour with chopped fresh herbs such as flat-leaf parsley, thyme, rosemary and coriander, and sparked by the live new savours of finely chopped garlic and fresh ginger, lemon grass and crushed dried chiles. Cream and butter are used in minimal quantities (the cream is usually crème fraîche for a lighter creaminess that does not separate in cooking). The butter (a tablespoon or two only) is whisked into the pan juices at the last minute of cooking, to create a shiny gloss, along with a splash or two of lime juice or Thai fish sauce for extra savour.

Pan-fried fruits are served as vegetables; bitter salad leaves, tossed for a moment only in an oiled pan, seasoned at the last minute with a little salt and lemon juice, sometimes replace more prosaic vegetables; 'minute' griddles (immediacy again) of julienned vegetables provide colour and freshness to grilled and poached fish and meats; as do single-layered golden 'crisps' of thinly sliced potato, sweet potato, new turnip, carrot or parsnip. I like, too, to use a flavour-dusting of brilliantly coloured baked ground orange peel, pounded toasted almonds and browned breadcrumbs, and the crisp-fried, almost transparent pancakes of finely minced vegetables that the French call 'croustillants'. Risottos, pastas, orzo, couscous and groats play their healthy part, too, in *New Great Dishes of the World*.

This is all made possible by the glorious new foods specially produced in this country or imported from around the world.

This is the big revolution: if we want to cook really well there is almost nothing to stop us.

New Basics

Oven-Roasted Lemons

Thin-skinned, untreated lemons are best for this recipe, which produces delicious Mediterranean-style roasted lemon quarters to serve with seafood or to use chopped in salad dressings and sauces for seafood and poultry.

**4 thin-skinned lemons,
   quartered
4 tablespoons sea salt
2 tablespoons sugar**

Preheat the oven to 190°C/375°F. Toss the lemon quarters with the sea salt and sugar. Place in a heatproof shallow baking dish, cover with aluminium foil and roast in the preheated oven for 1 to 1½ hours, until they feel soft when squeezed. Remove from the oven and allow to cool.

Moroccan Preserved Lemons

One of the prime ingredients of Moroccan cooking, preserved lemons can be bought ready-made in Morocco, packed in jars or loose, for use at home. But many Moroccan cooks prefer to make their own, from a mixture of small, thin-skinned lemons (*doqq*) and tart bergamot lemons (*boussera*). Outside of Morocco, look for ripe, smooth, thin-skinned lemons without flaws, for the best results. Thick-skinned lemons are not suitable.

Only the peel and the juice from the pulp (which is discarded) is used when you cook with preserved lemons, and the flavour is quite unique. The peel loses its bitter taste, and brings a different, pungent, even 'sexy' taste to countless Moroccan dishes.

**16 small, ripe, thin-skinned lemons
coarse salt
4 sprigs of fresh bay leaves
   (optional)
lemon juice**

To Soak the Lemons: Scrub the lemons with a stiff brush, then place them in a large container of glass, plastic, stainless steel or glazed earthenware. Cover with cold water and soak for 3 to 5 days, changing the water each day.

To Salt and Preserve the Lemons:
Insert the point of a sharp knife 6mm/¼in from the bud end of each soaked lemon and make four incisions lengthways to within 6mm/¼in of the other end. Cut into the incisions in each lemon so that the fruit is cut completely through but still held together at both ends.

Squeezing each lemon open, insert ¼ teaspoon coarse salt into the center. Arrange the salt-filled lemons in 4 sterilized preserving jars (such as Kilner or Mason). Sprinkle with 1 tablespoon of coarse salt per jar. Add the strained juice of 1 lemon to each jar, a sprig of bay if using, and pour in enough boiling water to cover.

Leave the lemons to steep in this mixture for at least 3 weeks before using them. You will find that the salty, oily pickling juice is honey-thick and highly flavoured. Use it in salads instead of vinegar; use it, too, to add savour to tagines. The lemons will keep in this mixture indefinitely if stored in a dry place.

To Use Preserved Lemons: Remove a lemon from the jar and rinse well under cold running water. Cut away the pulp from each quarter (squeezing the juice from the pulp to use in the recipe) and discard. Use the quartered preserved peel for delicious tagines of lamb, chicken or fish, or cut the peel into thin slices, julienne strips or tiny dice to use in vegetable tagines, with fish or in salads.

Never touch preserved lemons in the jar with an oily or greasy spoon, as fat will spoil the pickling mixture. Don't worry if a white film forms on the preserved lemons in the jar; just rinse it off before use.

Deep-Fried Lemon Zest

Fine threads of lemon zest macerated for 30 minutes in lemon juice and deep-fried to crisp golden curls make a wonderful flavour garnish. This is equally good made with orange or lime zest (use exactly the same procedure).

**2 lemons
salt
vegetable oil**

To Prepare the Lemons: Zest the lemons with a lemon zester lengthways into long thin threads. Squeeze the juice of the lemons into a flat bowl. Add the lemon threads and ½ teaspoon salt to the lemon juice. Toss the threads in the juice with your fingers and then allow to macerate for 30 minutes.

When Ready to Deep-fry the Lemon Zest: Pour vegetable oil into a small saucepan to 5cm/2in deep, place over a medium heat and heat to 190°C/375°F. If using an electric deep-fat fryer, follow the manufacturer's instructions.

Drain the lemon zests and pat dry between two pieces of kitchen paper. Drop half the zests by handfuls into the hot oil to deep-fry until crisp and golden: a matter of

seconds. With a slotted spoon, transfer the crisped zests to a strainer held over the pan to drain off the excess oil. Then put them on folded kitchen paper to continue draining. Repeat with the remaining zests. Use deep-fried lemon zest immediately.

Oven-Roasted Tomatoes

Oven-roasted tomatoes make wonderful accompaniments for broiled poultry or meats, for appetizer salads with broiled goat's cheese, or with waffles (see for example the delicious waffles from the Bathers Pavilion on page 30) for breakfast or brunch.

ripe tomatoes
vegetable oil

Preheat the oven to 190°C/375°F. Slice the tomatoes in half and place, cut-side up, on a baking tray. Sprinkle with a little vegetable oil, then roast in the preheated oven for about 1½ hours, until they have dried a little and caramelized.

Roasted Red and Yellow Peppers

Red and yellow peppers, their skins charred under a broiler or over a barbecue, make delectable appetizer salads when dressed with a full-flavoured vinaigrette and scattered with thinly sliced garlic, diced anchovies (in oil) and chopped flat-leaf parsley. Use, too, to garnish pasta, broiled or seared fish and Mediterranean recipes for grilled or casseroled chicken, lamb and veal. Green peppers can be roasted, too, but their thinner skin is harder to remove.

To Prepare Roasted Peppers: Wash and dry whole peppers. Place them under the broiler as close to the heat as possible (or on to the barbecue). Roast the peppers, turning them continually, until all the skin has charred and blistered.

Remove the peppers and put them in a plastic bag to cool.

When cool, rinse the peppers under cold running water rubbing the blackened skin off with your fingers. Use a sharp kitchen knife to peel off any skin that has not been touched by heat.

Cut each pepper into 4 to 6 lengths, rinse off the seeds and excess fiber and drain on kitchen paper. Then use as desired.

Garlic Croûtons

Crisp, golden, garlic-scented croûtons make a wonderful garnish for vegetable soups and purées, a country-style omelette, a salad, or even a Provençal daube or ragout.

4 slices day-old white bread
4 tablespoons olive oil
1 large clove garlic, sliced

To Prepare the Bread: Trim the crusts from the bread and discard. Cut the bread into even-sized dice.

To Make the Croûtons: Heat the oil in a large frying pan, then add the garlic and sauté until it turns pale gold. Use a slotted spoon to remove the garlic, and add the diced bread to the hot oil. Sauté, stirring constantly, until crisp and golden. Remove the croûtons from the pan and use immediately.

Potato Croûtons

This is a variation on the croûton theme, and is good to garnish a country vegetable soup or omelette.

2 baking potatoes
4 tablespoons vegetable oil
1 clove garlic, sliced

To Prepare the Potatoes: Peel the baking potatoes and cut them, lengthways, into 6mm/¼in-thick slices. Discard the two outer, rounded slices and cut the others into even-sized dice.

To Make the Potato Croûtons: Heat the oil in a large frying pan, then add the garlic and sauté until the garlic turns pale gold. Use a slotted spoon to remove the garlic, and add the diced potato to the hot oil. Sauté, stirring constantly, until crisp and golden and cooked through, making sure the heat is not too high and that the potatoes do not become brown before they are cooked. Remove the croûtons from the pan and use immediately.

Provençal Tapenade

This rich, dark and pungent Provençal spread takes its name from the local dialect word *tapeno*, which means caper.

50g/2oz pitted black olives
25g/1oz anchovy filets
25g/1oz tuna fish canned in oil
1–2 teaspoons Dijon mustard
50g/2oz capers
4–6 tablespoons olive oil
Cognac
freshly ground pepper

To Make the Tapenade: Pound the olives, anchovy filets and tuna fish to a smooth paste in a large mortar with Dijon mustard and capers. Add the olive oil, a little at a time, as for a mayonnaise. Season to taste with Cognac and pepper.

Force the mixture through a fine sieve, and it is ready to serve.

To Keep the Tapenade: Tapenade keeps well in a jar, and is excellent with hard-boiled eggs, or as a highly flavoured canapé spread.

Anchoïade

Starred in ancient Provence as a tasty open-fire-grilled paste spread on slices of bread, anchoïade is used today mainly as a topping for grilled or roasted fish, vegetables and poultry, or spread on fingers of toast as a garnish for Provençal soups or salads.

2 x 50g/2oz cans anchovy
   filets in oil, drained
1–2 large cloves garlic, chopped
2 tablespoons olive oil
100g/4oz slightly softened butter
few drops of lemon juice, Cognac
   or red wine vinegar
freshly ground pepper
pinch of dried herbes de
   Provence
crushed dried chiles
4–6 slices thick country bread

To Prepare the Anchoïade: Pound the anchovy filets, chopped garlic, olive oil and butter in a mortar until smooth. Season to taste with a few drops of lemon juice, Cognac or red wine vinegar, and freshly ground pepper, herbes de Provence and crushed dried chiles.

To Prepare the Bread: Cut the bread slices in half. Toast on one side only and, while still hot, spread anchoïade paste on the untoasted side, pressing the paste well into the bread. Toast in a hot oven or under the broiler for a few minutes just before serving.

Ligurian Pesto

Pesto is an age-old Ligurian green sauce, pungent with basil and pecorino cheese. In Italy it is used as a potent herb-flavoured sauce for pasta, to flavour country vegetable soups and as a topping for broiled or poached fish. In the early days of Mediterranean history, it travelled down the coast to Provence where it is a staple of that region's famous soup: pistou.

2–3 large cloves garlic, chopped
4–6 tablespoons finely chopped
   fresh basil
4–6 tablespoons finely chopped
   fresh flat-leaf parsley
2 tablespoons pine nuts
6–8 tablespoons freshly grated
   pecorino romano cheese, or
   Parmesan cheese
extra virgin olive oil
freshly ground pepper

Pound the chopped garlic, basil and parsley with the pine nuts and grated cheese in a mortar until smooth. Gradually add olive oil, little by little, whisking it in as you would for a mayonnaise, until the sauce is smooth and thick. Season to taste with freshly ground pepper. Use freshly made.

Polenta

Creamy yellow polenta takes up to 30 minutes, and a strong arm, to make well. 'Instant' polenta is quicker and easier to cook: try both and see which you prefer. Here is how to make polenta in the traditional manner.

1.1 litres/40fl oz salted water
450g/1lb yellow cornmeal
   (polenta)
½ crumbled vegetable stock
   cube, dissolved in 4 tablespoons
   melted butter
6–8 tablespoons freshly grated
   Parmesan cheese
salt and freshly ground pepper
freshly grated nutmeg
crushed dried chiles

To Prepare the Polenta: Bring 1.1 litres/40fl oz water to the boil. Pour the cornmeal in slowly, stirring constantly with a wooden spoon. Continue cooking for 20 to 30 minutes, stirring frequently, until the polenta is thick and soft and leaves the sides of the pan easily, adding a little more water if necessary.

To Season and Serve: Stir in the stock cube and melted butter mixture and the Parmesan cheese. Season to taste with salt (remembering that the stock cube has salt), freshly ground pepper, freshly grated nutmeg and crushed dried chiles. Serve spoonfuls of the hot polenta at once.

To Grill Polenta: Put the freshly made polenta into a tin, either wide and shallow or narrow and deep, to set. Allow to cool. When firm, cut into slices, brush with olive oil and grill on a preheated, ridged, cast-iron grill pan.

Sweet Onion Confit

This piquant sauce is excellent with pork, lamb and venison.

25g/1oz butter
50g/2oz sugar
225g/8oz onions, thinly sliced
4 tablespoons grenadine syrup
4 tablespoons red wine
4 tablespoons red wine vinegar
1–2 teaspoons dry sherry vinegar
salt and freshly ground pepper
crushed dried chiles

To Prepare the Onions: In a heavy frying pan, melt the butter and sugar. Add the sliced onions and simmer over a very low heat for 30 minutes or until soft.

To Finish and Serve: Add the grenadine syrup, red wine and both vinegars and continue to simmer for a further 30 minutes. Season to taste with salt, pepper and crushed dried chiles. Allow to cool completely before serving.

Pickled Ginger

Thin, pale pink, translucent slices of Chinese pickled ginger are often used in Pacific Rim cooking as a delicious, spicy garnish for broiled or poached fish, to top rillettes or tartares of raw salmon, tuna or scallops, or to give a sharp, light flavour-accent to stir-fries of seafood and vegetables.

100g/4oz fresh ginger
120ml/4fl oz rice wine vinegar
1–2 tablespoons lime juice
2–3 teaspoons Thai fish sauce

To Prepare the Ginger: Peel the fresh ginger. In a bowl, combine the rice wine vinegar with lime juice and Thai fish sauce to taste. Cut the ginger into the finest slices possible, crossways, using a mandolin or a sharp-bladed Japanese cleaver or chopper for the best results.

To Pickle the Ginger: Toss the thin ginger slices into the pickling mixture. Transfer the sliced ginger and juices to a sterilized preserving jar (such as Kilner or Mason). Seal tightly and refrigerate until ready to use: it will be ready to use after 3 days, and keeps in the refrigerator for at least 1 month.

Chile Jam

Clear, pink-tinted peppery Malaysian chile jam makes a wonderfully sweet–hot relish to accompany broiled venison, pork and lamb.

100g/4oz large, fresh, red chiles, seeded and very thinly sliced
225g/8oz red onions, very thinly sliced
25g/5oz sugar
450ml/15fl oz water
¼ teaspoon salt
1 clove garlic, finely chopped
1½ small lemons, thinly sliced

In a medium-sized saucepan, combine all the ingredients and cook over a high heat, with the saucepan uncovered, for about 20 minutes, or until the sauce thickens and the vegetables are tender.

Remove the saucepan from the heat and discard the lemon slices. Allow the jam to cool, then store in a sterilized jar in the refrigerator until ready to use.

Harissa

Harissa is a fiery condiment based on hot red chile peppers, olive oil and garlic, common to the Maghreb countries of Morocco, Tunisia and Algeria. An excellent flavour intensifier for saffron-flavoured fish soups and stews, I like to use it, too, to spice Moroccan couscous and tagines of meat and poultry, or meat and vegetable soups. I like to add a touch of harissa to a stew of tomatoes and red peppers used as a savoury base for poached eggs or the little fresh sausages called merguez.

2 red peppers, roasted and skinned (page 12)
25g/1oz fresh hot red chiles, or 1 teaspoon crushed dried chiles
2 cloves garlic, finely chopped
2 teaspoons cumin seeds
½ teaspoon coriander seeds
coarse salt
olive oil

Cut the skinned peppers into quarters, discarding stems but reserving seeds. Chop the flesh

coarsely and add to the seeds.

Slice the fresh chile pepper thinly; if using crushed dried chiles, soak them in hot water for a few minutes.

In a mortar, combine the chopped skinned fresh pepper, pepper seeds, sliced chile pepper (or soaked dried chiles, drained), garlic, cumin and coriander seeds, and salt to taste. Pound to a smooth paste, adding a little olive oil if desired.

Spoon into sterilized preserving jars (Kilner or Mason) and cover with a layer of olive oil, then seal the jars and refrigerate. A good harissa will be thick, with the consistency of a light mayonnaise. Serve it in a little side dish with a very small spoon.

Rouille

A rich chile sauce, thickened with breadcrumbs, rouille was invented by the fishermen of Provence, to enliven their meals of poached fish.

1 slice white bread, trimmed of crusts
2 large cloves garlic
1 tablespoon paprika
crushed dried chiles
2 tablespoons olive oil
2–4 tablespoons mayonnaise

Dip the bread in water and squeeze almost dry. Pound the bread, garlic, paprika and a pinch of dried chiles in a mortar until smooth. Add the olive oil and mayonnaise little by little, blending continuously, until you have a smooth aromatic paste.

Salsas

'*Salsa*' in Spanish is the word for sauce. Nothing could be simpler than that. In Mexico and in America's Southwest, the term refers to a variety of toppings and condiments, but usually it is a chunky red sauce featuring chopped chiles, tomatoes and

onions mixed with lemon juice or vinegar and fresh coriander or other herbs. Served as an appetizer with tortilla chips, or alongside the main dish, salsa adds flavour – and sometimes fire – to food.

Traditional salsas are served cold and as a garnish on the side of the plate. But the new salsas can be served hot, spooned on top of a main course of broiled or pan-seared meat, fish or poultry.

Don't go overboard when adding chopped hot chiles. A perfect salsa has a little heat, but not enough to overpower the flavour.

Salsa Fresca Chop some fairly mild New Mexican green chiles, ripe plum tomatoes and red onion. Combine them in a bowl. Add a little chopped fresh coriander for flavour and crushed dried chiles for heat. Finish the salsa with ground cumin, dried oregano, salt, lemon juice and olive oil to taste.

Avocado Salsa Peel and stone 1 ripe avocado and cut the flesh into dice. Chop ½ onion and 4 to 6 ripe tomatoes and stir gently into the diced avocado. Then add 1 or 2 chopped jalapeño peppers and 1 to 2 tablespoons chopped fresh coriander, and season to taste with salt, lemon juice and olive oil.

Red Onion Salsa Dice 1 large red onion and stir into 4 to 6 diced ripe plum tomatoes. Season with 1 or 2 chopped jalapeño peppers, 1 to 2 tablespoons chopped fresh coriander, and salt, lemon juice and olive oil to taste.

Pineapple and Sweetcorn Salsa Peel and core ½ fresh pineapple and cut the flesh into small dice. Add 1 small can of drained sweetcorn kernels and season to taste with diced red onion, chopped fresh coriander, salt, lemon juice and olive oil.

Christmas Salsa (half red and half green) Cut 1 large red pepper and 1 large green pepper into quarters. Remove the stem and core, cut the quarters into dice and combine with 2 diced ripe plum tomatoes. Season with 1 or 2 chopped jalapeño peppers and chopped fresh coriander, salt, lemon juice and olive oil to taste.

Jerk Seasoning

Jerk seasoning – a speciality of Jamaica – is one of the great flavour-giving mixes of all time. Use it for grilled pork, beef, lamb, chicken, lobster and other seafood. Even a plain grilled hamburger – or fish cake – will benefit from this potent mix.

8–10 allspice berries
2 scallions, green parts only, thinly sliced
2 tablespoons finely chopped garlic
pinch of finely chopped fresh ginger
pinch of freshly grated nutmeg
2 pinches of ground cinnamon
2–3 sprigs of fresh thyme, leaves only
2 Scotch Bonnet, Habañero, or other hot chiles, chopped
2 tablespoons soy sauce
4 tablespoons vegetable oil
3–6 tablespoons lime juice
½ teaspoon salt
freshly ground pepper

To Make the Jerk Seasoning: Crush the allspice in a mortar, or process in short bursts in a food processor. Add the scallions and pound (or process) until well mixed.

Add the finely chopped garlic and ginger, the nutmeg and cinnamon, thyme leaves and Scotch Bonnet peppers. (Note: Jamaicans like their jerk seasoning really hot; try using just one chopped hot pepper at first and then, if desired,

add the second one before seasoning the food to be grilled.) Mix the aromatic ingredients together well and then stir in the soy sauce, vegetable oil, lime juice and salt, and freshly ground pepper to taste.

To Use the Seasoning: Score the food to be grilled on all sides with a sharp knife. Rub the jerk seasoning mix well into the scored food and grill until crusty on the outside and moist and tender on the inside.

Moroccan Chermoula

This fragrant seasoning mix is equally good with fish or poultry, and minus the saffron makes an excellent seasoning for lamb and beef. Or omit the chopped fresh coriander, add cinnamon to taste, and you will have an aromatic 'flavourer' for squab and game in the Moroccan manner.

The object of the chermoula seasoning is not to mask the natural taste of the food but to enhance it. As the seasonings dissolve in the evaporating liquid of a tagine, for instance, during its long, slow cooking, they blend intimately with the food. Pan juices are then reduced over a high heat to complete the blending of flavours and oils, and spooned lovingly over the food to be served. Here, for fish, the marinade is rubbed well into fish steaks or pieces – or whole, slashed fish – and left to impart its flavours for at least 2 hours or, preferably, overnight.

The recipes for chermoula vary from family to family, from cook to cook. Almost all of them feature chopped parsley, coriander and onion and an assortment of spices. This first is my favourite.

1 large Bermuda onion, finely chopped
4 small or 2 large cloves garlic, finely chopped
½ teaspoon ground cumin
¼ teaspoon sweet paprika
½ teaspoon cayenne
1 pinch saffron threads
6 tablespoons finely chopped fresh coriander
6 tablespoons finely chopped fresh flat-leaf parsley
6 tablespoons olive oil
juice of ½ lemon
salt

Combine all the ingredients in a small bowl.

Quick Chermoula
2–3 small cloves garlic, finely chopped
½ teaspoon sweet paprika
½ teaspoon ground cumin
¼ teaspoon crushed dried chiles
4–6 tablespoons olive oil
2 tablespoons vinegar
2 tablespoons water

Mix all the ingredients together.

Chermoula with Preserved Lemon
2–3 cloves garlic, peeled and finely chopped
1 preserved lemon (page 10), peel only, finely diced
1 bunch of fresh flat-leaf parsley, finely chopped
1 large pinch saffron threads
½ teaspoon sweet paprika

¼–½ teaspoon crushed dried chiles
4–6 tablespoons olive oil
2 tablespoons lemon juice
2 tablespoons water

Mix all the ingredients together.

Wilted Salad Greens and Bitter Leaves
Today's salad leaves – especially the decorative bitter ones – have become a designer vegetable accompaniment, either wilted in a hot pan with melted butter or a tablespoon of extra virgin olive oil, or just tossed with a little lime juice and oil and served as they are. Better still, wilt the leaves in the hot pan juices of the meats, poultry or fish they are to accompany and add a splash of lemon or lime juice just before serving. I'm all for it.

If you want to take the easy way out, try the supermarkets for packets of washed and ready-to-eat salad herbs. They are excellent. But to take a little more trouble, use combinations of arugula, mâche, sorrel, frisée, watercress and bok choy, and add top sprigs of basil, purple basil, tarragon and coriander. Or try the following.

Watercress Sprigs: Toss in hot pan juices and then season with salt, crushed dried chiles and a splash of lemon just before serving.

Frisée, Arugula and Mâche: Toss in a hot oiled pan, and season with a pinch of finely chopped fresh garlic and ginger and lemon juice just before serving.

Baby Bok Choy Leaves: Blanch and then toss in hot pan juices with finely sliced red onion rings and a splash of soy or Thai fish sauce. Season to taste with salt, crushed dried chiles and a squeeze of lemon juice just before serving.

New Light Acidulated Olive Oil-Based Sauces

The new lighter, healthier cooking of today bans over-rich sauces and flavours, instead, adding a splash of extra virgin olive oil to the pan in which you have seared steaks, chops, fish or poultry cuts, or even vegetables. The sauce is then 'finished' by stirring in a little finely chopped chives, or basil or the stripped leaves of fresh thyme or oregano and a splash of fresh lime or lemon juice. Wonderfully fresh tasting, marvelously healthy. Made in seconds.

Another new way of sauce-making – coming to us from the Orient via the Pacific Rim – adds a pinch or two of finely chopped fresh garlic, ginger, lemon grass and chile pepper to the pan juices along with the extra virgin olive oil and lemon or lime juice to lend a zesty oriental flavour to your cooking.

I like, too, to add a splash of soy, sesame oil or Thai fish sauce along with the olive oil and lemon juice, for an even more intense flavour.

Or flavour the pan juices of seared meats, poultry or fish at the last minute with a dash of reduced white wine or dry Vermouth (boil 4 tablespoons dry white wine or Vermouth down to 1 tablespoon). Add a splash of extra virgin olive oil, a pinch of finely chopped garlic and/or chives and crushed dried chiles to taste, and you will have a new light 'sauce' of great flavour.

Infused Oils

Suspensions of finely chopped herbs, peppercorns or lemon zest in extra virgin olive oil are the new flavour agents, used to give extra colour and flavour to broiled or poached fish or shellfish and to drizzle in ribbons around plates of grilled or seared meat and poultry.

For Parsley Oil
3 tablespoons finely chopped fresh flat-leaf parsley
150ml/5fl oz extra virgin olive oil

For Basil Oil
3 tablespoons finely chopped fresh basil leaves
150ml/5fl oz extra virgin olive oil

For Rosemary Oil
2 tablespoons chopped fresh rosemary sprigs
150ml/5fl oz extra virgin olive oil

For Sage Oil
2 tablespoons chopped fresh sage leaves
150ml/5fl oz extra virgin olive oil

For Lemon Oil
2 tablespoons finely grated lemon zest
150ml/5fl oz extra virgin olive oil

For Pepper Oil
2 tablespoons cracked black pepper
150ml/¼ pint extra virgin olive oil

Heat the finely chopped leaves of fresh herb, the zest or the cracked pepper in a small saucepan with the olive oil until the oil starts to sizzle. Remove the pan from the heat and swirl the oil around until the sizzle stops. Then pour through a muslin-lined sieve into a sterilized bottle or jar, pressing the ingredients down in the sieve with the back of a spoon to release all the flavour. Leave to cool, then seal tightly and refrigerate. The flavoured oil will keep for 1 week in the refrigerator.

Minute-Grilled Vegetable Strips

Serve minute-grilled strips for a gala vegetable accompaniment, chock full of colour and flavour. Cut your choice of carrots, zucchini, turnips, potatoes, sweet potatoes, parsnips and cucumber into thin julienne strips. Serve just one variety on its own, or a combination of three, such as carrots, unpeeled zucchini strips and turnips, or two, such as potatoes and sweet potatoes, or carrots and cucumber. Blanch the vegetable strips before cooking them in 4 tablespoons of vegetable stock and 50g/2oz butter on a hot griddle or in a nonstick frying pan. Season the vegetables with salt, freshly ground pepper or crushed dried chiles, and a squeeze of lemon or lime just before serving.

Pan-Seared or Broiled Fruits

Some of the new light 'vegetable' accompaniments are pan-seared fruits. I like the following:

Sliced Quinces: Flavour with a little brown sugar and finely chopped garlic tossed in buttery pan juices until golden and tender.

Halved Small Pears: Steam for a minute and then toss in the pan juices of the meat or game they are to be served with … or until golden brown and well flavoured.

Ripe Figs: Halve, brush with melted butter, season with salt, freshly ground pepper and crushed dried chiles, and broil or pan-grill. Serve with sprigs of fresh mint.

Unpeeled Apple Slices: Toss in butter with a little brown sugar until golden, then season with salt, freshly ground pepper and chopped fresh oregano.

Slices of Banana or Plaintain: Pan-fry and serve with fish or meats in the Caribbean manner.

Seedless White Grapes: Pan-sear in butter, then sprinkle with minced mint and cracked black pepper.

Fresh Pineapple Slices or Wedges: Toss in butter with a pinch or two of sugar until golden, then season with a spark of lemon juice and dust with ground cinnamon.

Perfect Green Salad

Never out of favour. There are two secrets to perfect salad dressing: the preparation of the salad itself and the preparation of the dressing. Salad leaves must be thoroughly washed and dried and preferably chilled before being mixed with the dressing. No water should be allowed to drip from the leaves into the dressing. If you do not own a salad spinner, an easy way to dry well-washed leaves is to pile them loosely in the center of a clean dish towel and then gently pat them dry. Gather up the edges and corners of the towel, shake out any remaining drips of water over the sink and chill in the refrigerator until crisp.

Chopped garlic is often a must. Rub a cut clove of garlic around the bowl at the outset, then chop the garlic and add it to the salad before the final tossing.

As for the dressing, I usually prefer to mix mine directly in the salad bowl – a wooden one, of course, and washed as seldom as possible – blending olive oil and vinegar or citrus juice with freshly ground pepper, salt, garlic and chopped fresh herbs, before I add the salad leaves. Break the leaves into the salad bowl: leaves should be left whole, or torn, never cut. Add the remaining ingredients, toss well, a final toss to ensure that every leaf is glistening with the dressing, a final check for flavour, and the salad is ready to serve.

Fresh Tarragon Vinaigrette

This dressing could well become one of your house specialities. It is excellent for pulse vegetables and summer salads of all kinds, and it doubles and triples successfully for large parties.

6–8 tablespoons extra virgin olive oil
2 tablespoons freshly squeezed lime juice
1 tablespoon balsamic vinegar
leaves from 3 sprigs of fresh tarragon
1–2 tablespoons finely chopped fresh chives
salt and freshly ground pepper
crushed dried chiles

In a bowl, combine the first 5 vinaigrette ingredients. Season to taste with salt, freshly ground pepper and crushed dried chiles.

Croustillants

French cooks like to serve single-layered golden 'crisps' (hence the name 'croustillants') of very thinly sliced potato, new turnip, carrot or parsnip deep-fried in oil until crisp and golden. For greater finesse, you can process the raw vegetables, bind them with a little seasoned flour and beaten egg (to make small, paper-thin crisp 'pancakes' – 3 to 4 per serving) and then pan-fry or deep-fry them for seconds only just before serving. Delicious. And different.

Couscous, Orzo, Barley or Groats as a Vegetable

Couscous makes a wonderful vegetable on its own when steamed until tender and seasoned with a hint of salt, ground cinnamon, cumin, ginger, paprika and cayenne (not enough to taste any of these spices, but just enough to give flavour to the couscous). Fork in a little freshly grated Parmesan cheese just before serving. Chopped fresh chives and/or flat-leaf parsley, or a flavour dusting of chopped baked orange, almond and breadcrumbs make a fine flavour additive (see Michel Bras' baked orange powder, below).

I like to serve orzo (little 'grains' of pasta) cooked exactly like a risotto or saffron risotto as a flavoursome vegetable accompaniment. Or try barley or buckwheat groats (kasha), cooked in the same manner but for longer. For groats, mushrooms or raisins make a good flavour additive.

Michel Bras' Baked Orange Powder with Pounded Juniper Berries, Toasted Almonds and Browned Breadcrumbs

Michel Bras, one of the truly creative great cooks of the world – his famous restaurant at Laguiole in southwestern France is one of the gourmet meccas of French gastronomy – makes a wonderful mix of baked orange zest, crushed juniper berries, toasted almonds and browned breadcrumbs to serve with roast lamb or pork. I like to use this flavoursome mix as a

'dusting', too, to give an elusive but exciting flavour to rice, couscous, orzo or barley, cooked as above, or to a lightly dressed salad of mixed bitter leaves.

25g/1oz thinly pared orange zest strips, about 6cm/2½in long by 1.5cm/¾in wide
75g/3oz sugar
300ml/10fl oz water
7 juniper berries
1 teaspoon ground almonds, toasted
50g/2oz soft white breadcrumbs
25g/1oz butter
5 tablespoons peanut oil

To Make the Orange Powder:
Make sure there is no pith left on the orange zests. Dissolve the sugar in the water over a low heat and simmer until it is a thick syrup. Add the pared zests and cook until they are quite soft. Remove the pan from the heat and allow the zests to cool in the syrup.

Preheat the oven to 190°C/375°F. When the orange zests are quite cool, drain them, pulling them one by one through your fingers to remove excess syrup. Place on a lightly buttered baking tray and bake in the preheated oven for 20 minutes, or until cooked through but still slightly supple when you take them out of the oven. Keep flat by covering with another baking tray and allow to harden to a glass-like finish.

Place the glass-like zests on a clean towel on a flat working surface and crush to a powder with a rolling pin. Transfer to a bowl.

To Finish the Flavour Mix: Finely chop or process the juniper berries and then pass through a sieve into the bowl. Add the toasted ground almonds and mix well.

Brown the breadcrumbs in the butter and oil stirring constantly, until they are a uniform golden brown. Using a slotted spoon,

transfer to paper towel and squeeze them quite dry. Michel Bras recommends that you squeeze the breadcrumbs at least twice in paper towel to ensure that all the excess fat is removed. Then stir them into the orange, almond and juniper mixture.

Jill Dupleix's Quick Crusty Pizza Base

My friend Jill Dupleix, glamorous young food editor of the *Sydney Herald* and *Australian Elle Magazine*, is changing the culinary face of Australia. Bright, cheery and a superlatively imaginative cook, this is her quick-style version of a thin, crusty, pizza base.

50g/2oz butter
350g/12oz self-raising flour
240ml/8fl oz milk
1 teaspoon lemon juice

To Prepare the Base: Preheat the oven to 200°C/400°F. Dice the butter and process with the flour in a food processor on a stop-start, stop-start basis until the mixture resembles fine breadcrumbs.

Add the milk and the lemon juice and process again, as above, until the dough gathers into a ball. Add a little more flour if the mixture seems too wet.

To Bake the Pizza: Turn the dough out on to a floured board and knead it lightly. Then roll or pat it out to a round or square shape, pinching the edges slightly to make a rim.

Place the base on a baking tray, add your choice of toppings, drizzle with a little olive oil and bake in the preheated oven for 5 minutes. Then remove the tray and bake the pizza directly on the oven shelf for another 5 minutes or so, until the base is crisp and the topping is perfect.

Makes 1 pizza base

Great Breakfasts

Russian Blini with Caviar or Smoked Salmon

Diminutive buckwheat blini, puffed and golden, make a great special breakfast treat. I like to serve them hot from the pan, topped with real black caviar, melted butter and sour cream. Excellent, too, with smoked salmon and crème fraîche, or diced cooked beetroot in a garlic and watercress vinaigrette with sour cream.

570ml/20fl oz milk
1 tablespoon sugar
1 tablespoon dried yeast
100g/4oz buckwheat flour
100g/4oz plain flour
½ teaspoon salt
3 egg yolks
2 tablespoons melted butter,
    plus extra for greasing
3 egg whites, stiffly beaten

To Serve
black caviar (not lumpfish),
    or substitute red caviar, or
    smoked salmon or sturgeon
melted butter
sour cream
lemon wedges

To Make a Yeast 'Sponge': Heat half the milk until lukewarm and pour into a warm bowl. Add the sugar and yeast and allow the yeast to soak for a few moments before stirring, then leave it to sit for 10 minutes. (Note: Some yeasts can be added directly to dry ingredients, and do not need to be left to froth up. See the packet instructions.)

Warm another mixing bowl and sift in the flours, together with the salt. Make a well in the center and strain in the yeast and milk mixture. Then rock the bowl gently so that some of the flour falls into the liquid, and shake an equal thickness of flour over the top so that the yeast is bedded warmly in the middle of the bowl of flour.

Cover the mixing bowl with foil and then with a clean towel. Leave it in a warm place for about 20 minutes to start the yeast working.

Beat the egg yolks and whisk into the remaining warm milk. Add the melted butter and pour into the raised sponge mixture. Beat well, mixing in the remaining flour, then let stand, covered as above, for 30 minutes more.

When Ready to Serve: Fold in the stiffly beaten egg whites. Cook 3 or 4 blini at a time on a lightly buttered hot griddle or large nonstick frying pan. The blini should not be more than 5–8cm/2–3in in diameter. Cook until small bubbles form on the top of each little pancake; then turn over to cook on the other side. Remove the blini from the pan and keep them warm while you prepare the others.

Serve blini hot with black or red caviar, or smoked salmon or sturgeon, and accompany with melted butter, sour cream and lemon wedges.

Makes 24 to 36 small blini

American Popovers with Rumbled Eggs

'Rumbled eggs' is the name of a nineteenth-century breakfast dish mid-way between an omelette and a scramble. To achieve its meltingly moist quality, the eggs are 'rumbled' in soft folds to the back of the pan as the still-uncooked egg mixture is allowed to cook for seconds only before also being gently pushed (rumbled) in its turn to the back of the pan.

The modern touch: a scattering of bits of crème fraîche at the end of the cooking process to enrich the softly 'rumbled' eggs. Serve them on their own with smoked salmon for a superb breakfast or brunch dish, or in crisp golden American popovers when you want to show off.

For the American Popovers
450ml/15fl oz milk
½ teaspoon salt
2 tablespoons melted butter
5 eggs, lightly beaten
225g/8oz flour, sifted

For the Rumbled Eggs
10 eggs
salt and freshly ground pepper
crushed dried chiles
25–50g/1–2oz butter
1 tablespoon olive oil
2–4 tablespoons crème fraîche

To Make the Popovers: Preheat the oven to 220°C/425°F. Combine the milk, salt, butter and eggs in a mixing bowl. Add the flour and beat until smooth. The batter should have the consistency of thick cream.

Butter a 12-hole deep bun tray and half-fill the hollows with the batter. Bake in the preheated oven for 15 minutes, then reduce the temperature to 190°C/375°F and bake for 15 to 20 minutes longer, or until the popovers are well risen and golden brown.

To 'Rumble' the Eggs: Break the eggs into a medium-sized bowl. Season to taste with salt, freshly ground pepper and a pinch of crushed dried chiles, and beat with a whisk until well mixed.

When ready to cook, melt 25g/1oz butter with the olive oil in a large nonstick frying pan. Pour in the eggs and, with a wooden spatula, gently push the egg mixture to the back of the pan, tipping the pan forward to allow the liquid, still-uncooked eggs to come to the front. Continue this process – pushing eggs to the back of the pan, and tipping the pan forward to allow uncooked egg to come to the front and into contact with the hot pan, adding a little more butter around the edges as you cook.

When the eggs are still moist and a little undercooked on the surface, dot the rumbled eggs with crème fraîche and serve immediately, with hot popovers.

Serves 4

Joyce Molyneux's Crab Cakes at the Carved Angel

Pan-seared crab cakes with a sprightly touch of lime zest and juice make wonderful fare for breakfast or brunch. But serve them, too, as a light first course, or a tasty main course with a salad of cucumber, sour cream and chives, or a salsa of diced vegetables served in leaves of chicory. Joyce Molyneux's renowned restaurant, the Carved Angel, is in Devon.

225g/8oz prepared crab
  (½ brown meat and ½ white
  meat)
1 egg, beaten
1 tablespoon mayonnaise or
  sour cream
2 teaspoons grain Dijon
  mustard
2 teaspoons chopped scallions
a little chopped fresh coriander
freshly grated zest of 1 lime
juice of ½ lime
salt and freshly ground pepper
crushed dried chiles
50g/2oz soft white
  breadcrumbs

To Make the Crab Mixture: In a mixing bowl, combine the crab, beaten egg, mayonnaise or sour cream, mustard, chopped scallions and coriander, and lime zest and juice. Season generously with salt, freshly ground pepper and dried chiles and leave to stand for 1 hour.

To Make the Cakes: Shape the mixture into round cakes and coat with soft breadcrumbs. Bake in a 200°C/400°F oven for 10 minutes, or shallow-fry until golden brown on both sides. Serve hot.

Serves 4

Champagne Fruits

Champagne at breakfast can be addictive, especially when it is the fizzing ingredient of a fresh-tasting fruit salad for a gala Sunday breakfast, or (halving the quantities) a special 'morning-after' breakfast starter for two.

1 medium-sized pineapple
4 pears, peeled, cored and
   sliced
4 Cox's Orange Pippin apples,
   peeled, cored and sliced
4 plums, pitted and sliced
4 bananas, peeled and sliced
1 bunch of grapes, halved and
   seeded
4 fresh apricots, halved and
   pitted
confectioners' sugar
2 tablespoons brandy
2 tablespoons lemon juice
¼ bottle Champagne

To Prepare the Fruit: Peel the pineapple, core and slice into rings. Reserve the top. Slice each ring in half and combine with the sliced pears, apples, plums and bananas and halved grapes and apricots in a mixing bowl. Dust with confectioners' sugar to taste, moisten with the brandy and lemon juice, toss and chill.

When Ready to Serve: Transfer the fruit to a serving bowl, pour the Champagne over and decorate with the pineapple top.

Serves 4

Red Fruit Bowl

This brilliantly coloured summer fruit salad – a stunning combination of reds and blues – makes a great morning 'freshener': serve it chilled with a dollop of crème fraîche or as a sparkling fresh-fruit garnish for a slice of old-fashioned hot French toast. Choose perfectly ripe fruit.

225g/8oz dark red cherries
1–2 pints small strawberries
½ pint redcurrants
½ pint raspberries
½ pint blueberries
juice of 1–1½ lemons,
   flavoured with a little
   Cognac and confectioners'
   sugar

To Prepare the Fruits: Pit the cherries, hull the strawberries and strip the stems from the redcurrants. Clean the fruit as necessary.

To Finish: Combine the fruits in a bowl. Add the Cognac-flavoured, sweetened lemon juice and toss lightly. Marinate in the refrigerator for at least 30 minutes before serving.

Serves 4

Oranges and Prunes in Orange-Tea Syrup

Oranges and prunes are healthy foods. And we need healthy beginnings to our days. This amber-tinted, tea-scented concoction makes the perfect morning eye-opener for great breakfasts. Serve it, too, as the refreshing first course for a lazy Sunday brunch. Follow with the waffles on page 30 or American popovers with rumbled eggs (page 25), and the day is made.

3 navel oranges, peeled and sliced

For the Prunes
20 large Californian prunes
4 strips thinly pared orange zest
1 orange pekoe tea bag

For the Orange Syrup
100g/4oz sugar
2–3 short cinnamon sticks
150ml/5fl oz orange juice
liquid from prunes
1 tablespoon pink peppercorns

To Prepare the Prunes: Soak the prunes, orange zest and tea bag in boiling water to cover for about an hour, or until the prunes are plump. Remove the tea bag and drain the prunes and the orange zest, reserving the liquid.

To Make the Orange Syrup: In a medium-sized saucepan, combine the sugar, cinnamon sticks, orange juice and liquid from the prunes and bring to the boil. Lower the heat and simmer for 5 minutes. Then add the pink peppercorns and the drained prunes and orange zest and cook for 10 more minutes. Remove from the heat.

To Complete the Dish: Arrange the orange slices in a shallow bowl and add the prunes and hot orange syrup. Allow to cool, then chill until ready to serve.

Serves 4

Cheese and Scallion Waffles with Herbed Mascarpone and Roasted Tomatoes

The Bathers Pavilion Restaurant on Balmoral Beach just outside Sydney is famous for its inventive cooking style and its laid-back approach to casual dining. On a recent visit I enjoyed a morning meal of crisp-baked waffles served with delicious herb-flecked mascarpone and the sharp note of roasted ripe tomatoes. The cheese and scallion flavouring of the waffles takes this dish out of the ordinary breakfast class and makes it a great dish for a Sunday breakfast, a light lunch or an intimate late night supper.

At the Bathers Pavilion they use a waffle iron to cook these crisp cakes. If you do not have one, cook them in a frying pan using small metal rings such as egg or crumpet rings. The roasted tomatoes make an extra-special accompaniment.

For the Cheese and Scallion Waffles
175g/6oz self-raising flour
3 tablespoons freshly grated Parmesan cheese
3 tablespoons freshly grated Cheddar cheese
3 scallions, finely sliced
sea salt and freshly ground pepper
2 eggs, lightly beaten
450ml/15fl oz milk
melted butter, for cooking

For the Herbed Mascarpone
225g/8oz mascarpone
2 tablespoons mixed chopped fresh herbs (parsley, chives, basil, oregano)
sea salt and freshly ground pepper

For the Roasted Tomatoes
12 oven-roasted tomato halves (page 12)

To Prepare the Waffle Batter: In a medium-sized bowl, combine the flour, cheeses, sliced scallions, and salt and freshly ground pepper to taste. Make a well in the center.

In a separate bowl, mix the eggs and milk. Pour the egg mixture into the flour mixture, whisking to make a batter. Reserve.

To Prepare the Herbed Mascarpone: In a small bowl, combine the mascarpone with the herbs and seasoning. Mix well. Reserve.

To Prepare the Roasted Tomatoes: Preheat the oven to 170°C/325°F. Place the roasted tomato halves on a baking tray and warm through in the oven: about 30 minutes.

To Cook the Waffles: Heat a waffle iron and brush with a little melted butter. Cook the waffles according to the waffle-iron manufacturer's instructions. (See introduction, above, if you do not have a waffle iron.)

To Serve: Top each serving of waffles with a spoonful of the herbed mascarpone and 2 or 3 roast tomato halves. Serve immediately.

Serves 4 to 6

Spiced Sausage Patties with Cranberries Cumberland

The crisp, spicy flavour of these homemade sausage patties from America's Creole bayous will make you forget any sausage you've ever eaten. They are fabulously easy to make … and even tastier to eat. You can also use the mixture to fill sausage casings for highly flavoured sausages, although I prefer it made into these little sausage patties.

For the Spiced Sausage Patties
675g/1½lb lean pork
350g/12oz fat salt pork
2 cloves garlic, chopped
1 teaspoon salt
1 bay leaf, crumbled
¼–½ teaspoon ground
   allspice
¼–½ teaspoon ground
   coriander
1 teaspoon cracked pepper
crushed dried chiles
2 tablespoons olive oil, plus
   more for sautéing
1 egg, beaten
1 Spanish onion, finely
chopped
leaves from 2–3 sprigs of fresh
   thyme
2 tablespoons finely chopped
   fresh flat-leaf parsley

**For the Cranberries
Cumberland**
225g/8oz raw cranberries,
   chopped
240ml/8fl oz boiling water
100g/4oz sugar
finely grated zest of 1 orange
240ml/8fl oz orange juice
2 teaspoons Dijon mustard
2–4 tablespoons port (optional)

To Prepare the Patties: Put the meat through the finest blade of your mincer, or have it minced by your butcher.

In a mortar, combine the chopped garlic, salt and crumbled bay leaf with ground allspice and coriander to taste. Add the cracked pepper, a pinch of crushed dried chiles and the olive oil and pound to a smooth paste.

Add this mixture to the minced meat with the beaten egg, and chopped onion, thyme and parsley. Mix thoroughly and form into small balls. Flatten each ball into a small patty and refrigerate until ready to serve.

To Make the Cranberries Cumberland: In a medium-sized saucepan, combine the chopped cranberries, boiling water, sugar and orange zest. Bring to the boil and stir until the sugar has completely dissolved. Simmer for about 10 minutes or until the berries are soft.

Stir in the orange juice and Dijon mustard, and the port if using. Continue to cook for 5 minutes more. Then remove from the heat and cool to room temperature. Pour into small bowls or molds and refrigerate until ready to serve.

When Ready to Serve: Sauté the patties in olive oil until cooked through but not dry. Serve immediately with cranberries Cumberland and/or scrambled eggs.

Serves 4 to 6

Tunisian Adja with Eggs

Adja – a Tunisian blend of onions, tomatoes and red peppers with North African spices – is a richly sauced dish. Poach an egg per person in it for a colourful and delicious breakfast with a difference.

4 large eggs

For the Tunisian Sauce
2 Spanish onions, thickly sliced
10 tablespoons olive oil
4 medium-sized ripe tomatoes, sliced
2 medium-sized red peppers, sliced
1 green pepper, cut into large dice
100g/4oz canned Italian plum tomatoes, chopped
1–2 cloves garlic, finely chopped
salt and freshly ground pepper
large pinch each of paprika and cayenne pepper
4 large eggs

For the Garnish
ground cumin and paprika
sprigs of fresh coriander

To Prepare the Vegetables: In a large frying pan, sauté the thickly sliced onions in 6 tablespoons olive oil until golden. Add the sliced tomatoes and red peppers, diced green pepper, chopped plum tomatoes and finely chopped garlic. Simmer the vegetables for 15 to 20 minutes, or until soft and cooked through.

Add the remaining olive oil to the pan and season with salt, freshly ground pepper, paprika and cayenne. Simmer for a further 5 minutes. Divide the vegetables among 4 large ramekins (10–12cm/4–5in diameter).

To Finish and Bake the Adja: Preheat the oven to 170°C/325°F.

Make a shallow depression in the center of the vegetables in each ramekin with the back of a tablespoon. Carefully break an egg into each one.

Place the ramekins in a roasting tin. Cover each one with a small saucer and pour boiling water into the roasting tin to come about halfway up the ramekins. Bake for 10 minutes, or until the eggs are just set. Remove the saucers.

To Serve: Place each ramekin on its saucer and sprinkle the eggs with fine trails of ground cumin and paprika. Garnish with sprigs of fresh coriander and serve immediately.

Serves 4

Congee

In Hong Kong, I got used to comforting bowls of gently seasoned rice with fish and prawns in a subtly flavoured thickened stock. If you love the tastes of ginger, scallions, chiles and coriander, you will love congee.

100g/4oz rice
1 litre/35fl oz light chicken stock
1 tablespoon Thai fish sauce
175g/6oz white fish filets
6 raw tiger prawns, peeled
2 thin slices of fresh ginger, peeled and finely chopped
1 clove garlic, finely chopped
4 scallions, thinly sliced
salt and white pepper
crushed dried chiles, or ½ small fresh red chile, thinly sliced
4 sprigs of fresh coriander

To Prepare the Rice: Rinse and drain the rice. In a large saucepan, combine the drained rice with the chicken stock and half the fish sauce. Bring to the boil. Skim off any impurities, then lower the heat and simmer for at least 1 hour, or until the rice is a soft pulp.

To Make the Congee: Thinly slice the fish filets and tiger prawns and add to the rice. Boil for 3 minutes, then add the chopped ginger and garlic, the remaining fish sauce and half the thinly sliced scallions. Cook for a further 10 minutes. Season with salt, white pepper and crushed dried chiles to taste (or the sliced fresh chile).

To Serve: Pour the congee into soup bowls, garnish with the remaining scallion rings and the coriander sprigs, and serve immediately.

Serves 4

Vegetable Kedgeree

A cool morning kedgeree of diced vegetables and rice, garnished with chopped hard-boiled egg whites and watercress leaves, is topped with a dusting of mimosa (freshly grated or sieved hard-boiled egg yolks) just before serving.

100g/4oz basmati rice
2 hard-boiled eggs
25–50g/1–2oz butter
2 sticks celery, finely sliced
½ Spanish onion, finely
    chopped
½ red pepper, cut into dice
½ yellow pepper, cut into dice
6 button mushrooms, cut into
    quarters
1–2 tablespoons ketchup
4 tablespoons chopped
    watercress leaves
salt and freshly ground pepper
crushed dried chiles

To Prepare the Rice and the Eggs: Boil or steam the rice in the usual way until tender but not mushy. Chop the whites of the hard-boiled eggs. Set the yolks aside.

To Make the Kedgeree: Melt the butter in a medium-sized sauté pan or frying pan. Add the cooked rice, the sliced celery and the chopped onion, and sauté until the onion is translucent. Then add the diced peppers and quartered mushrooms. Stir in the ketchup and toss lightly over a medium heat until the rice and vegetables are heated through. Stir in the chopped egg white and watercress leaves and correct the seasoning, adding a little salt, freshly ground pepper and a pinch of crushed dried chiles.

To Serve: Grate the egg yolks to make mimosa. Dust the kedgeree with the mimosa and serve immediately.

Serves 4

Jamaican Salt Fish and Ackee

Ackee – the fruits of a Jamaican tree – when fully ripe (and that is the only time they are safe to eat) are the most wickedly sensuous fruits I have ever seen. Their glossy black pits and moist golden flesh literally burst out of the dusty, rich red skins when this beautiful breakfast fruit is ripe. Jamaican cooks in this country use canned ackee (not unlike soft scrambled eggs in aspect and texture) to make this exotic breakfast dish – and so do I.

450g/1lb salt cod, soaked
   overnight in cold water
   and drained
2 tablespoons vegetable oil
1–2 cloves garlic, chopped
1 green pepper, chopped
1 Scotch Bonnet, Habañero, or
   other hot chile, sliced
4 scallions, thinly sliced
1 large Spanish onion, sliced
2 large tomatoes, peeled,
   seeded and sliced
1 x 400g/14oz can ackee
1–2 pinches of freshly ground
   pepper
hot pepper sauce, such as
   Tabasco (optional)

For the Garnish
sautéed sliced plantains
toasted corn bread or olive
   ciabatta

To Prepare the Cod: Place the drained salt cod in a saucepan. Add just enough cold water to cover the fish and bring gently to the boil. Remove from the heat and allow the fish to steep in the hot water for 10 minutes, or until tender. Drain, remove the skin and any bones, and cut the fish into cubes or large flakes.

To Cook the Dish: In a large sauté pan or frying pan, combine the vegetable oil with the chopped garlic and green pepper, and the sliced Scotch Bonnet, Habañero or other hot chile, scallions and Spanish onion. Cook over a medium heat, stirring, for 3 to 5 minutes, or until the peppers and onions are just tender.

Then put in the poached salt cod and continue to cook, stirring, for 2 minutes. Add the sliced tomatoes and the ackee and cook, stirring gently, for about 3 minutes, or until the ackee is heated through. Just before serving add freshly ground pepper and a little hot pepper sauce, if desired.

To Serve: Spoon salt fish and ackee on to hot plates and garnish with sautéed sliced plantains and toasted corn bread or olive ciabatta.

Serves 4 to 6

Great Brunches

Super Salmon, Tomato and Basil Stack

Oven-roasted rounds of fresh salmon filet brushed with Thai dressing and crisp Parmesan-coated bread vie for top flavours with fat slices of pan-seared tomato in this towering appetizer stack of surprising colour and flavour. Serve it with a homemade Béarnaise sauce.

4 x slices of white bread, 2.5cm/1in thick, cut into 8cm/3¼in rounds
4 tablespoons freshly grated Parmesan cheese
4 salmon filets
salt and crushed dried chiles
2 large vine-ripened tomatoes, peeled

For the Thai Dressing
6 tablespoons olive oil
1 teaspoon Thai fish sauce
2 teaspoons lime juice
pinch of cayenne pepper

For the Garnish
8 sprigs of fresh basil
4 tablespoons slivered fresh basil leaves
1 x recipe quantity hot Béarnaise sauce (page 249)

To Prepare the Roasted Bread Rounds: Preheat the oven to 200°C/400°F.

Combine the ingredients for the Thai dressing, then brush some dressing lightly over the top and sides of the bread rounds. Roll the sides of the bread rounds in freshly grated Parmesan and sprinkle a little more on top. Place on an oiled baking tray and set aside.

To Prepare the Roasted Salmon Filets: With a small sharp knife, remove and discard the skin and any bones from the salmon filets. Using a large pastry cutter about 8cm/3¼in in diameter, cut out a circle from the center of 1 filet. Continue with the remaining filets. (Reserve trimmings for use in another recipe.) Brush the rounds of salmon with a little of the Thai dressing. Place on the oiled baking tray alongside the bread rounds (or on another tray). Season to taste with salt and crushed dried chiles. Set aside.

To Prepare the Pan-seared Tomato Slices: Cut the tops and bottoms off each peeled tomato. Cut each tomato into 2 slices, about 2cm/¾in thick. Place in a nonstick frying pan, brush with Thai dressing and season to taste with salt and crushed chiles.

To Cook: About 12 minutes before you are ready to serve, place the baking tray(s) in the preheated oven and cook for 9 to 10 minutes, or until the bread is crisp and the salmon filets are cooked through.

In the meantime, pan-sear the tomato slices on one side in the nonstick frying pan for 2 to 3 minutes. With a metal spatula, turn the tomatoes over and cook for 2 to 3 minutes on the other side, or until the tomatoes are well coloured.

To Assemble and Serve: Place 1 roasted bread round on each of 4 heated salad plates. Garnish with 1 sprig of fresh basil.

With a metal spatula, transfer the salmon to a bread round. Repeat with the other 3 filets.

Garnish each salmon round with a sprig of fresh basil. Then, using a metal spatula, transfer a pan-seared tomato slice to the top of the salmon on each stack. Garnish each stack with a mound of slivered basil leaves and spoon over a little Béarnaise sauce. Serve the remaining sauce separately.

Serves 4

Creamed Finnan Haddie

From the coastal villages of Scotland comes this golden cream of smoked haddock served with crisp fried croûtons. A hint of turmeric adds colour and spice. Serve it on its own in a soup bowl or accompany it with saffron- or turmeric-flavoured rice. (Illustrated on page 39.)

1kg/2lb smoked haddock
milk
40g/1½oz butter
3 tablespoons flour
450ml/15fl oz heavy cream
1 large pinch saffron threads
¼ teaspoon ground turmeric
freshly ground pepper
freshly grated nutmeg
triangles of bread, sautéed in
   butter

To Prepare the Fish: Soak the haddock in water to cover for 2 hours. Drain.

   Put the drained haddock in a heavy saucepan. Cover with equal amounts of milk and water and bring to a fast boil. Remove from the heat and allow to stand for 15 minutes. Drain the haddock and reserve the stock.

To Make the Sauce: Melt the butter in the top of a double boiler. Stir in the flour and cook for 3 minutes, stirring continuously. Add the heavy cream, saffron, turmeric (for colour) and 300ml/½ pint of the reserved haddock stock, and continue to cook, stirring from time to time, until the sauce is reduced to the consistency of heavy cream. Season to taste with freshly ground pepper and a little freshly grated nutmeg.

To Finish and Serve: Remove the skin and bones from the haddock and break the flesh into pieces. Fold the haddock pieces into the sauce and simmer gently until ready to use. Scrve in a shallow dish or dishes surrounded by triangles of bread sautéed in butter.

Serves 4 to 6

Red Bean and Macaroni Soup

Soup for brunch? The Chinese do it, so why not the Mexicans? Try this recipe for what I like to call Mexican minestrone when next you have friends round for an informal breakfast/lunch. Or serve it as a hot first course for an informal dinner.

200g/7oz dried red kidney
   beans
1.7 litres/60fl oz chicken stock
4 tablespoons olive oil
1 large Spanish onion, chopped
1 clove garlic, finely chopped
1 x 400g/14oz can Italian plum
   tomatoes, seeded and
   chopped
2 bay leaves
1–2 sprigs of fresh rosemary
2 teaspoons sugar
salt and freshly ground pepper
150g/5oz elbow macaroni,
   cooked
2 roasted red peppers (see
   page 12), cut into dice

For the Garnish
chopped fresh flat-leaf parsley
   and coriander, or thinly
   sliced scallion
freshly grated Parmesan
   cheese

To Prepare the Beans: Rinse the dried beans and pick out any impurities. Place the beans in a medium-sized heatproof casserole and add water to cover by 5cm/2in. Bring to the boil and boil vigorously for 10 minutes. Remove the pot from the heat and allow the beans to soak, covered, for 1 hour.

Drain the beans, return them to a clean casserole and cover with half the chicken stock. Bring to the boil, skimming off any impurities from the surface of the stock, then reduce the heat to low. Simmer the beans until they begin to be tender: 1 to 1½ hours.

To Prepare the Vegetables: Heat the olive oil in a large frying pan, add the chopped onion and garlic and sauté until the vegetables just begin to take on colour. Stir in the chopped tomatoes, bay leaves, rosemary, sugar, and salt and freshly ground pepper to taste, and continue to cook until the mixture begins to bubble. Then transfer the contents of the frying pan to the beans.

To Finish the Soup: Add the remaining chicken stock to the beans and vegetables, cover the casserole and continue to simmer very gently until the beans are tender: up to 1 hour more.

Five minutes before serving, add the cooked macaroni and diced roasted peppers.

To Serve: Transfer the contents of the casserole to a heated soup tureen, sprinkle with chopped parsley and coriander, or thinly sliced scallion, and serve immediately with the Parmesan cheese.

Serves 4 to 6

Ziang Scallion Cakes

One of the pleasures of a Hong Kong breakfast party is this crisp scallion-flavoured puffy pancake, served with Chinese plum jam (available in supermarkets and Chinese stores) or homemade chile jam (page 14).

For the Pastry
150g/6oz self-raising flour
½ teaspoon granulated sugar
½ teaspoon salt
50g/2oz lard, cut into dice
4 tablespoons iced water

For the Scallion Filling
1 tablespoon lard or cooking
   oil
75g/3oz scallions, green
   parts only, cut into
   6mm/¼in segments
½ teaspoon soy sauce
½ teaspoon sesame oil

oil for deep-frying

To Make the Pastry: In a mixing bowl, mix the flour, sugar, salt and lard with your fingers, as you would for any pastry. Add the iced water and mix to a smooth dough.

Sift flour over a pastry board and roll out the pastry to a circle about 23cm/9in in diameter.

To Prepare the Filling: In a wok or frying pan, heat the lard or cooking oil until smoking hot, then immediately add the scallions and stir-fry for 1 minute. Add the soy sauce and sesame oil, toss well, and remove from the wok. Drain off excess juices.

To Make the Cakes: Sprinkle the scallions over the pastry. With your hands, roll up the pastry into a long sausage-shape. Cut across into 4 equal-sized pieces and, with a rolling pin, roll each piece into a circle 7.5cm/3in in diameter. Deep-fry the scallion cakes in hot oil until crisp and golden.

Cut each cake into quarters and serve immediately.

Serves 4

Asian Samosas

These crisp golden pastry triangles packed with a savory spinach filling make delicious hot finger food, a savory first course, or a light luncheon dish with Asian overtones. Use filo pastry.

6 sheets filo pastry
1 egg, beaten
lime wedges

For the Samosa Filling
4 tablespoons vegetable oil
1 large Spanish onion, finely
    chopped
2 cloves garlic, finely chopped
1 fresh red chile, finely
    chopped
6 scallions, cut into
    6mm/¼ in segments
225g/8oz potatoes, diced
1 teaspoon curry powder
½ teaspoon ground coriander
¼ teaspoon ground ginger
2 tablespoons tomato paste,
    dissolved in 4 tablespoons
    water
100g/4oz young spinach
    leaves, cooked
juice of ½ lemon
2 tablespoons fresh chives,
finely chopped

To Make the Filling: In a large frying pan, heat the vegetable oil. Add the finely chopped onion, garlic and chile and the white parts of the scallions and cook, stirring continuously, until the vegetables begin to colour. Add the diced potatoes, spices and tomato paste mixture. Continue to cook, stirring from time to time, until the moisture has almost evaporated and the potatoes are cooked through. Then stir in the spinach, the green parts of the scallions, the lemon juice and the chopped chives. Cover the pan, remove from the heat and reserve.

To Prepare the Filo Pastry: Cut each filo pastry sheet in half lengthways. Fold both long sides of each piece of pastry over to the center to make a narrow strip about 5cm/2in wide with 2 strengthening 'hems'.

To Make the Samosas: Place 2 teaspoons of the vegetable mixture at the top of a strip of pastry. Fold one corner over to make a triangle shape at the top, then turn the triangle over at the base, and continue to fold in the same way until you reach the end of the pastry strip and have a fat triangle-shaped samosa.

Brush the inside of the last fold of pastry with a little beaten egg (with your finger) and seal the samosa.

Continue with the other pastry strips. Place the samosas on a baking tray and reserve.

To Cook and Serve: Preheat the oven to 180°C/350°F. Bake the samosas in the preheated oven for 25 to 30 minutes, or until puffed and golden brown, then serve immediately with wedges of lime.

Serves 4 to 6

Salade Niçoise in Croûton Baskets

This pointy croûton basket is a lovely idea from Australia's food doyenne, Joan Campbell.
I like to use it for a light salade niçoise, as here, or as a hot, crisp 'carrier' for pan-seared spicy
tiger prawns.

For the Croûton Baskets
1 one-day-old white sandwich
  loaf, unsliced
1–2 cloves garlic, halved
olive oil
6 tablespoons freshly grated
  Parmesan cheese
1–2 teaspoons paprika
salt

For the Salad
mixed salad leaves and sprigs
  of fresh herbs, as desired
8–12 plum tomato wedges
8–12 strips of red pepper
8–12 strips of green pepper
2–3 hard-boiled eggs, cut into
  quarters
8–12 black olives
4–6 anchovy filets
200g/7oz can tuna, drained
4–6 hard-boiled quail's eggs
  in their shells (optional)

**For the Garlic and Herb
Vinaigrette**
120ml/4fl oz extra virgin olive
  oil
2–3 tablespoons fresh lime
  juice
1–2 cloves garlic, finely
  chopped
2 tablespoons finely chopped
  fresh basil
2 tablespoons finely chopped
  fresh flat-leaf parsley
salt and freshly ground pepper

To Prepare the Croûton Baskets: Preheat the oven to 190°C/375°F.

With a sharp serrated knife, remove the end crusts from the
sandwich loaf and cut the loaf into 4 to 6 equal slices approximately
6cm/2½in thick. Trim the crusts from each thick slice to form a
square and then cut each square into a triangle shape.

Choose a small cookie cutter to fit well within each bread triangle
and press down to cut out the center section of each one. Discard
the center sections.

Rub the cut surface of each croûton basket with the garlic, then
brush the same area liberally with olive oil. In a small bowl, combine
the grated Parmesan and the paprika and season with salt to taste.
Dust the cut surfaces with the seasoned Parmesan.

Place the baskets on a baking tray and bake in the preheated oven
for 10 minutes, or until the bread is crisp and golden.

To Prepare the Salad: Place the salad leaves in a bowl. Combine all
the ingredients for the vinaigrette, mixing well, and add half the
dressing to the leaves. Toss well. In another bowl, combine the
tomato wedges and red and green pepper strips, add the remaining
dressing and toss well.

To Serve: Arrange the salad leaves in each basket, then garnish each
attractively with 2 tomato wedges, red and green pepper strips, hard-
boiled egg segments and olives, along with an anchovy filet and a
chunk or two of canned tuna. If you like, add a hard-boiled quail's
egg too. Serve immediately.

Serves 4 to 6

Deep-Fried Mussel Brochettes with Béarnaise Sauce

This is one of my favourite starters, but it was not until I served it at a Sunday late-breakfast-cum-lunch that I realized its full potential, especially when served with freshly made Béarnaise sauce and wild rice.

1kg/2¼lb mussels
2 tablespoons finely chopped shallots
2 sprigs of fresh thyme
2 sprigs of fresh parsley
1 bay leaf
salt
150ml/5fl oz dry white wine
225g/8oz unsmoked bacon, 1 thick slice
freshly ground pepper
melted butter
1 x recipe quantity Béarnaise sauce (page 249)

To Prepare the Mussels: Scrape, beard and wash the mussels, discarding any that are cracked or open. Place the cleaned mussels in a heavy saucepan with the finely chopped shallots, thyme, parsley and bay leaf. Season lightly with salt and moisten with the white wine. Cover the saucepan and steam for 3 to 5 minutes over a high heat, shaking the pan frequently, until the shells are all open. Discard any mussels that do not open, then remove the remaining mussels from their shells. Make the Béarnaise sauce and keep it hot over simmering water.

To Make the Brochettes: Preheat the broiler. Cut the bacon into mussel-sized pieces. Thread the mussels on to small skewers (2 per person) with pieces of bacon between them, then season with freshly ground pepper and brush with a little melted butter. Cook under a medium-hot broiler until the bacon is golden, turning the skewers from time to time.

To Serve: Strain the freshly made Béarnaise sauce through a fine sieve and serve at once with the mussel brochettes.

Serves 4

Austrian Krapfen

When I was very young I took weekly violin lessons from an Austrian music teacher whose wife was a wonderful cook. After the lesson we would enjoy her delicate deep-fried Austrian pastries (a sort of indented yeast dumpling) with tart apricot jam and a blanched almond. I serve them today as a deliciously nostalgic breakfast or brunch treat… but with someone else playing the violin on the CD player.

180ml/6fl oz milk
1 tablespoon active dry yeast
2 tablespoons sugar
225g/8oz flour, sifted
2 tablespoons vegetable oil
1 egg yolk, beaten
1 teaspoon vanilla essence
oil for deep frying

For the Decoration
1 jar (approximately 450g/1lb)
   apricot jam
24 blanched almonds
confectioners' sugar

To Prepare the Krapfen: In a saucepan, warm the milk, removing it from the heat before it boils. In a medium-sized bowl, combine the yeast with 6 tablespoons of the warm milk and stir to dissolve the yeast. When the yeast bubbles, blend in the sugar and just enough of the flour to make a thick paste. Cover the bowl with a dish towel and leave in a warm place for 15 minutes.

Add the vegetable oil, beaten egg yolk, remaining milk, vanilla essence and flour to the frothy yeast, and mix until you have a dough. Knead the dough for 5 minutes or until it leaves the sides of the bowl. Shape the dough into a ball and place in an oiled mixing bowl. Cover with a dish towel and leave to rise in a warm place for 1 hour.

Roll the dough out thinly on a lightly floured surface and, using a cookie cutter, cut out circles 5–6cm/2–2½in in diameter. Leave the circles to rise in a warm place for 30 minutes.

When Ready to Cook: Heat the oil in a deep-frying pan or a shallow heatproof casserole. With your fingers and thumb, make a slight indentation in each of 4 to 6 rounds of dough and slide them gently into the hot oil. Cook the krapfen until they are puffed and golden. Take each out of the hot oil with a slotted spoon and leave to drain on paper towels. Continue in the same manner with the remaining circles of dough. As soon as the krapfen in each batch are cool enough to handle, place a spoonful of apricot jam in each indentation and press a blanched almond into the jam. Just before serving, dust lightly with confectioners' sugar.

Serves 4 to 6

The Bathers Pavilion's Chile Salt Squid

The new Australian cooking is famous for its super-light dishes – perfect for breakfasts, brunches and sun-filled lunches by the sea. On my visit to the Bathers Pavilion on Balmoral Beach in Sydney, I loved the lightly cooked little 'rolls' of deep-fried squid tossed with colourful pepper strips and fresh coriander sprigs in a hot, sweet and sour dressing. This fabulous spicy squid salad, served by Victoria Alexander and Genevieve Harris at the beautiful beach-side restaurant, would be great, I thought, for a company breakfast or brunch, or as the high-flavoured starter for a special lunch party. Tender young squid are readily available now in the supermarkets. The trick here is to lightly score the squid on the underside to make it even more tender and to make it 'roll' attractively. Another plus: the squid is cooked for exactly one minute just before serving.

450g/1lb squid, cleaned
3 peppers: 1 green, 1 red,
    1 yellow
1 large fresh red chile
1 large carrot
1 small red onion
vegetable oil, for frying
large bunch of fresh coriander

For the Dressing
2 fresh tiny hot (birdseye)
    chiles
700ml/25fl oz rice vinegar
225g/8oz sugar
2 tablespoons lime juice

For the Seasoned Flour
5 tablespoons flour
1 tablespoon chile powder
½ tablespoon freshly ground
    pepper
1 tablespoon onion powder
1 tablespoon garlic powder
½ tablespoon salt

To Prepare the Dressing: Cut the tiny chiles in half lengthways. Place the rice vinegar, sugar and chile peppers in a saucepan over a medium heat. Stir to dissolve the sugar and then simmer for about 20 minutes or until the mixture has reduced to a thin syrup. Remove from the heat and add the lime juice. Strain and allow to cool.

To Prepare the Seasoned Flour: Mix the flour and spices together and set aside.

To Prepare the Chile Salad: With a sharp knife, score the underside of the squid lightly into a criss-cross pattern. Cut the peppers and the large chile into thin strips. Cut the carrot into thin strips. Finely slice the onion. Combine the vegetables in a bowl.

In a large frying pan, pour vegetable oil to a depth of 5cm/2in. Heat until hot (when a small cube of bread turns golden brown in 1 minute). Dip the squid in the seasoned flour until well coated and then fry in the hot oil for 1 minute until the flour crust is crisp. Drain, then slice into 1cm/½in rings.

To Serve: Add the squid to the prepared vegetables and pour over the dressing. Toss, serve on to individual plates and garnish with plenty of coriander leaves.

Serves 6

Chinese Salad in Lettuce Shells

This is one of those seemingly intricate recipes from China that is actually very easy to prepare: a fresh-tasting 'salad' of thinly sliced vegetables, ham, squab or chicken breast and Chinese mushrooms. Served hot in a crisp lettuce shell, it makes a great light brunch dish; served cold it also makes an intriguing first-course salad or light luncheon dish.

2 slices fresh or canned bamboo shoot
4 sticks celery
4 carrots
50g/2oz canned abalone
75g/3oz cooked ham
150g/6oz breast of squab or chicken, poached in stock
6 Chinese dried black mushrooms
salt, sugar and crushed dried chiles
1–2 teaspoons light sesame oil
4–8 crisp curled lettuce leaves, such as radicchio or iceberg

To Prepare the Ingredients: Cut the bamboo shoot crossways into thin slices and then cut the slices into matchstick-thin strips. Cut the celery into segments and then the segments into matchstick-thin strips. Peel the carrots, cut lengthways into thin slices and then into matchstick-thin strips. Cut the canned abalone, cooked ham and poached squab or chicken into thin strips. Soak the dried black mushrooms in a little boiling water. Squeeze dry, remove tough stems and then cut the caps into thin strips.

Combine all the prepared ingredients in a medium-sized bowl. Season to taste with salt, sugar and crushed dried chiles. Add the light sesame oil and toss until the flavours impregnate all the ingredients. Chill until ready to serve.

To Serve: Place 1 or 2 (according to size) crisp, curled, lettuce-leaf 'shells' on each of 4 salad plates, fill with the Chinese salad and serve immediately.

Serves 4

American Corn 'Oysters'

A delicious sweetcorn and red pepper fritter called an 'oyster' is a fond memory of my grandmother's kitchen where we used to enjoy superb Sunday morning meals of corned beef or salmon hash, griddled sweetcorn 'oysters' and thick slices of country ham from the farm. Today, I bring this old favourite spankingly up-to-date with an avocado salsa (page 16).

2 egg yolks
225g/8oz fresh, canned and
   drained, or frozen and
   defrosted sweetcorn kernels
25g/1oz fresh breadcrumbs
4 tablespoons diced roasted
   red pepper (page 12)
juice of ¼ lemon or lime
½ teaspoon baking powder
salt and freshly ground pepper
crushed dried chiles
3 egg whites

To Prepare the Batter: In a medium-sized bowl, beat the egg yolks until light coloured. Stir in the sweetcorn kernels, breadcrumbs, diced roasted pepper, lemon or lime juice and baking powder. Season to taste with salt, freshly ground pepper and crushed dried chiles.

In a clean bowl, whisk the egg whites until stiff. Fold gently into the sweetcorn batter mixture.

To Cook the Corn 'Oysters': Heat a large griddle or nonstick frying pan and brush with olive oil. Drop the batter mixture by the tablespoon on to the hot griddle or pan and cook until the 'oysters' are lightly browned on both sides, turning them once. Drain on kitchen paper and keep warm while you cook the remaining 'oysters'. Serve immediately, with avocado and tomato salsa.

Serves 4 to 6

Great Starters

Tomato Cups with Green Dressing

This is a recipe for the late summer months when large, ripe, full-flavoured tomatoes are readily available. The green garnish of stand-up asparagus spears, scallions and watercress sprigs is most attractive with its fragrant green dressing.

For the Tomatoes
4–6 large ripe tomatoes
salt and freshly ground pepper

For the Garnish
4–6 asparagus spears
8–12 sprigs of watercress
2 scallions, white parts
    only, sliced into thin rings

For the Dressing
6 tablespoons chopped
    watercress leaves
6 tablespoons sliced scallion
(green parts only)
2 tablespoons chopped fresh
    chives
1 clove garlic, chopped
6 tablespoons fresh soft
    breadcrumbs
2–3 tablespoons wine vinegar
8–12 tablespoons olive oil
salt and freshly ground pepper
cayenne pepper

To Prepare the Tomatoes: Dip the whole tomatoes into boiling water, then immediately into iced water, to loosen the skins. This way they will not partially cook or disintegrate. With a sharp knife, peel them. Cut off the top third of each tomato. Carefully scoop out the tomato seeds and flesh from each base to form cups and place, cut-side up, on a serving platter. Season the insides generously. Cut the tomato tops into small dice. Chill.

To Prepare the Garnish: Poach the asparagus in boiling salted water until *al dente*. Drain, cool and chill.

To Prepare the Dressing: Combine the watercress, scallion, chives, garlic and breadcrumbs with the diced tomato tops in a small bowl. Add the vinegar and oil. Mix well and season with salt, freshly ground pepper and cayenne pepper. Chill until ready to use.

To Serve: Spoon the dressing into the tomato cups. Cut each asparagus spear into 4 equal lengths, and use as small upstanding 'spears' to garnish the tomatoes along with watercress sprigs and scallion rings.

Serves 4 to 6

Japanese Seared Beef with Fresh Ginger

A thin strip cut from 2.5cm/1in-thick sirloin steak, seared on the edges in a hot nonstick frying pan, is the prime ingredient of this delicious Japanese appetizer. Serve it on its own as a light first course of distinction, or as part of a combination of dishes served together. I like to serve the beef just seared on the edges – very rare – but it can be cooked more if desired. A vegetarian version can be made with thin strips of pan-seared eggplant.

16 long thin slices rare beef (20 by 5cm/8 by 2in): cut from a 2.5cm/1in-thick sirloin steak that has been seared in a hot pan

3–4 tablespoons sesame oil

32 julienne strips of carrot, blanched

32 x 5cm/2in fresh chive strips, blanched

For the Marinade

2.5cm/1in piece of fresh ginger

juice of 1 lime

4 tablespoons orange blossom honey

4 teaspoons soy sauce

To Make the Marinade: Peel the ginger and cut into julienne strips. In a small bowl combine the lime juice, honey and soy sauce. Add the julienne of ginger and leave for 2 hours.

To Serve: Brush the strips of beef with sesame oil. Fold one short edge into the center, then fold the other edge over it, making 3 layers. You will have an approximately 5cm/2in square. Repeat with the remaining beef strips.

Place 4 pieces of beef on each of 4 individual serving plates, with julienne of ginger and its marinade in the center. Garnish each beef square with 2 pieces of carrot and chive, crossed diagonally.

Serves 4

Oysters in Champagne with Caramelized Scallions

Here's a fabulous way to present oysters literally just warmed through in a Champagne sauce. This glamorous starter uses only 3 or 4 oysters per serving, presented on the half shell, bathed in an amber-tinted Champagne sauce and garnished with caramelized scallions.

12–16 oysters

For the Caramelized Scallions
20 large scallions
salt
25g/1oz butter
4–6 tablespoons of Champagne
    from a ¼ bottle
splash of balsamic vinegar

For the Sauce
25g/1oz butter
1 tablespoon flour
¼ fish stock cube, crumbled
150ml/5fl oz crème fraîche
pinch of sugar
½–1 teaspoon soy sauce
½–1 teaspoon Thai fish sauce
remaining Champagne from
    the ¼ bottle used above
salt and freshly ground pepper

To Prepare the Oysters: Open the oysters over a large bowl (to catch the liquid). With a small, sharp knife, remove the oysters from their shells and put in the bowl with their liquid. Rinse the deep oyster shells (discarding the top shells) and scrub off any impurities.

To Caramelize the Scallions: Trim the roots from the scallions and cut off the green tops, leaving about 7.5cm/3in of the white part. Place in a saucepan, cover with boiling water, add salt and cook for 3 minutes. Drain and transfer to a bowl of iced water to preserve the texture. When cold, drain again and cut in half lengthways.

Brown the scallions lightly on the cut sides in the butter in a nonstick frying pan. When golden-brown on the cut sides, add the Champagne and balsamic vinegar, and swirl the pan around until the liquid has almost disappeared and the scallions are caramelized. Remove the scallions from the pan and keep warm; reserve the pan.

To Prepare the Sauce: Add the butter to the pan in which you caramelized the scallions. Place over a medium heat and stir until the butter has melted into the pan juices. Stir in the flour and crumbled fish stock cube and continue to cook, stirring, until the flour is cooked through without changing colour. Stir in the crème fraîche and sugar, the soy sauce and Thai fish sauce to taste, and continue to cook, stirring, until the sauce is well blended and slightly thickened. Add the reserved oyster liquid (saving the oysters for later) and just enough of the Champagne to make a smooth sauce with the consistency of thick cream. Season with salt and pepper and reserve.

To Finish the Dish: Heat the oven to 110°C/225°F and warm the reserved oyster shells. Heat the sauce in a pan over a low heat (without allowing it to come to the boil). Add the oysters and warm through for about half a minute. Remove from the heat and reserve.

To Serve: Place 3 (or 4) hot oyster shells on each of 4 heated salad plates. Spoon 1 oyster into each shell, with 1 or 2 scallion segments. Garnish each dish with the remaining scallion segments and spoon over the creamed oyster sauce. Serve immediately.

Serves 4

Artichoke Hearts with Foie Gras

This is one of the all-time greats: it came from La Mère Brazier of Lyons. The artichoke hearts are seasoned with fresh tarragon vinaigrette while still warm, chilled in the dressing until ready to serve on a bed of bitter leaves, and then topped with slices of pâté de foie gras and sprinkled with extra fresh tarragon.

8 large artichokes

juice of 1 lemon

2 x recipe quantity tarragon vinaigrette (page 20) made ½ during preparation, ½ before serving

bitter salad leaves to choice, such as watercress, mâche, frisée, radicchio

salt and freshly ground pepper

8 thin rounds of pâté de foie gras

1 tablespoon chopped fresh tarragon

To Prepare the Artichokes: Cut off the stalks and tough outer leaves of 1 artichoke. Slice through the leafy part down to the last rows of leaves nearest the stalk. Pare off the remaining leaves until only the heart and 'choke' is left. Remove the 'choke' with a knife or sharp-edged teaspoon, and discard. Place the heart in cold water with the juice of a lemon added to preserve colour, while you prepare the remaining 7 artichokes.

Drain the artichoke hearts, then poach in boiling salted water for about 30 minutes. Drain again, and allow the artichoke hearts to dry while you prepare the vinaigrette. Toss the still-warm artichoke hearts in the first half of the vinaigrette dressing and allow to cool, then chill in the refrigerator for at least 45 minutes, or else overnight.

To Serve: Arrange the bitter salad leaves in 4 individual dishes and season with salt and freshly ground pepper. Dress with the freshly made vinaigrette. Remove each artichoke heart from its vinaigrette bath with a slotted spoon and, allowing 2 hearts per person, arrange on the bed of leaves. Place 1 slice of pâté de foie gras on each heart, sprinkle with fresh tarragon and serve immediately.

Serves 4

Tortillons of Sole with Sculpted Vegetables

This recipe is as easy as wrapping filets of sole around your finger. Fasten the sole 'twists' with toothpicks and poach in well-flavoured stock for 2 to 3 minutes. Garnish each dish just before serving with small sculpted balls of poached carrot, turnip and cucumber and diced raw tomato. Beautiful.

8 filets of lemon sole
50g/2oz butter
6 tablespoons finely chopped
   onion
8 fresh basil leaves
6 sprigs of fresh tarragon,
   leaves only
300ml/10fl oz fish stock
1 fish stock cube, crumbled
juice of ½ lemon
salt and freshly ground pepper

For the Vegetable Garnish
4 medium carrots, peeled and
   lightly poached
2 medium turnips, peeled and
   poached
½ cucumber, peeled and seeded
1 large beefsteak tomato

To Prepare the Tortillons: Cut each filet of lemon sole in 2, lengthways. Twist a strip of filet around your index finger until it resembles a coiled spring. Secure with a wooden cocktail stick and reserve. Continue with remaining filets.

To Prepare the Vegetable Garnish: Using a small melon-ball cutter, cut 8 small balls each from the carrots, turnips and cucumber. Then, with a sharp kitchen knife, cut 8 sticks 7.5cm/3in long of each vegetable. Blanch in boiling water until *al dente*, then keep warm. Peel, seed and dice the large tomato, and reserve.

To Cook the Tortillons: Melt 25g/1oz butter in a wide, shallow saucepan and sauté the chopped onion until translucent. Add the basil and tarragon leaves, fish stock and fish stock cube. Bring to the boil and reduce to a simmer.

Place the tortillons of sole in the stock. Cover the pan and cook for 2 to 3 minutes. When cooked, remove the sole from the stock with a slotted spoon and keep warm.

Add the remaining butter to the stock and add lemon juice to taste. Check the seasoning and add a little salt and freshly ground pepper if necessary. Strain the sauce through a sieve over the sole and garnish with the cooked vegetables and the diced raw tomato. Serve immediately.

Serves 4

Tomato, Mozzarella and Basil Stack with Balsamic Vinegar and Lime Vinaigrette

This towering new-age salad of tomato, mozzarella and basil leaves, served with a balsamic vinegar, lime and basil vinaigrette, is at its best when vine-ripened tomatoes are in the shops.

16 thin rounds fresh buffalo
  mozzarella cheese
4 large, vine-ripened tomatoes,
  chilled
16–24 large fresh basil leaves

For the Balsamic Vinegar and
Lime Vinaigrette
150ml/5fl oz extra virgin olive
  oil
1 tablespoon balsamic vinegar
2–3 tablespoons lime juice
fresh basil leaves, cut into thin
  slivers
salt and freshly ground pepper
crushed dried chiles

For the Garnish
4 sprigs of fresh basil
black olives

To Prepare the Vinaigrette and Marinate the Cheese: In a large, wide bowl, combine the extra virgin olive oil, balsamic vinegar and lime juice to taste. Add slivered basil leaves and season to taste with salt, freshly ground pepper and crushed dried chiles. Mix well, then add the sliced mozzarella cheese, spooning the dressing over the slices. Chill until ready to serve.

To Prepare the Tomatoes: Cut the tomatoes, one by one, into 6mm/¼in slices, including the tops and bottoms. Re-form each tomato.

To Assemble the Stacks: With a slotted spoon, remove the marinated mozzarella slices from the dressing (reserve the dressing). Alternate slices of tomato and mozzarella to create a stack on each plate, garnishing each layer of cheese with a leaf or two of basil and ending each stack with a tomato 'cap' (see photograph). Spoon the dressing over. Garnish each plate with a sprig of basil and a few olives, and serve immediately.

Serves 4

Rillettes of Smoked Eel with Tiny Diced Vegetables

The brilliantly coloured 'dice' of cooked and raw vegetables give this delicious loose pâté of smoked trout and eel its distinctive look. At Carrier's, my restaurant in Camden Passage, Islington, I used to form egg shapes of the rillettes mixture with two tablespoons. For a more simple approach, serve the rillette mixture in small ramekins, accompanied by strips of toast.

450g/1lb fresh smoked eel
1 fresh smoked trout
(450g/1lb)
salt and freshly ground pepper
cayenne pepper
150ml/5fl oz heavy cream
lemon juice

For the Mustard Vinaigrette
2 tablespoons wine vinegar or
lemon juice
¼ teaspoon Dijon mustard
salt and freshly ground pepper
6–8 tablespoons olive oil

For the Garnish
4 small radishes, washed
2 thin slices cooked beetroot
1 medium carrot, cooked until
crisp-tender
tiny sprigs of frisée or mâche
1 tablespoon finely chopped
fresh tarragon
1 tablespoon finely chopped
fresh flat-leaf parsley

To Prepare the Fish: Skin the eel, and skin and filet the trout. Purée one third of the eel and all of the trout in a blender or food processor. Season to taste with salt, freshly ground pepper and cayenne pepper. Add half the heavy cream and the juice of quarter of a lemon and process until smooth. Add the remaining heavy cream and season with more lemon juice, salt and freshly ground pepper if desired. Continue to process until well mixed. Transfer the mixture to a bowl.

Cut the remaining eel into thin strips about the size of matchsticks and fold gently into the eel and trout mixture. Reserve.

To Prepare the Mustard Vinaigrette: Mix together the wine vinegar or lemon juice and Dijon mustard, and season to taste with salt and freshly ground pepper. Add the olive oil and beat with a fork until the mixture emulsifies.

To Prepare the Garnish: Cut the radishes, beetroot and carrot into tiny dice. Marinate each vegetable separately in a little of the vinaigrette until needed.

To Serve: Shape the 'rillettes' mixture into 4 to 6 oval shapes using 2 tablespoons dipped in hot water (shapes should resemble eggs), and serve on individual plates. Garnish each plate with tiny sprigs of frisée or mâche, and spoon out small heaps of the diced radish, beetroot and carrot around the rillettes.

Drizzle the remaining dressing over the salad greens and vegetables, sprinkle each rillette 'egg' with finely chopped tarragon and parsley, and serve immediately.

Note: Do not use frozen eel or trout – they produce too much moisture.

Serves 4 to 6

Terrines of Rouget with Champagne Sauce

You will need ramekins to make this dish. With its ambrosial rich sauce, this is the perfect first course for a perfect dinner.

100g/4oz filet of rouget (red
   mullet)
100g/4oz filet of turbot or
   sole
2 egg whites
salt and freshly ground pepper
350ml/12fl oz heavy cream

For the Champagne Sauce
15g/¼oz butter
2 shallots, finely chopped
4 button mushrooms,
   finely chopped
sprig of fresh tarragon
¼ teaspoon tomato paste
6 tablespoons dry white wine
6 tablespoons Champagne
pinch of saffron threads
salt and white pepper
300ml/10fl oz heavy cream

To Prepare the Fish: In a blender or food processor, work the rouget and turbot or sole until fine. Add the egg whites, season to taste with salt and freshly ground pepper and process until smooth. Add the heavy cream and continue to blend for a further few seconds. Do not overwork. Correct the seasoning and then transfer to a bowl. Cover and chill for at least 20 minutes.

Preheat the oven to 190°C/375°F.

Grease 8 ramekins and fill them with the fish mixture. Cover each ramekin with foil and place in a roasting pan. Pour in boiling water to come part-way up the sides of the molds. Set the pan over a high heat until the water comes to the boil again, then cook in the preheated oven for 20 minutes.

To Make the Champagne Sauce: In a thick-bottomed frying pan, melt the butter and sauté the finely chopped shallots and mushrooms with the tarragon and tomato paste until the vegetables are soft. Add the dry white wine, Champagne and saffron threads, and season to taste with salt and white pepper. Continue to cook until the sauce is reduced to a quarter of its original quantity.

Add the heavy cream and correct the seasoning, adding a little more salt and pepper and a little more tomato paste (diluted in a little water) for added colour if desired. Continue to cook until the sauce is thick and smooth. Strain through a fine sieve.

To Serve: Have ready 4 heated serving plates. Turn the terrines out on to the plates and spoon Champagne sauce over and around each terrine. Serve immediately.

Serves 4

New Potato Salad with Black Olive, Tomato and Shallot Confit Dressing

Whole small new potatoes cooked in their skins and then peeled and tossed while still warm in a chopped black olive, diced tomato and shallot confit vinaigrette makes a great summer salad. Use this colourful dressing, too, for a cold macaroni salad.

1kg/2¼lb small new potatoes

For the Dressing
6 tablespoons chopped black Greek-style olives
4 tablespoons peeled, seeded and diced plum tomatoes
4 tablespoons finely chopped shallots, softened in 25g/1oz butter
4 tablespoons puréed canned plum tomatoes, or passata
6–8 tablespoons extra virgin olive oil
2–4 tablespoons lemon juice
salt and freshly ground pepper
crushed dried chiles

To Prepare the Potatoes: About 2 hours before serving, cook the new potatoes (skins on) in boiling salted water until just tender. When cool enough to handle, carefully remove the skins with a small sharp kitchen knife.

Put the peeled potatoes in a glass salad bowl and set aside.

To Make the Dressing: In a medium-sized bowl, combine the first 6 ingredients and season to taste with salt, freshly ground pepper and crushed dried chiles.

To Serve: Add the dressing to the still-warm potatoes and toss gently. Serve at room temperature.

Serves 4 as an appetizer, or 4 to 6 as a vegetable accompaniment to broiled or poached fish, poultry or meat

Stir-Fried Crab Cream

This is imperial banquet fare. It accomplishes the impossible: stir-frying cream. You will love its light, airy consistency with its subtle crab flavouring. You just have to try it.

175ml/6fl oz heavy cream
2 teaspoons cornflour
4 tablespoons milk
¼ teaspoon sugar
½ teaspoon salt
50g/2oz cooked white crab meat, shredded
peanut oil for frying
25g/1oz vermicelli noodles
2 tablespoons pine nuts (optional)
4 egg whites

For the Garnish
2 tablespoons crab roe (optional) or 4 to 8 fresh coriander leaves

To Prepare the Cream: Bring the heavy cream to the boil in a small saucepan. Remove from the heat. Combine the cornflour, milk, sugar and salt in a small bowl, stir until smooth and add to the hot cream. Cook the cream, stirring constantly, until it thickens.

Pour the cream into a medium-sized mixing bowl and add the cooked crab meat. Leave to steep until ready to use.

To Deep-fry the Vermicelli: Pour 7.5cm/3in peanut oil into a wok and heat until very hot. Drop in the vermicelli noodles and fry for half a minute, or until the noodles swell up and crisp in the hot oil. Remove the noodles immediately with a slotted spoon and drain well on paper towel.

To Deep-fry the Pine Nuts: Scoop up the pine nuts, if using, in the slotted spoon, dip into the hot oil and fry until golden. (Unless the spoon is slotted, the hot oil won't reach the pine nuts.) Remove immediately and drain. Pour off excess oil, leaving the entire inside of the wok lightly oiled.

To Fry the Crab Meat in 3 Easy Steps: Whisk the egg whites until stiff and fold into the crab and cream mixture.

Place the oiled wok over a low flame. Pour in a third of the crab cream and rotate the wok rapidly so the mixture rolls around the sides of the hot wok and cooks on the oiled surface, at the same time pushing the cooked mixture loosely up the sides of the wok. Continue until all the liquid has cooked in loose folds. Keep the cooked crab cream warm by transferring to a hot plate set over simmering water. Cover.

Wash and dry the wok and oil it again. Pour half the remaining cream mixture into the wok and cook as above. Again, transfer the cooked mixture to the hot plate and cover, then cook the remaining cream in a clean and oiled wok in the same way.

To Serve: Spoon the steamed crab cream into 4 bowls, surround with crisp-fried vermicelli, sprinkle with pine nuts and garnish with crab roe or fresh coriander. Serve immediately.

Note: Crab cream must not brown, just be allowed to thicken slightly while cooking (between a custardy mixture and shirred eggs).

Serves 4

Chinese Steamed Scallops with Black Bean Sauce

Perhaps the most perfect of Chinese 'little' dishes: individual shells of steamed scallop and scallion with a delicate clear sauce of soy and black bean. This version shows Thai and Japanese influences. (Illustrated on page 55.)

12 small scallops, cleaned (reserve 4 scallop shells if you have them)
½ teaspoon finely chopped fresh ginger
½ teaspoon finely chopped shallots
1 clove garlic, finely chopped
2–3 tablespoons fermented black beans, rinsed to remove excess salt
1 tablespoon peanut or grapeseed oil
3 tablespoons freshly squeezed lime juice
1 teaspoon Thai fish sauce
1 teaspoon Japanese soy sauce
1 tablespoon mirin (Japanese rice wine)
¼ teaspoon finely chopped fresh red chile

For the Garnish
2 scallions, green parts only, thinly sliced

To Steam the Scallops: In an ovenproof serving bowl that will hold the scallops in one layer (and fit inside your steamer), combine the scallops, ginger, shallots and garlic and toss well. Top with the black beans, peanut or grapeseed oil, lime juice, Thai fish sauce, soy sauce, mirin and finely chopped chile.

Preheat the oven to 110°C/225°F.

Heat the bowl over a small pan of steaming water until it is quite hot. Then place a rack in a larger pan filled with boiling water to a depth of 5cm/2in, and place the bowl on the rack (or place the bowl in your steamer). Cover the pan and turn up the heat. Steam for 12 minutes.

To Serve: While the scallops are steaming, scrub 4 scallop shells and place them, or 4 individual porcelain scallop shells or other small dishes, in the preheated oven to warm. Serve the scallops and their juices in the heated shells or dishes, garnished just before serving with thinly sliced scallions.

Serves 4

Great Salads

Perfect Green Salad

There are some things in a restaurant that have to be just perfect. It is not the more complicated dishes that one has to worry about, it is the simple ones. A perfect green salad is one of the most difficult to achieve in its perfect simplicity. This is my version.

2 romaine lettuce hearts
12 sprigs of baby frisée
12 sprigs of mâche
12 sprigs of watercress
12 sprigs of fresh coriander
12 sprigs of fresh tarragon
2 sprigs of fresh flat-leaf
    parsley

For the Vinaigrette
1 large clove garlic, thinly
sliced
½ teaspoon sea salt (ideally
    from Guérandes)
2 coriander roots (optional)
6–8 teaspoons extra virgin
    olive oil
2 tablespoons lime juice
¼ – ½ teaspoon Thai fish sauce
freshly ground pepper
crushed dried chiles

To Prepare the Greens: Wash all of the salad greens in cold running water. Transfer the greens carefully to a colander to drain and then spin them in a salad spinner. Wrap the greens loosely in a clean dish towel and chill until ready to use.

To Make the Vinaigrette: In a mortar, mash the garlic with the sea salt and coriander root (if using) into a paste. Add the olive oil, lime juice, Thai fish sauce, freshly ground pepper to taste, and just a pinch of crushed dried chiles. Mix well with a spoon, making sure the garlic paste is incorporated totally into the dressing.

To Serve the Salad: Put the prepared salad greens into a chilled salad bowl, arranging the sprigs of herbs on top. Pour the vinaigrette over and toss gently with the greens. Correct the seasoning, adding a little more lime juice, sea salt or freshly ground pepper if necessary. Serve on individual salad plates.

Serves 4

Ballon Rouge's Franschhoek Farm Salad

The Ballon Rouge Restaurant in the sleepy wine village of Franschhoek, near Cape Town, serves a delicious salad of crisp leaves and lightly poached and raw vegetables.

For the Salad Leaves
12 small frilly Red Leaf lettuce
   leaves
12 small crinkly Green Leaf
   lettuce leaves
12 baby arugula leaves
4 butterhead lettuce hearts
4 red Oak Leaf lettuce hearts

For the Baby Vegetables
12 julienne strips of carrot
12 julienne strips of yellow
   zucchini
12 julienne strips of green
   zucchini

For the Dressing
4 tablespoons balsamic vinegar
2 teaspoons Dijon mustard
1 teaspoon granulated sugar
8 tablespoons extra virgin
   olive oil
2–4 tablespoons finely
   chopped fresh chives
salt and freshly ground pepper
crushed dried chiles

For the Garnish
orange, red and yellow cherry
   tomatoes
12 x 7.5cm/3in segments
   scallion
borage flowers
sprigs of fresh red basil
sprigs of fresh green basil

To Prepare the Leaves: Wash the salad leaves and lettuce hearts in cold water. Shake or spin dry. Wrap loosely in a dish towel and chill in the refrigerator.

To Prepare the Baby Vegetables: Poach the vegetable strips in lightly salted water until just crisp-tender. Drain and chill.

To Prepare the Dressing: In a small bowl, combine the balsamic vinegar, Dijon mustard and sugar and mix well. Whisk in the olive oil and finely chopped chives, and season to taste with salt, freshly ground pepper and crushed dried chiles.

To Assemble and Serve the Salad: Toss the salad leaves and baby vegetables in the dressing and arrange the leaves and vegetables on chilled individual salad plates. Top each salad with lettuce hearts and garnish with cherry tomatoes, scallion segments, borage flowers and sprigs of red and green basil. Spoon over the remaining dressing and serve immediately.

Serves 4

Caesar Salad

A Caesar salad with a difference – Parmesan-crisped fingers of focaccia with long romaine lettuce leaves and thin strips of anchovy in a special Caesar dressing made (in the classic manner) using free-range organic eggs. If you are not sure of the source of your eggs, make a lightly flavoured garlic mayonnaise, thickened with chopped hard-boiled egg, instead. Both versions are delicious.

2 heads of romaine lettuce
12 thin strips of focaccia bread
extra virgin olive oil
8 tablespoons freshly grated
   Parmesan cheese, of which 4
   are lightly flavoured with
   paprika
6 anchovy filets in oil, drained
   and halved lengthways
freshly ground pepper

For the Classic Caesar Dressing
juice of 1½ lemons
2 tablespoons garlic oil (slice
   1 clove garlic into a little
   olive oil and leave for
   2 hours, then remove the
   garlic)
1½ teaspoons Worcestershire
   sauce
6 tablespoons vinaigrette
   (page 20)
1 free-range organic egg

To Prepare the Lettuce: Wash, dry and break the romaine lettuce leaves into fairly big pieces. Wrap in a clean dish towel and chill in the refrigerator until ready to serve.

To Prepare the Focaccia Strips: Preheat the oven to 190°C/375°F. Brush the focaccia strips with extra virgin olive oil and dust with the paprika-flavoured Parmesan, then place in the hot oven and bake for 3 minutes or until crisp and golden brown. Reserve.

To Prepare the Classic Caesar Dressing: In a medium-sized bowl, combine the lemon juice, garlic oil, Worcestershire sauce and vinaigrette.

Immerse the egg (with its shell) in barely simmering water for 3 minutes. Immediately the time is up, lift the egg out of the water with a slotted spoon. Break the egg in half over the dressing and scoop out the runny yolk and almost runny white into the bowl with a spoon. Whisk the soft-cooked egg into the sauce until well blended.

To Serve: Place the salad greens in a large salad bowl. Pour over the salad dressing and toss until each leaf is coated and there is no dressing left in the bottom of the bowl. Add the Parmesan-crisped focaccia strips and the anchovy strips. Sprinkle with freshly ground pepper and freshly grated Parmesan cheese and serve immediately.

Note: The consumption of raw or partly cooked eggs can carry a risk of salmonella, particularly for pregnant women, very young children and the elderly.

Serves 6

Paella Salad

Chilled paella salad is an innovative twist on a traditional Spanish favourite. It has all the ingredients of a classic paella, but is served cold, with a garlicky vinaigrette dressing.

For the Rice
225g/8oz arborio rice
1.2 litres/40fl oz boiling salted water
1 generous pinch saffron threads
¼ teaspoon ground turmeric
1 chicken stock cube

For the Shellfish
24–36 mussels (or raw tiger prawns)
150ml/5fl oz water
150ml/5fl oz white wine
½ onion, finely chopped
½ teaspoon dried thyme

For the Garnish
1 red and 1 yellow pepper, cut into julienne strips
12 thin slices chorizo, sautéed in 25g/1oz butter
2 tablespoons finely chopped fresh flat-leaf parsley

For the Vinaigrette
½ Spanish onion, finely chopped
1–2 cloves garlic, finely chopped
2 tablespoons wine vinegar
6 tablespoons olive oil
salt and freshly ground pepper
crushed dried chiles

To Prepare the Rice: Cook the rice in the boiling salted water with the saffron, turmeric and chicken stock cube until tender, but still firm: about 15 minutes. Drain thoroughly, reserving 300ml/10fl oz liquid, and allow the rice to cool.

To Prepare the Shellfish: Scrape, beard and wash the mussels. Place in a heavy saucepan with the water, white wine, chopped onion and dried thyme. Cover the pan and steam for 3 to 5 minutes over a high heat, shaking the pan frequently, until the mussels have opened. Discard any mussels that do not open.

Remove the mussels from the pan, shaking back any liquid trapped in their shells. Reserve the liquid in the pan. Allow the mussels to cool and then remove from their shells.

If using tiger prawns, cook them in the mixture of water, dry white wine, chopped onion and dried thyme for 3 to 5 minutes. Remove them, reserving the liquid. When cool enough to handle, peel the prawns.

To Finish the Paella: Filter the liquid from the mussel pan (or prawns) through a sieve lined with fine muslin or filter paper and then return to the rinsed-out pan. Add the red and yellow pepper strips and saffron rice liquid and simmer for 5 minutes.

In a large salad bowl, combine the rice and mussels (or prawns). Add the pepper strips and pan juices to the bowl, together with the slices of chorizo and finely chopped parsley. Cool.

To Serve: Blend the vinaigrette ingredients in a bowl, beating with a fork until they form an emulsion. Pour over the salad, toss lightly and chill before serving.

Serves 4

New York Salad I

I like this creamy Roquefort-flavoured dressing with its garnish of chopped hard-boiled eggs, crisp-fried crunchy bacon and chopped chives. Use this dressing, too, for a plum tomato side salad to accompany grilled fish or steak.

2 romaine lettuces
6–8 tablespoons olive oil
2 tablespoons vinegar
2 tablespoons heavy cream
2 tablespoons Roquefort cheese, crumbled
freshly ground pepper
Tabasco sauce
2 hard-boiled eggs, finely chopped
2 thick slices crisp-cooked bacon, crumbled
4-6 tablespoons of fresh chives, cut into even-sized snippets

To Prepare the Lettuces: Wash the lettuces and shake dry in a salad spinner, or dry each leaf carefully in a dish towel. Wrap in a dry dish towel and allow to crisp in the refrigerator until ready to use.

To Make the Dressing: Combine the olive oil and vinegar (3 to 4 parts olive oil to 1 part vinegar), add the cream and crumbled Roquefort cheese, and whisk until smooth. Add freshly ground pepper and Tabasco to taste, and stir in half the chopped hard-boiled egg, bacon and chive snippets.

To Serve: Arrange the lettuce in a salad bowl. Pour the dressing over and toss the salad until each leaf is glistening. Garnish with the remaining chopped egg, bacon and chives, and serve.

Serves 4 to 6

New York Salad II

Tender young spinach leaves make a crisp salad with a New York touch when teamed with sliced ripe avocado, quartered hard-boiled eggs and delicate red onion rings.

450g/1lb young spinach leaves
6–8 tablespoons olive oil
1–3 teaspoons vinegar
2 tablespoons fresh lime juice
1 clove garlic, finely chopped
2 tablespoons finely chopped fresh flat-leaf parsley
salt and freshly ground pepper
crushed dried chiles

For the Garnish
1 ripe avocado
2 hard-boiled eggs, quartered
1 small red onion, thinly sliced

To Prepare the Leaves: Wash the spinach leaves in cold water. Cut off the stems, drain and chill until ready to use.

To Prepare the Dressing: Combine the olive oil and vinegar, to taste, with the lime juice and finely chopped garlic and parsley. Season with salt, freshly ground pepper and crushed dried chiles.

To Serve: Halve, pit, peel and slice the avocado. Arrange the chilled spinach leaves in a salad bowl. Pour over the dressing and toss until each leaf glistens. Taste and correct the seasoning of the salad, then garnish with the sliced avocado, quartered hard-boiled egg and onion rings, and serve immediately.

Serves 4 to 6

Nine Herb Salad

This salad – a herb salad to end all herb salads – was the pride of my eighteenth-century kitchen garden at Hintlesham Hall in Suffolk. I still serve it – garden fresh – for really special occasions.

1 romaine lettuce and
  1 extra romaine lettuce
  heart
12–18 sprigs of mâche
12 sprigs of fresh tarragon
  (about 2.5cm/1in long)
12 sprigs of fresh basil
  (about 2.5cm/1in long)
12 sprigs of fresh purple basil
  (about 2.5cm/1in long)
12 sprigs of purslane
  (about 2.5cm/1in long)
12 sprigs of arugula
  (about 2.5cm/1in long)
12 sprigs of fresh flat-leaf
  parsley (about 2.5cm/1in
  long)

For the Mustard Vinaigrette
2 tablespoons lime juice
1 tablespoon Dijon mustard
6–8 tablespoons extra virgin
  olive oil
salt and freshly ground pepper
crushed dried chiles

For the Garnish
coarsely chopped fresh herb
  fennel
coarsely chopped fresh chives
coarsely chopped fresh
  flat-leaf parsley

To Prepare the Lettuces and Herbs: Wash the romaine lettuce and lettuce heart. Wash the mâche sprigs carefully, removing the root ends. Shake the lettuces and mâche sprigs dry in a salad basket, or dry carefully with kitchen paper. Wrap in a clean dish towel and chill.

Arrange the lettuces, mâche sprigs and tarragon, basil, purple basil, purslane, arugula and flat-leaf parsley sprigs in a salad bowl.

To Make the Vinaigrette: Combine the lime juice and the mustard. Add the olive oil, then season to taste with salt, freshly ground pepper and chiles. Beat or shake until the mixture emulsifies.

To Serve: Pour the dressing over the salad ingredients, add the fennel, chives and parsley and toss until all the ingredients glisten. Serve at once.

Serves 4 to 6

Truffled Chicken Salad

This truffled chicken appetizer, with its hidden cargo of finely shredded lettuce and diced tuna, requires finely chopped black truffles for its full impact, as I used to serve it at my Islington restaurant, Carrier's. It can be made with bottled black truffles from a supermarket, flavoured with truffle oil from an Italian delicatessen, or with French canned black truffles in their own juice (from a French delicatessen).

Substitute a julienne of lightly poached celeriac for the chicken in this recipe and it becomes a delicious foil for cold roast duck, goose or pork.

4–6 tablespoons mayonnaise
truffle juice, or truffle oil and
    lime juice
salt, celery salt and freshly
    ground pepper
2 tablespoons finely chopped
    black truffles
1 lettuce, finely shredded
450g/1lb cooked chicken
    breast meat, sliced into thin
    strips
3 hard-boiled eggs, finely
    chopped
4 sticks celery, diced
1 200g/7oz can tuna fish,
    drained and flaked

For the Garnish
finely chopped fresh flat-leaf
    parsley
bitter leaves: arugula, mâche,
    frisée and watercress, tossed
    with a little truffle oil and
    lime juice

To Prepare the Salad: Thin the mayonnaise with juice from a small can of black truffles (if you are using them) or truffle oil and lime juice (if using dry-packed truffles). Season to taste with salt, celery salt and freshly ground pepper. Add the finely chopped black truffles. Combine the sauce with the shredded lettuce, strips of cooked chicken breast, chopped eggs and diced celery and tuna fish. Mix well. Add more mayonnaise and seasoning if desired. Chill.

To Serve: Arrange the salad in a mound on individual salad plates. Sprinkle with finely chopped parsley and garnish each plate with a cordon of bitter leaves (arugula, mâche, frisée and watercress) tossed in a little truffle oil and lime juice. Serve immediately.

Serves 4 to 6

Green Papaya Salad with Rockpool's Famous Nam Jim Dressing

The first time I dined at Neil Perry's Rockpool Restaurant overlooking Sydney Harbour, I was bowled over by the flavours of a green papaya and braised pork hock salad, garnished with slivered Vietnamese mint and Thai basil and tossed in a fabulous salad dressing in which palm sugar, fresh lime juice, Thai fish sauce and thinly sliced green chiles played their amazingly subtle parts. Since then I have met this same sauce – sweet, sour, salt and hot – used to enhance barbecued squid, seared sea scallops and even pan-seared oysters. Try it with this crisp Pacific Rim salad of green papayas or mangoes (you can buy them in Asian and Chinese food shops, and often in supermarkets – papaya is also called pawpaw), cucumber and fresh bean sprouts, garnished with shredded coriander and mint leaves and crushed roasted peanuts. Rockpool's Nam Jim sauce is one of the great flavourings of the Pacific Rim cuisine. Make it your own. (Illustrated on page 71, at the top.)

2 small green papayas or green mangoes, or a combination of the two, peeled and cut into fine julienne strips

⅓ unpeeled cucumber, seeded and cut into fine julienne strips

100g/3½oz bean sprouts, trimmed

3 cloves garlic, sliced and fried in oil until crisp and golden

3 tablespoons fresh coriander, leaves shredded

3 tablespoons fresh mint, leaves shredded

4 tablespoons peanuts, roasted and lightly crushed

For the Nam Jim Dressing
2 cloves garlic
2 coriander roots, or 6 stems
1 teaspoon sea salt
4–6 small fresh green chiles
2 tablespoons palm sugar
3 tablespoons Thai fish sauce
6 tablespoons fresh lime juice
4 shallots, thinly sliced

To Prepare the Salad: In a large salad bowl, combine the thin strips of papaya and/or mango, cucumber, bean sprouts and crisp-fried garlic. Chill.

To Prepare the Nam Jim Dressing: Place the garlic, coriander roots (or, failing that, the coriander stems) and sea salt in a mortar and pound until well crushed. Do not reduce to a paste. Add the green chiles and crush lightly. If you crush too much at this stage, the sauce will get hotter, so be careful. Mix in the palm sugar, fish sauce, lime juice and thinly sliced shallots. According to Neil Perry, if you leave the Nam Jim to sit for a while, the flavour intensifies.

To Serve: Remove the salad from the refrigerator. Pour the dressing over it and toss well. Garnish with the shredded coriander and mint and the crushed roasted peanuts, then toss lightly once more. Serve immediately.

Serves 4 to 6

Great Soups

Paul Bocuse's Soupe aux Truffes Elysées

This recipe for truffled chicken soup is a show-stopper. Created for French president Valéry Giscard d'Estaing, Bocuse served it at a luncheon given at the Elysées Palace when he was awarded the prestigious Cross of the Legion of Honour as ambassador of French gastronomy. The soup, with its ballooning puff-pastry crust, created an immediate sensation with the world press. It has become one of the great classic inventions of our time.

2 teaspoons each diced carrots, celery and mushrooms, softened in butter

50g/2oz fresh black truffles, thinly sliced

20g/¾oz pâté de foie gras, diced

240ml/8fl oz well-flavoured rich chicken consommé

50–75g/2–3oz flaky pastry (page 251)

1 egg yolk, beaten

To Prepare the Soup Ingredients: Combine the diced simmered vegetables, thinly sliced truffle and diced pâté de foie gras in an individual heatproof porcelain soup bowl (the kind called *gratinée lyonnaise*), or a 250g/8oz soufflé mold, or any heatproof bowl with a 10cm/4in diameter. Pour in the rich chicken consommé.

To Prepare the Pastry: Roll the flaky pastry into a round large enough to fit over the soup bowl, allowing for an overlap of 2cm/¾in all round. Brush the edges with beaten egg yolk and fix the pastry, brushed side down, on to the rim by pinching it. Chill in the refrigerator for 30 minutes.

To Bake and Serve: Preheat the oven to 200°C/400°F.

Brush the top of the pastry with egg yolk and bake in the center of the preheated oven for 10 minutes, or until the pastry has risen into a dome. Lower the heat to 190°C/375°F and bake for a further 12 minutes, or until golden brown.

The pastry dome is dramatic, but it is also practical – it holds in the flavour and heat of the soup. As you break the dome with a spoon at the table, an aromatic puff of steam arouses your tastebuds and sets your gastric juices flowing. But be gentle as you break the crust open – the pieces of feather-light pastry will drop into the soup, adding flavour and texture.

Serves 1 (repeat 3 more times to serve 4)

Mediterranean Fish Soup with Rouille

Along the southern reaches of Provence – from Marseilles to Monte Carlo – fish soup reigns supreme. I give you here a classic recipe for one of the best *soupes de poissons* to be found along the coast. But remember: unless you are lucky enough to be preparing your soup on the shores of the Mediterranean, many of the little fishes that give the soup its unique savour will not be available. I suggest that you use a combination of pieces of small rouget (red mullet), red snapper and sea bass (cleaned but complete with heads and bones – they give the flavour), plus a small crab and a slice or two of eel to capture some of the warmth and flavour of Provence. (Illustrated on page 83.)

8–12 tablespoons olive oil (2 tablespoons per person)
2 Spanish onions, sliced
2–3 cloves garlic, chopped
6 ripe tomatoes, seeded and coarsely chopped
1 bouquet garni (parsley, thyme, rosemary, dried fennel)
1 bay leaf
1.2kg/2½ lb small fish, small crab and eel (see introduction), cleaned and scaled if necessary, roughly sliced if large
1.5 litres/50fl oz salted water
1 generous pinch saffron threads
½ teaspoon crushed dried chiles

To Serve
freshly grated cheese, such as Gruyère
stale French bread, rubbed with garlic
rouille (page 14)

To Prepare the Soup: Heat the olive oil in a large heatproof casserole, and sauté the sliced onions in the oil until transparent. Add the garlic, chopped tomatoes, bouquet garni and bay leaf, and simmer, stirring frequently, until slightly reduced. Add the fish, small crab and eel and continue to cook, stirring constantly, until the fish are soft.

Add the salted water, saffron threads and crushed dried chiles, and bring to the boil, skimming off the froth. Cook over a fairly high heat for 20 minutes. Strain into a clean saucepan, pressing all the fish and vegetable juices through the sieve back into the soup.

To Serve: Reheat the soup and serve it in large soup bowls, accompanied by bowls of freshly grated cheese, rounds of stale French bread rubbed with garlic, and rouille.

Serves 4 to 6

Gordon Ramsay's Cappuccino of Haricots Blancs with Morels

Another great creation – nearer home this time – is Gordon Ramsay's witty 'cappuccino' made of an unbelievably airy froth of white beans scented with truffle oil. Secret touch: cooked wild and cultivated mushrooms and white beans lurking in its depths. If you follow this recipe, and the one on page 84 for truffled soup, to the letter, you'll be the best cook on the block.

A Bamix gives you a superb froth, but in the absence of one of these you can use a hand-held blender instead. I did for the photograph.

800g/1¾ lb small dried white
   haricot or navy beans,
   soaked overnight
salt
1 small onion
1 carrot
1 fresh bouquet garni
   (fresh thyme, flat-leaf
   parsley and rosemary)
400ml/14fl oz well-flavoured
   vegetable stock
150ml/5fl oz heavy cream
trickle of truffle oil
sea salt and freshly ground
   pepper
pat of ice-cold butter

For the Garnish
100g/4oz fresh morels, or
   other wild mushrooms,
   sliced if large
50g/2oz butter
1–2 teaspoons truffle oil

To Prepare the Beans: Drain the soaked beans, put in a saucepan and cover with lightly salted water. Add the onion, carrot and bouquet garni and bring to the boil. Boil for 10 minutes, then lower to a simmer and cook for about 25 to 30 minutes until soft. Using a slotted spoon, remove about 100g/4oz of the beans and reserve as garnish. Continue cooking the remainder for a further 10 minutes until very soft.

Drain and discard the onion, carrot and bouquet garni. Blend the beans in a blender or food processor to a fine purée. (At Gordon Ramsay's Aubergine restaurant in London, for absolute perfection they rub the purée through a sieve with the back of a ladle.)

Clean the saucepan and add the vegetable stock. Bring to the boil and cook to reduce for 5 minutes.

To Prepare the Garnish: Sauté the morels (or other wild mushrooms) in the butter until just cooked, then stir in a little truffle oil. Set aside with the reserved beans.

To Finish the Soup: Using a Bamix or hand-held blender, mix the reduced stock into the bean purée until it is smooth, then whisk in the cream and a trickle of truffle oil. Add sea salt and freshly ground pepper to taste.

To Serve: Divide the reserved beans and morels among 6 warmed soup bowls or large breakfast coffee cups. Check the seasoning of the soup, then reheat to boiling. Using the Bamix again, whisk in a pat of ice-cold butter and froth up. Spoon the 'cappuccino' froth over the beans and morels. Serve immediately.

Serves 6

Oyster and Spinach Bisque with Red Caviar

This is a special-occasion recipe. The bisque can be prepared the day before and chilled until ready to serve. The garnish of poached oysters and little spinach 'oysters' can then be heated in a few tablespoons of fish stock just before serving.

75g/3oz butter
1 Spanish onion, coarsely
    chopped
1 stick celery, coarsely chopped
1 carrot, coarsely chopped
4 sprigs of fresh parsley,
    coarsely chopped
4 tablespoons flour
850ml/30fl oz hot fish stock
6 oysters
2 tablespoons dry white wine
175g/6oz spinach leaves
350ml/12fl oz heavy cream
½ lemon
salt and freshly ground pepper
50g/2oz red caviar (not red
    lumpfish roe)
cayenne pepper (optional)

To Prepare the Bisque: Melt 50g/2oz of the butter in a thick-bottomed saucepan and gently sauté the chopped onion, celery, carrot and parsley until the vegetables are soft, but not coloured.

Add the flour and cook for 2 to 3 minutes, stirring continuously. Pour in a little hot fish stock and stir until blended, then add the remaining stock. Simmer, stirring from time to time, until smooth and well blended. Pour the bisque through a fine sieve into a large bowl, pressing the vegetables with a wooden spoon to release their flavour. Allow the strained bisque to cool, then refrigerate.

To Prepare the Oysters: Remove the oysters from their shells over a thick-based pan (a small enamelled cast-iron frying pan is good for this) to catch any juices. Reserve the shells for the garnish. Add the oysters to the pan, together with the dry white wine. Simmer the oysters for 1 minute only, them remove them from the pan with a slotted spoon and keep warm. Reserve the cooking liquid.

To Prepare the Spinach 'Oysters': Melt the remaining butter and turn the spinach in it until the leaves wilt. Make 12 parcels the size of the oysters by folding the leaves inwards to resemble green oysters. Brush each parcel with a little melted butter and keep warm.

To Prepare the Oyster Shell Garnish: Scrub the outsides of 6 oyster half-shells with a stiff brush. Whip 120ml/4fl oz of the heavy cream until thick. Season to taste with a squeeze of lemon juice and with salt and freshly ground pepper. Whip again to blend the flavours. Place 1 to 2 tablespoons of flavoured whipped cream in each oyster half-shell and top with a little red caviar.

To Finish and Serve: Add the remaining heavy cream to the bisque, pour into a heavy saucepan and bring just to the boil. Add the reserved liquid from the oysters and correct the seasoning, adding lemon juice, salt and freshly ground pepper or cayenne.

Place 1 poached oyster in each of 6 heated shallow soup bowls. Pour in the hot bisque and place 2 spinach parcels in each bowl. Just before the guests are called to the table, put 1 cream-and-caviar-filled oyster half-shell in each bowl as a garnish.

Serves 6

Italian Leek and Pumpkin Soup

Pumpkin is one of the great new ingredients, and this leek and pumpkin soup created by Roman chef/proprietor Vernon Jarrett shows pumpkin off at its best. Try it. It's a revelation.

50g/2oz butter
1 Spanish onion, chopped
450g/1lb peeled pumpkin
  flesh, diced
225g/8oz potatoes, diced
100g/4oz fresh broad beans,
  shelled
600ml/20fl oz milk
salt
cayenne pepper
100g/4oz leeks
600ml/20fl oz hot chicken stock
150ml/5fl oz heavy cream
100g/4oz steamed white rice
2–3 tablespoons chopped fresh
  chervil or flat-leaf parsley

To Prepare the Soup: Melt half the butter in a large saucepan and cook the chopped onion gently until golden.

Add the diced pumpkin, potatoes, beans and milk to the pan and bring to the boil. Reduce the heat and simmer for 45 minutes, stirring from time to time to prevent scorching, adding a little more milk if the mixture becomes too dry.

To Finish the Soup: Sieve the soup into a clean saucepan, pressing the vegetables through with a wooden spoon or passing them through a food mill. Season to taste with salt and cayenne pepper.

Cut the leeks into fine strips and cook in the remaining butter. Add half the leeks to the soup, along with the chicken stock, and bring slowly to the boil.

To Serve: Stir in the heavy cream, steamed white rice and chopped chervil or parsley. Heat through then transfer to a heated soup tureen, or individual serving bowls, and garnish with the remaining leek strips. Serve immediately.

Serves 4 to 6

Italian Mama's Comfort Soup

Ask any Italian man whom he loves most in the world and he'll tell you: his Mama. And this is why. A wonderfully comforting soup that includes a lot of love in the recipe as well as homemade chicken soup and pumpkin-filled tortellini. Of course you can use commercial tortellini. But Mama wouldn't.

Tortellini means 'navel'. You get the message I'm sure. Fat and firm little circles of pasta dough, filled on one side with a cheese-flavoured vegetable or meat filling, folded over like a tiny savoury apple turnover, and twisted around your finger into a perfect little ring. Or navel.

**1.5 litres/50fl oz rich
chicken stock or consommé**
**225g/8oz fresh spinach,
carefully washed, tough
stems removed**
**6–8 tablespoons freshly grated
Parmesan cheese**
freshly ground pepper

For the Fresh Pasta Dough
8 egg yolks
2 whole eggs
4 tablespoons olive oil
2 teaspoons salt
8 tablespoons cold water
450g/1lb flour

For the Tortellini Filling
**225g/8oz cooked pumpkin
flesh (or yellow-fleshed
sweet potato), peeled and
diced**
200ml/7fl oz heavy cream
1 egg yolk
2 tablespoons truffle oil
salt and crushed dried chiles

To Make the Pasta Dough: In the bowl of a food processor, combine the ingredients for the pasta dough and process, in short bursts at first, and then in a continuous buzz, until a smooth dough is formed.

Roll out the dough as thin as possible (or put it through a pasta machine at the thinnest cut). Stamp out at least 12 rounds, 6.5cm/2½in in diameter. Cover with a damp dish towel and reserve.

To Prepare the Tortellini Filling: In the bowl of a food processor, combine the cooked pumpkin flesh (or sweet potato) and the heavy cream and blend to a smooth purée. Add the egg yolk and truffle oil, season to taste with salt and crushed dried chiles, and process again. Transfer to a bowl and, if necessary, allow to cool.

To Make and Cook the Tortellini: Spoon a teaspoon of filling on to each pastry round, a little off-center. Fold one side of the circle over the filling (like an apple turnover) and press around the edges to seal. Wrap the straight side around your finger to form a circle, joining the edges together. Repeat until all the pasta and filling is used up. (If you make more than 12, keep the extra in the refrigerator for use at another meal. Best within 3 days.)

Cook the stuffed fresh pasta in boiling salted water for 3 minutes. Drain and reserve to warm up in the soup.

To Serve: Pour the stock or consommé into a saucepan and bring to the boil over a medium heat. Add the spinach leaves and pasta and bring back to the boil. Serve immediately with the freshly grated Parmesan and freshly ground pepper.

Serves 4 to 6

Pea and Sorrel Soup

A pale green purée of peas, garnished just before serving with fine strips of cooked cucumber, sorrel and peas, makes a lovely beginning to an elegant meal.

50g/2oz butter
675g/1½lb frozen peas,
    defrosted
1.2 litres/40fl oz chicken stock
1 cucumber, peeled
2 large egg yolks
150ml/5fl oz heavy cream
2 teaspoons lemon juice
salt and freshly ground pepper
cayenne pepper
6–8 sorrel leaves, stalks
    removed, cut into narrow
    strips

To Prepare the Peas: Melt half the butter in a medium-sized saucepan and add the frozen peas and 2 tablespoons of the chicken stock. Cover and cook the peas, stirring occasionally, until just tender.

Reserve one third of the peas for the garnish. Purée the remainder in a blender with half of the remaining stock. Press the purée through a sieve with a wooden spoon into a bowl.

To Prepare the Cucumber Garnish: Cut the peeled cucumber into 4cm/1½in lengths. Halve them and remove the seeds. Then cut the flesh into small sticks. In a small pan, simmer these cucumber sticks in the remaining butter for about 3 minutes or until tender. Remove with a slotted spoon and reserve.

To Make the Soup: Beat the egg yolks with the heavy cream. Mix well and add to the pea purée.

Bring the remaining stock to the boil, remove from the heat and stir in the creamy pea purée. Return to the heat and cook gently, stirring continuously, until the soup is smooth and thick. Do not let it come to the boil or it will curdle.

To Serve: Add the lemon juice and salt, freshly ground pepper and a little cayenne pepper to taste. Garnish with the reserved peas, cucumber sticks and strips of sorrel leaves. Serve immediately.

Serves 4

Saffron Soup with Fresh Herbs

Years ago, when I owned Carrier's in Islington and Hintlesham Hall in Suffolk, hot saffron soup with caviar was one of our winter standbys. And the same soup, served chilled with a lemon 'float' of crème fraîche topped with bright green chopped herbs, was a summer favourite. Gunther Schlender, who was my head chef at Carrier's for many years, now owns his own restaurant, Mansfield's in the delightful little town of Cuckfield, West Sussex. His lighter version of this Carrier classic is worth a visit on its own. (The chilled soup is illustrated on page 82.)

450g/1lb leeks, coarsely chopped
225g/8oz potatoes, peeled and coarsely chopped
50g/2oz butter
1.2 litres/40fl oz chicken stock
pinch of saffron threads
4 tablespoons dry white wine
salt and freshly ground pepper
150ml/5fl oz crème fraîche

For the Fresh Herb Garnish
2 tablespoons finely chopped fresh parsley and chives, or fresh tarragon
4–6 very thin lemon slices
2–3 tablespoons crème fraîche

For the Black Caviar Garnish
2 tablespoons black caviar, not lumpfish roe
4–6 very thin lemon slices
2–3 tablespoons crème fraîche

To Prepare the Soup: Sauté the coarsely chopped leeks and potatoes in a large pan with the butter. Then add the chicken stock and a pinch of saffron threads and simmer gently, uncovered, until the vegetables are soft.

Leave the soup mixture to cool a little, then purée it in a blender or food processor. Rub the mixture with a wooden spoon through a sieve into a large bowl and return to the rinsed-out pan. Stir in the remaining saffron threads, which you have warmed through in the dry white wine, season to taste with salt and freshly ground pepper and heat through gently. Remove the pan from the heat and reserve.

To Serve Chilled: Allow the soup to cool, then strain it into a bowl. stir in the crème fraîche and chill in the refrigerator. Before serving, pour the chilled soup into bowls and garnish each serving with a lemon slice topped with crème fraîche and sprinkled with chopped fresh herbs.

To Serve Hot: Stir in the crème fraîche and heat through gently. Pour into heated bowls and garnish each serving with a lemon slice topped with crème fraîche and sprinkled with black caviar.

Serves 4 to 6

Seafood Laksa

Malaysian in origin, Australian by choice, laksa, whether based on seafood or chicken, or even vegetarian, is a prime example of the new food coming to us from down under. Malaysian shrimp paste – highly pungent and, I am afraid, mighty smelly until cooked – is available from Asian food shops. If at first you are in doubt, substitute 1 or 2 mashed anchovies to add punch to this delicious soup and noodle meal.

For the Laksa Paste
1 teaspoon each finely chopped garlic, fresh ginger, lemon grass and coriander root
2 fresh red chiles, finely chopped
1 teaspoon shrimp paste
½ teaspoon ground turmeric
2–3 tablespoons vegetable oil

For the Noodle Soup Base
4 tablespoons vegetable oil
½ Spanish onion, finely chopped
24 fresh mussels, scrubbed and bearded
6 tablespoons dry white wine
12 raw tiger prawns, peeled and deveined
2 kaffir lime leaves, thinly sliced (or the finely grated zest of 1 lime)
600ml/20fl oz vegetable stock (or fish stock)
300ml/10fl oz coconut milk
350g/12oz fresh Chinese egg noodles
1–2 teaspoons soy sauce
1–2 teaspoons Thai fish sauce

For the Garnish
fresh coriander leaves
2 scallions, green parts only, finely sliced, or a handful of fresh bean sprouts

To Prepare the Aromatic Laksa Paste: For the best flavour, place all the ingredients in a mortar and, using a pestle, pound to a smooth paste. Or blend in a food processor. Reserve.

To Prepare the Noodle Soup Base: In a large saucepan, heat 2 tablespoons of vegetable oil and add the finely chopped onion, the mussels and the dry white wine. Cover the pan and cook for 2 to 3 minutes, or until the mussels open. Remove the saucepan from the heat. With a slotted spoon, transfer the mussels to a plate and reserve (discard any that do not open). Keep the mussel juices in the saucepan for later use.

In a frying pan, sauté the laksa paste in the remaining vegetable oil until fragrant. Add the prawns and lime leaves (or grated lime zest) and sauté for 1 minute more. With a slotted spoon, transfer the prawns to the dish with the mussels. Reserve.

Add half the vegetable stock (or fish stock) to the juices and aromatics in the frying pan; stir well and bring to the boil. Then transfer the contents of the frying pan to the saucepan in which you cooked the mussels. Add the remaining stock and the coconut milk and simmer over a low heat, stirring constantly, until the soup is smooth and heated through.

To Prepare the Chinese Egg Noodles: Place the noodles in a bowl, add enough boiling water to cover and leave until the noodles soften, then drain and rinse under cold water.

When Ready to Serve: Add the drained noodles to the soup and heat through. Season the soup with soy sauce and Thai fish sauce, to taste. Top with the reserved mussels and prawns, garnish with coriander and scallions or bean sprouts, and serve immediately.

Serves 4

Note: A delicious chicken laksa can be prepared in the same way: substitute thin strips of cooked chicken breast for the seafood, use vegetable or chicken stock and proceed as above.

Moroccan Harira with Kefta

Harira – a subtle mix of lamb broth, lamb, lentils, chickpeas, chopped tomatoes, onion, garlic, fresh herbs and spices, thickened at the last minute with a little flour, or beaten eggs – is the traditional 'breakfast' soup of Ramadan: warming, fortifying and inexpensive. In Morocco today it is often served, in a lighter version, as a much-loved first course for evening meals – or as a supper on its own, with a squeeze of fresh lemon juice added by each guest to his own portion at the table. This version uses small spicy minced lamb balls called kefta instead of the classic diced lamb.

For the Kefta Balls
350g/12oz minced lamb
salt and freshly ground pepper
crushed dried chiles

For the Harira Broth
1–2 scallions, cut into
    6mm/¼in segments
1 stick celery, with leaves, cut
    into 6mm/¼in segments
1 Spanish onion, coarsely
    grated
175g/6oz lentils
100g/4oz dried chickpeas *and*
    175g/6oz dried broad beans,
    soaked overnight and
    drained
1 generous pinch saffron
    threads
1 litre/35fl oz water
salt and freshly ground pepper
4 tablespoons olive oil
2 tablespoons flour
3 tablespoons each chopped
    fresh coriander and flat-leaf
    parsley
4 large, ripe tomatoes, skinned
    and finely chopped
½ preserved lemon (page 10)
    peel only, diced
lemon quarters

For the Rice
850ml/30fl oz water
50g/2oz rice
salt

To Prepare the Kefta Balls: Season the minced lamb to taste with salt, freshly ground pepper and crushed dried chiles. Mix well. Roll the lamb into small balls 1cm/½in in diameter. Poach in a little boiling water for 5 minutes, then drain and reserve.

To Prepare the Harira Broth: In a large saucepan or casserole, combine all the ingredients up to and including the water. Season with salt and freshly ground pepper to taste.

Bring to the boil, skimming all the froth from the surface as the water begins to bubble, then add the olive oil. Turn down the heat and simmer, covered, for 1 hour, adding a little water if necessary.

To Prepare the Rice: Bring the water to the boil in a saucepan and add the rice with salt to taste. Cover, and cook the rice until tender but not mushy: it will not absorb all the water. Drain the cooked rice, reserving the liquid, and add the rice to the broth.

To Finish and Serve the Soup: Combine the flour with 150ml/5fl oz of the reserved rice liquid, then pour into a small saucepan. Stir in the fresh herbs, chopped tomatoes and diced preserved lemon peel. Simmer, stirring from time to time, for 15 minutes, until the flour is cooked. Stir into the soup. Add the kefta balls and heat through. Taste and correct the seasoning.

Serve the soup immediately with lemon quarters. Guests squeeze a little lemon juice, to taste, into each serving.

Serves 6

David Wilson's Vegetable and Herb Broth with Lobster and Prawns

David Wilson, chef-proprietor of the Peat Inn in Fife, Scotland, is a shy man with unbounded talent. His tiny restaurant was one of the most interesting stop-offs on my signature-recipe tour of the British Isles for Granada Television. His recipe for vegetable and herb broth is a mouth-tingling winner, with or without the lobster and prawns.

1 450g/1lb freshly cooked lobster, meat removed from shells and brought to room temperature
6 small langoustines, or tiger prawns, cooked, shelled and brought to room temperature

For the Broth
2–3 tablespoons olive oil
1 tablespoon finely chopped shallots
1 clove garlic, finely chopped
1 teaspoon chopped fresh thyme
1 bay leaf
25g/1oz chopped carrot
25g/1oz chopped fennel
25g/1oz chopped celery
25g/1oz chopped leek, white part only
50g/2oz unsalted butter, diced
25g/1oz pearl barley
2 tablespoons crème fraîche
1 teaspoon tomato paste
1 litre/35fl oz vegetable stock
1 tablespoon finely chopped fresh tarragon
1 tablespoon finely chopped fresh basil
1 tablespoon finely chopped fresh chervil or flat-leaf parsley
salt and freshly ground pepper

To Prepare the Broth: Warm the olive oil in a large frying pan over a low heat. Add the finely chopped shallots and garlic and cook for 3 to 4 minutes or until soft. Stir in the thyme and bay leaf, and add the chopped carrot, fennel, celery and leek, along with the butter. Cook, stirring occasionally, until the vegetables 'sweat' and soften.

Stir in the barley, crème fraîche and tomato paste, and combine well. Then pour in the vegetable stock and add half the quantity of fresh herbs. Bring to the boil, reduce the heat and simmer for about 20 minutes or until the vegetables are tender. Season to taste with salt and freshly ground pepper.

To Serve: Put the prepared shellfish into warm soup bowls. Pour over the boiling broth, sprinkle with the remainder of the fresh herbs and serve immediately.

Serves 4 to 6

Great
Vegetables

Stuffed Zucchini with Primavera Garnish

Fresh young zucchini stuffed with peas and scallions, and surrounded by a medley of spring vegetables, are a great accompaniment to tender roasts of lamb, chicken or beef.

6 zucchini (10cm/4in long)

For the Stuffing
2 x 450g/1lb packets frozen
    small green peas
3 sprigs of fresh flat-leaf
    parsley, coarsely chopped
6 scallions, green parts
    only, chopped
6 tablespoons heavy cream
salt and freshly ground pepper
freshly grated nutmeg
cayenne pepper
melted butter

For the Primavera Garnish
3 large carrots
3 young turnips
18 snow peas
½ chicken or vegetable stock
    cube, crumbled
25g/1oz butter
6 tablespoons small green peas
    (reserved from stuffing)
salt and freshly ground pepper
cayenne pepper

To Prepare the Zucchini: Blanch the zucchini in simmering water for 1 minute, then remove them with a slotted spoon and dip them immediately into cold water. Add the frozen small green peas (reserving 6 tablespoons for the primavera vegetable garnish) to the simmering water and cook for 2 minutes. Drain. Slice the zucchini in half lengthways and carefully scoop out the seeds with the point of a teaspoon.

To Stuff and Bake the Zucchini: Preheat the oven to 200°C/400°F. Combine the cooked peas, parsley, scallions and heavy cream in a blender and blend until the mixture is a slightly grainy purée. Add salt, pepper, nutmeg and cayenne to taste.

Fill the 12 zucchini halves with the pea mixture, rounding the mixture high in each zucchini half to reform a whole 'zucchini'. Brush each lightly with melted butter and place on a baking tray. Bake in the preheated oven for 20 minutes.

To Prepare the Garnish: Cut each carrot and turnip into 6 sticks 10cm/4in long. Trim the snow peas.

Put the carrot and turnip sticks into a frying pan with the crumbled stock cube, butter and just enough water to cover. Bring gently to the boil, then simmer for 6 minutes. Remove the vegetables with a slotted spoon, reserving the liquid in the pan.

Just before serving, add the reserved small green peas, the carrot and turnip sticks and the snow peas to the pan and heat through. Drain and season to taste with salt, freshly ground pepper and cayenne.

To Serve: Garnish the freshly baked zucchini with the primavera vegetables and serve at once.

Serves 6

Terrine of Winter Vegetables

This is a wonderful terrine to make. Fresh-tasting and attractive, it is at its best when served with a mustard mayonnaise (add 1 to 3 teaspoons Dijon mustard to 300ml/½ pint homemade mayonnaise) or cucumber cream (add half a cucumber, peeled and diced, to 300ml/½ pint crème fraîche).

For the Vegetables
550g/1½ lb young carrots
600ml/20fl oz hot vegetable
   stock, made with a cube
450g/1lb young turnips
225g/8oz *haricots verts* (extra
   fine green beans)
1 bunch green asparagus
   (upper halves only)

For the Mayonnaise Aspic
2x11.7g packets/4 tablespoons
   flavoured powdered gelatin
450ml/15fl oz boiling water
6 tablespoons light cream
6 tablespoons homemade
   mayonnaise
¼ teaspoon cayenne pepper
lemon juice

To Prepare the Vegetables: Trim and scrape the carrots and cut lengthways into quarters or eighths, according to size. Poach in the boiling vegetable stock until just tender, then remove with a slotted spoon and cool.

Trim and peel the turnips and cut into thin strips. Poach in the boiling stock as above; remove and cool.

Cook the *haricots verts* in the stock for 5 minutes; remove and cool.

Cook the asparagus in the stock for 5 minutes; drain and cool.

To Make the Mayonnaise Aspic: Dissolve the flavoured powdered gelatin in the boiling water, stirring well. When the gelatin is completely dissolved and the mixture has cooled, add the cream and blend well. Then add the mayonnaise, cayenne pepper, and lemon juice to taste, and beat until well blended. Strain the mixture into a bowl and allow to set in the refrigerator until quite syrupy. In the meantime, put the terrine together.

To Assemble the Terrine: Line the base of a 1.4-litre/2½-pint rectangular terrine mold or loaf pan with parchment paper. Arrange a layer of *haricots verts* over the bottom of the pan, then place a layer of carrot strips (using half the quantity of strips) on top. Place the turnip strips on top of the carrots, and the asparagus spears on the turnips. Top with the remaining carrots.

Holding the vegetables gently in place with your fingertips, carefully pour the syrupy mayonnaise aspic into the terrine. Allow to set in the refrigerator.

To Serve: Unmold the terrine then cut gently into slices using a dampened serrated knife. Serve with mustard mayonnaise or cucumber cream (see introduction).

Serves a variable number of guests, depending on how served

Char-Grilled Mediterranean Vegetables with Lemon and Pepper Oils

The healthiest starter or main course or vegetable accompaniment imaginable, this recipe for grilled peppers, tomatoes and red onions, at its simplest, takes on new glamour when green and yellow zucchini slices are added, or even parsnips and carrots, or baby eggplants. Wonderful hot. Gorgeous cold. Serve it like it is, marinated in the flavoursome dressing that is used as a basting sauce while the vegetables are on the grill, or dress it up with twin bands of flavoured oils: lemon and pepper.

2 red peppers
2 green peppers
2 beefsteak tomatoes
1 red onion
1 medium-sized eggplant
2 green zucchini (optional)
2 yellow zucchini (optional)

For the Dressing
8 tablespoons olive oil
½ teaspoon light soy sauce
1 tablespoon lime juice
1 clove garlic, finely chopped
2 tablespoons chopped red
   onion
lemon juice
salt and freshly ground pepper
crushed dried chiles

For the Garnish
small cherry tomatoes
finely chopped fresh
   flat-leaf parsley
sprigs of fresh basil, tarragon
   and arugula
infused lemon oil (optional;
   page 18)
infused pepper oil (optional;
   page 18)

To Prepare the Dressing: Combine the first 5 dressing ingredients in a small bowl. Add lemon juice, salt, freshly ground pepper and crushed dried chiles, to taste.

To Prepare the Vegetables: Cut the red and green peppers in half, remove the seeds and cut into thick strips. Slice the tomatoes thickly. Peel the onion and slice into rings. Cut the eggplant lengthways into slices. Cut off the ends of the green and yellow zucchini and cut lengthways into slices or across into rings.

To Char-grill: Using a ridged cast-iron char-grill pan or, if cooking outside, a barbecue, first get the pan or the fire hot (on a hot pan, splashed water dances and quickly disappears), then put on the onion slices and the pepper strips and brush with the dressing. Cook until the onions and peppers are tender and tinged with brown, brushing with more dressing as necessary, then turn over to brown the other side. Then add the eggplant and tomato slices and, if using them, the zucchini slices, brushing with dressing and cooking in the same way.

To Serve: Arrange the char-grilled vegetables on individual serving plates, garnish with cherry tomatoes and fresh herbs and, if desired, spoon overlapping ribbons of lemon and pepper oils around the vegetables on each plate.

Serves 4

Marinated Mushrooms en Brioche

The smallest button mushrooms you can find are necessary for this spectacular course of spicy, wine-marinated mushrooms served in oven-crisped brioches flavoured with paprika and butter. It's a great vegetable course on its own, or an elegant accompaniment for poached or pan-seared fish, chicken or veal.

675g/1½ lb small button mushrooms

For the Bouillon
juice of 1 lemon
½ Spanish onion, finely chopped
16 coriander seeds
8 black peppercorns
thin strip of lemon zest
8 tablespoons olive oil
300ml/10fl oz dry white wine
salt

For the Cases
6 small brioches
3 tablespoons melted butter
paprika
salt

To Finish
1–2 tablespoons olive oil
lemon juice
2 tablespoons mixed finely chopped fresh coriander and flat-leaf parsley

To Prepare the Bouillon: In a saucepan, combine the lemon juice, finely chopped onion, coriander seeds, peppercorns, lemon zest, olive oil and dry white wine. Season with salt. Place over a high heat and bring to the boil. Skim the surface, then reduce the heat and simmer for 10 minutes.

To Prepare the Mushrooms: Wash and trim the mushrooms, leaving small button mushrooms whole, and cutting larger ones in half. Add the mushrooms to the bouillon, with enough water to ensure the mushrooms are covered. Simmer uncovered for 10 minutes, or until the mushrooms are tender. Transfer the mushrooms and bouillon to a bowl, leave to cool and then chill, if wished, until needed.

To Make the Brioche Cases: Preheat the oven to 180°C/350°F. Cut a slice from the top of each brioche and carefully scoop out two-thirds of the insides. Place the cases and tops on a baking tray. Brush with melted butter seasoned with paprika and salt to taste, and bake for 5 minutes.

To Finish and Serve: Using a slotted spoon, remove the mushrooms from their liquid and set aside. Stir the olive oil, lemon juice to taste, and coriander and parsley into the liquid. Sprinkle 1 tablespoon of liquid into each baked brioche case, then fill each case with the mushrooms, scattering a few remaing mushrooms on each plate. Sprinkle with the remaining liquid, add the brioche tops and serve at once.

Serves 6

Creamed Onion Tart

Sweet Spanish onions, finely sliced and cooked until meltingly soft in butter and oil, provide the base for this creamy custard tart with its delicate cheese and nutmeg flavouring.

50g/2oz butter
1 tablespoon olive oil
900g/2lb Spanish onions, very
   finely sliced
a 25cm/10in pre-baked
   fingertip pastry crust
   (page 251)

For the Sauce
300ml/10fl oz milk
1 bay leaf
1 clove
3–4 black peppercorns
½ chicken stock cube, crumbled
15g/½ oz butter
1½ tablespoons flour
3 egg yolks
2 tablespoons freshly grated
   Parmesan cheese
salt and freshly ground pepper
freshly grated nutmeg

To Prepare the Onions: Melt the butter with the olive oil in a thick-bottomed saucepan. Add the finely sliced onions and sauté gently, stirring constantly with a wooden spoon, for 4 to 5 minutes, until the onions have softened. Then cover the pan, reduce the heat even further and 'sweat' the onions for 10 to 15 minutes longer, stirring occasionally. They should be meltingly soft but not coloured. Set aside.

Preheat the oven to 180°C/350°F.

To Prepare the Sauce: Bring the milk to the boil in a small saucepan with the bay leaf, clove, peppercorns and stock cube. Remove the pan from the heat, cover and leave the milk to infuse for 10 to 15 minutes. Strain into a jug.

In a large saucepan, melt the butter, add the flour and stir over a moderate heat for 2 to 3 minutes to form a pale roux. Stir in the infused milk slowly and carefully – to avoid making the sauce lumpy – and when it is smooth, simmer for 2 minutes until it thickens and loses its raw, floury taste.

Remove the pan from the heat and beat in the egg yolks, one at a time, followed by half the Parmesan cheese. Season generously with salt, freshly ground pepper and a pinch of freshly grated nutmeg.

To Make the Tart: Drain off any liquid that may have collected in the pan with the onions and stir the onions gently into the sauce. Pour the mixture into the pre-baked pastry crust and sprinkle with the remaining Parmesan.

Bake the tart in the preheated oven for 25 to 30 minutes, or until the filling is set and golden brown on top. Serve hot or warm.

Serves 6

Yellow and Green Zucchini Coins

Thin rounds of green and yellow zucchini, pan-fried in butter and water and flavoured with half a vegetable stock cube and a pinch or two of crushed dried chiles, are all you need to create this quickly cooked and colourful vegetable accompaniment. Garnish, if you will, with mini cherry tomatoes or diced vine-ripened tomatoes, and segments of scallion.

2–4 yellow zucchini
2–4 green zucchini
4–6 tablespoons olive oil
½ vegetable stock cube, crumbled
salt and crushed dried chiles

For the Garnish
12–18 mini cherry tomatoes or 1 large vine-ripened tomato, seeded and diced
2 scallions, green parts only, cut into 6mm/¼in segments
juice of ½ lemon
chopped or whole coriander leaves (optional)

To Prepare the Zucchini: Cut the ends from the zucchini and slice them as thinly as you can.

When Ready to Cook: Heat the olive oil in a large nonstick frying pan. Add the crumbled stock cube, stir until well blended, then add the thinly sliced zucchini and sauté, stirring constantly over a medium heat, until the zucchini take on an intense yellow and green colour in the hot pan. When the zucchini are done, season to taste with salt and crushed dried chiles.

Note: If the zucchini slices start to brown, the heat is too high.

To Serve: Transfer the zucchini to a warm serving plate and garnish with the cherry tomatoes or diced tomato and the scallions. Sprinkle with lemon juice and, if desired, sprinkle with coriander leaves. Serve immediately.

Serves 4 to 6

Caviar of Eggplants with Black Olives

Eggplant caviar or 'poor man's caviar', as it is often called, is a favourite summer appetizer all along the Mediterranean coast – a smooth eggplant purée highly flavoured with pounded black olives, garlic and lemon juice. To be sure of success, however, use firm, fresh, shiny eggplants; if they are stale, you will never be able to rid them of their metallic aftertaste. Serve eggplant caviar with pita bread, focaccia or ciabatta, and more olive oil, if desired.

2 large purple eggplants
100g/4oz Greek-style black olives, pitted and chopped
2 cloves garlic
sea salt and freshly ground pepper
6 tablespoons olive oil
1 tablespoon lemon juice
pinch of paprika

For the Garnish
8 black olives
sprigs of coriander
lemon quarters

To Prepare the Eggplants: Preheat the oven to 200°C/400°F. Wash and dry the eggplants, but do not peel them. Lay them on a baking sheet and bake for 15 to 20 minutes, or until very soft, turning them once or twice.

When the eggplants are mushy, remove from the oven. Cut them in half and scoop out the pulp with a spoon. Pound the pulp in a large mortar or rub through a sieve. Leave to cool.

To Make the Eggplant Caviar: In a large mortar, pound the olives to a paste with the garlic and ½ teaspoon sea salt. Stir in 2 tablespoons of the olive oil.

Stir the olives into the cooled eggplant purée until well blended, then add the remaining olive oil gradually, beating constantly as for a mayonnaise. Season to taste with lemon juice, salt, freshly ground pepper and a pinch of paprika. Turn into a serving dish and chill.

When Ready to Serve: Serve chilled with whole olives, sprigs of fresh coriander, lemon quarters, and bread of your choice (see introduction).

Serves 4 to 8

Rice and Black Olive Towers with Confit of Tomatoes

An olive- and avocado-studded pilaf of rice, with a highly flavoured tomato confit, is molded into little towers to make an attractive vegetable garnish.

For the Rice
50g/2oz butter
2 tablespoons finely chopped onion
225g/8oz basmati rice
4 tablespoons white wine
700ml/25fl oz vegetable stock
salt

For the Garnish
25g/1oz butter
100g/4oz tomatoes, peeled, seeded and diced
½ teaspoon finely chopped garlic
¼ teaspoon dried herbes de Provence
salt and freshly ground pepper
100g/4oz avocado, diced
50g/2oz black olives, pitted and chopped
strips of orange zest, to finish

To Prepare the Rice: Preheat the oven to 180°C/350°F. Melt the butter in a heatproof casserole and sauté the finely chopped onion for 1 minute. Add the rice and stir for another minute. Pour in the wine and vegetable stock, and season with salt. Bring to the boil, then cover the casserole and transfer to the preheated oven to simmer for 20 minutes. Stir once only with a fork.

To Prepare the Garnish: Melt the butter in another heatproof casserole or a large saucepan and sauté the diced tomatoes and finely chopped garlic for 1 minute. Add the herbes de Provence and season to taste with salt and freshly ground pepper. Let simmer for 5 minutes. Add the diced avocado and the olives, and gently stir into the finished rice.

This much of the recipe may be prepared ahead of time.

To Serve the Towers: Butter 6 individual ramekins. Fill them with the rice mixture and place them in a roasting tin. Pour in boiling water to come halfway up and simmer over a medium heat until the rice towers are heated through. Unmold and serve at once, with orange zest scattered over the top of the towers.

Serves 6

Portobello Mushrooms à la Bordelaise

Portobello mushrooms with their 'meaty' flesh and rich brown interiors make a gourmet meal in themselves – whether you are a vegetarian or a hearty carnivore. Just sauté the flat caps in olive oil augmented with finely chopped garlic and half a crumbled vegetable stock cube for extra savour. Turn the mushrooms once before adding a splash of red wine and a hint of lemon juice to the pan juices. Once the pan juices come to the sizzle again, turn the mushrooms over again. And if you want the wine-infused *jus* to be extra sumptuous, whisk a little diced chilled butter into the pan juices after transferring the mushrooms to a heated serving dish. Then pour the glossy juices over the mushrooms and serve immediately.

8 medium-sized portobello mushrooms
2–3 tablespoons olive oil, plus extra if required
½ vegetable stock cube, crumbled
2 cloves garlic, finely chopped
150ml/5fl oz wine
salt and freshly ground pepper
crushed dried chiles
2 tablespoons finely diced butter (optional)
juice of ½ lemon

For the Garnish
snippets of chopped chives
whole chives (optional)

To Prepare the Mushrooms: There are two ways of serving portobello mushrooms: either whole, or thickly sliced, according to their size.

In 1 large or 2 small frying pans, heat the olive oil. Add the crumbled vegetable stock cube and stir to blend well. Then add the mushroom caps (or slices), sprinkle with finely chopped garlic and sauté over a high heat for about 3 minutes, shaking the pan to keep them from sticking and adding a little more oil if necessary.

With a spatula, turn the mushroom caps over (or, with a wooden spoon, stir the mushroom slices). Add the red wine and shake the pan for 1 minute until the pan juices come to the sizzle again. Season to taste with salt, freshly ground pepper and crushed dried chiles. Cook the mushrooms for 3 minutes more, or until they are well browned and tender.

To Serve: Transfer the mushrooms to a heated serving dish. Stir the pan juices over a high heat for a minute or two until the liquids are reduced to 4 to 8 tablespoons: 1 to 2 tablespoons of *jus* per serving. Then stir the diced butter into the pan juices, if desired, to make the *jus* thick and glossy. Pour the thickened *jus* over the mushrooms. Sprinkle with lemon juice and chopped chives. Add a garnish of crossed whole chives, if desired, and serve immediately.

Serves 4

Potato 'Apples and Pears'

When Richard Shepherd, fresh from training at La Réserve de Beaulieu on the Côte d'Azur, first opened the restaurant at David Levin's Capitol Hotel on Basil Street in London, he enchanted us with his deep-fried potato croquettes formed into the shape of diminutive apples and pears. This is my idea of how it was done.

450g/1lb cold, mashed
   potatoes
salt
4-6 tablespoons freshly grated
   Parmesan cheese
100g/4oz butter, softened
1 egg yolk
2 thin slices cooked ham, cut
   into very fine dice
freshly ground pepper
short strips of dried mushroom
   (to serve as 'stems')

For the Coating
2 egg whites, beaten
salt
flour
homemade dry breadcrumbs,
   sieved, or polenta (maize)
oil for frying

To Prepare the Potato Purée: Using a balloon whisk, gradually beat the freshly grated Parmesan, the softened butter, the egg yolk, and the finely diced ham into the mashed potato. Season generously with salt and freshly ground pepper.

To Form the 'Apples' and 'Pears': Shape the potato purée into small balls. Take half of the balls and form each one into an 'apple' by slightly flattening it and with your thumb making an indentation in the top. Push a short thin strip of dried mushroom into the top of each fruit to make a stem.

To make pears, use your fingers to pull the top of each remaining ball upwards to a point to form a 'pear' shape. Use dried mushroom strips as before to make the stems.

Place the apples and pears on a tray in the freezer for 30 minutes to firm up before deep frying.

To Coat the 'Fruit' and Deep-fry: In a flat bowl, whisk the egg whites with a pinch of salt until they foam. Dip each 'fruit' in flour to coat lightly, then brush with the beaten egg whites and pat on a coating of fine dry breadcrumbs or polenta (maize).

Heat oil in a deep-fat fryer to 180°C/350°F. Deep-fry the croquettes until golden brown; drain on kitchen paper. Keep warm in the oven until ready to serve.

Serves 4

French Peas à l'Ancienne

This is a recipe for a loved one only. But oh what a recipe! Fresh pea pods, both ends clipped, are blanched for minutes only in a frying pan containing just enough water to cover them, and then stripped with your fingers – crisp, highly flavoured little peas and their green juices – into another pan containing a little melted butter and some chopped scallions (green parts only). You have no idea what a great flavour this simple dish can have. Suffice to say that it was lovingly created in the French court by none other than Louis XV for his beloved Pompadour.

You will find out why it is a recipe only for one (or maybe two) loved ones when you strip the boiling hot peas from their pods with your bare fingers, helped only by a clean dish towel and a dish of iced water to cool your fingers between pods. But try it … the results are amazing.

450–675g/1–1½ lb fresh peas in their pods
sea salt
50g/2oz unsalted French butter, melted
2–3 scallions, green parts only, cut into 6mm/¼ in segments
freshly ground pepper

To Prepare and Cook the Pea Pods: With a pair of scissors, snip off both ends of each pea pod. This is to allow a little of the boiling water to enter the pods as they cook.

Place the pea pods in a large frying pan and add enough cold water just to cover them. Sprinkle with a little sea salt, and bring to the boil over a high heat. Remove the pan from the heat the minute the water comes to the boil. Drain off the water and leave the peas in the hot pan to keep warm.

Have ready another large frying pan with the butter and green scallion tops.

To Strip the Peas from their Pods: Have ready a clean dish towel (to protect the fingers of one hand while you strip the hot pods) and a bowl of iced water (to cool the fingers of your other hand between pods). Strip the peas and green juices into the pan of butter and scallions. Place the pan over a high heat and toss the peas in the butter and scallions for 1 minute or until they are warmed through. Serve immediately. To cheers.

Serves 2 or, if you are a martyr, 3

Great Pasta

Penne alla Puttanesca, Summer Version

There is a famous dish in Naples dedicated to the ladies of the evening who had, it seems, wonderful appetites – for pasta as well as for love – and found great pleasure in sharing platters of penne alla puttanesca after a hard night on the tiles. This is my lighter version, for the balmy summer nights of Naples. After all, a girl's gotta eat!

450g/1lb penne, or other ribbed pasta
salt

For the Sauce
450g/1lb plum tomatoes, seeded and diced
24 black olives in oil, drained, pitted and halved or chopped
4 shallots, softened in 2 tablespoons olive oil
4 tablespoons fresh basil leaves coarsely chopped
salt and freshly ground pepper
crushed dried chiles
extra virgin olive oil

To Prepare the Sauce: In a medium-sized bowl, combine the diced tomatoes, halved or chopped black olives, softened shallots and chopped fresh basil leaves. Mix well and season to taste with salt, freshly ground pepper and crushed dried chiles. Pour over enough extra virgin olive oil to cover. Reserve.

To Cook the Pasta: Bring a large saucepan of salted water to the boil, add the spaghetti and cook for 7 to 10 minutes until *al dente*: just tender, but not overcooked. Drain the pasta and transfer to a heated, deep serving dish. Add the marinated vegetable mixture and toss. The hot pasta will heat the sauce. Serve immediately.

Serves 4

Note: This dish is also delicious served cold. Chill the sauce and drained pasta separately, after tossing the pasta in a little olive oil, until you are ready to eat.

Quadretti with Lemon and Vodka

Tired of spaghetti, tagliatelle or penne? Yet in love with pasta? Quadretti (attractive little pasta squares made out of fresh egg pasta lasagne sheets) will make an intriguing addition to your pasta repertoire. Serve the quadretti with traditional bolognese sauce (page 129), cheese sauce or pesto, or with this delicious vodka and lemon sauce, spiked with ketchup and softened, if desired, with a dollop of crème fraîche.

450g/1lb fresh egg lasagne
   sheets
salt
freshly grated Parmesan
   cheese

For the Lemon Vodka Sauce
2 lemons
75g/3oz butter
2–3 tablespoons vodka
4–6 tablespoons ketchup
4 tablespoons crème fraîche
   (optional)
salt and freshly ground pepper
crushed dried chiles

To Prepare the Quadretti: Cut the fresh lasagne sheets (4 at a time) in half lengthways and then cut each half into 3 squares. Repeat with the remaining lasagne sheets. Reserve the quadretti.

To Prepare the Sauce: Scrub the lemons with a brush under running water and dry thoroughly. Then, with a sharp knife, cut the zest of each lemon into long thin strips. Cut each strip lengthways into long thin zesty threads.

Melt the butter in a pan. Add the lemon threads and cook over a medium heat for 3 minutes. Do not allow the butter to colour. Stir in vodka to taste and enough ketchup to colour the sauce. If a richer sauce is desired, stir in a little crème fraîche. Season to taste with salt, freshly ground pepper and crushed dried chiles, and remove the pan from the heat. Reserve.

To Cook the Pasta: Bring a large saucepan of salted water to the boil, add the pasta squares (quadretti) and cook for about 5 minutes or until *al dente*: just tender, but not overcooked.

To Serve: Drain the pasta and transfer to a large frying pan. Add the lemon and vodka sauce and toss over a high heat until the pasta and sauce are warmed through. Correct the seasoning and serve immediately, with an accompanying bowl of freshly grated Parmesan.

Chinese Egg Noodles with Crisp Vegetables

Chinese egg noodles, sold fresh or dried in supermarkets across the country, make a welcome addition to our menus, whether served in a Thai bouillon, tossed in lime juice, sesame oil and soy sauce and served as a bed for grilled tiger prawns, or, as here, served as a very special base for vegetables crisp-cooked in the Chinese manner.

225g/8oz Chinese egg noodles

4 stems of Chinese broccoli, cut into thin diagonal sprigs, blanched

100g/4oz bean sprouts, trimmed

6–8 cherry tomatoes, cut in half

12–16 young spinach leaves

2 scallions, cut into 6mm/¼in segments

crushed dried chiles

For the Chinese Flavourings
1 tablespoon fresh ginger, finely chopped
2 cloves garlic, finely chopped
3 tablespoons peanut oil
1 tablespoon light sesame oil
1–2 teaspoons light soy sauce
pinch of crushed dried chiles

To Cook the Noodles: Bring a large saucepan of salted water to the boil, add the noodles and cook for 3 minutes or until tender. Drain.

To Stir-fry the Ingredients: Heat a wok or large frying pan. When hot, add all the Chinese flavouring ingredients and stir-fry for 30 seconds. Then add the Chinese broccoli and stir-fry for 3 minutes. Add the bean sprouts, cherry tomatoes and spinach leaves and stir-fry for 1 minute more.

Tip in the drained noodles, add the scallions, and toss together in the hot pan for 1 to 2 minutes until the noodles are heated through. Season to taste with crushed dried chiles and serve immediately.

Serves 4

Pasta e Fagioli

Pasta e fagioli – macaroni or penne with borlotti, or pinto or navy beans – is a lovely concoction from the Veneto. Try it, too, using red kidney beans as a colourful variation. Half soup/half starter, this earthy pasta dish has been a favourite of mine since I was eight years old. That's quite a recommendation.

225g/8oz dried borlotti, red kidney, pinto or navy beans
1 beef marrow bone, about 10cm/4in long (optional)
4 tablespoons tomato paste
2.4 litres/80fl oz cold water
1 Spanish onion, finely chopped
1 clove garlic, finely chopped
3 tablespoons olive oil
3 tablespoons finely chopped fresh flat-leaf parsley
1 teaspoon salt
2 teaspoons dried oregano
freshly ground pepper
crushed dried chiles
225g/8oz macaroni or other small dried pasta shapes
2 tablespoons freshly grated Parmesan cheese

The Night Before: Soak the dried borlotti, red kidney, pinto or navy beans overnight in cold water. Drain.

The Day of Serving: Combine the soaked beans, marrow bone (if using), tomato paste and water in a large saucepan. Bring to the boil and skim off any froth, then reduce the heat, cover and simmer for 1 hour, skimming from time to time as necessary.

Sauté the onion and garlic in the olive oil until the onion is translucent. Add to the soup together with the finely chopped parsley, salt and dried oregano. Season to taste with freshly ground pepper and crushed dried chiles. Leave to simmer, covered, for about 20 minutes. Then add the pasta and continue to cook until the pasta is *al dente*. Serve in a heated soup tureen, sprinkled with freshly grated Parmesan cheese.

Serves 6 to 8

Gnocchi alla Romana

Your own homemade gnocchi – diminutive Roman dumplings made with ricotta cheese, softened butter, egg yolks and flour, seasoned with freshly grated Parmesan cheese – will soon become your *specialità della casa*.

50g/2oz softened butter
8 tablespoons freshly grated
Parmesan cheese
3 egg yolks, beaten
225g/8oz ricotta cheese,
pressed through a sieve
4 tablespoons flour
salt and freshly ground pepper
freshly grated nutmeg
50g/2oz butter, melted,
to serve

To Prepare the Gnocchi: In a mixing bowl, combine the softened butter, half the freshly grated Parmesan and all the egg yolks. With a wooden spoon or whisk, beat until well mixed. Stir in the sieved ricotta alternately with the flour, and season to taste with salt, freshly ground pepper and freshly grated nutmeg.

To Cook the Gnocchi: Preheat the broiler to high, and bring a large saucepan of salted water to the boil. Butter a shallow baking dish large enough to take the gnocchi in a single layer, and set aside.

Spoon the gnocchi mixture into a piping bag fitted with a 1cm/½in nozzle and hold over the saucepan. Force the mixture through the nozzle, cutting it into 2.5cm/1in pieces with scissors. Poach the gnocchi over a low heat for 6 to 7 minutes or until cooked through. Remove with a slotted spoon and drain on kitchen paper.

Arrange the gnocchi in the buttered dish and spoon the melted butter over. Sprinkle with the remaining Parmesan cheese and broil for 10 minutes or until the butter is bubbling and the gnocchi are golden brown. Serve immediately.

Note: Sometimes I serve the gratineed gnocchi with a bowl of well-flavoured, hot tomato sauce (page 248) and some extra grated Parmesan cheese, so that my guests can help themselves.

Serves 4

Pasta with Green Vegetables and Saffron Cream

The brilliant yellow, highly flavoured sauce which dresses this party dish of pasta sets off the jewel tones of the poached vegetables to perfection.

450g/1lb fresh tagliarini or tagliatelle
salt
25g/1oz butter
freshly ground pepper
crushed dried chiles
freshly grated Parmesan cheese

For the Vegetable Garnish
8–12 spears fresh asparagus, tough stems removed, cut into segments and blanched
16 sugarsnap peas, blanched
16 snow peas, blanched
16 broccoli florets, steamed
100g/4oz fresh peas
2–4 small zucchini, cut into thin rounds
2oz/50g butter
1 thin slice cooked ham
½ vegetable stock cube, crumbled
150ml/5fl oz cold water

For the Saffron Cream
1 x 400ml/14fl oz tub crème fraîche
1 pinch saffron threads
½ vegetable stock cube, crumbled
4–6 tablespoons cooking water from pasta
freshly ground pepper
crushed dried chiles

To Prepare the Vegetable Garnish: In a large frying pan, combine the blanched asparagus segments, sugarsnap peas, snow peas, steamed broccoli florets, fresh peas and thin zucchini rounds. Add the butter, cooked ham (for flavour), crumbled vegetable stock cube and cold water and bring rapidly to the boil. Then turn down the heat and simmer for a few more minutes until the vegetables are crisp-tender. Remove the slice of ham and discard; it has served its purpose. Turn off the heat, drain the vegetables and keep them warm in the pan.

To Cook the Pasta: Bring a large saucepan of salted water to the boil, add the tagliarini or tagliatelle (or pasta ribbons of your choice) and cook for 3 to 5 minutes (for fresh pasta), 7 to 11 minutes (for dry pasta) until *al dente*: just tender, but not overcooked. While the pasta is cooking, prepare the saffron cream. When the pasta is ready, drain and reserve, keeping a little of the pasta water to soften the saffron cream.

To Prepare the Saffron Cream: In a small saucepan, combine the crème fraîche, saffron threads, crumbled vegetable stock cube and 4 to 6 tablespoons of the cooking water from the pasta. Cook over a medium heat, stirring until the sauce is heated through. Season to taste with freshly ground pepper and crushed dried chiles, and continue to simmer the sauce over a very low heat until the sauce is thick and creamy.

To Assemble the Dish and Serve: In a large clean saucepan, melt the butter. Add the drained pasta, season to taste with salt, freshly ground pepper and crushed dried chiles and cook over a high heat, stirring constantly, until the pasta is heated through. Transfer the pasta to a heated serving bowl. Strain the saffron cream sauce over the pasta and garnish with the colourful, buttery vegetables. Serve immediately with an accompanying bowl of freshly grated Parmesan.

Serves 4

Lasagne al Forno

This light version of a Bolognese classic – baked meat lasagne – uses chopped mortadella sausage instead of the minced pork and beef in the traditional recipe.

450g/1lb lasagne
salt
175g/6oz mozzarella cheese, diced
175g/6oz cooked mortadella sausage, coarsely chopped
3 hard-boiled eggs, sliced
50g/2oz Parmesan cheese, freshly grated
225g/8oz ricotta cheese
salt and freshly ground pepper
crushed dried chiles
butter

For the Tomato Sauce
1.4kg/3lb tomatoes, coarsely chopped
3 tablespoons tomato paste
3 large carrots, coarsely chopped
1 Spanish onion, coarsely chopped
3 sticks celery, coarsely chopped
2 cloves garlic, chopped
2 tablespoons finely chopped fresh flat-leaf parsley
finely grated zest of ½ lemon
salt and freshly ground pepper
2 tablespoons olive oil
25g/1oz butter

To Prepare the Tomato Sauce: In a thick-bottomed saucepan, combine the tomatoes with the tomato paste and chopped carrots, onion and celery. Stir in the garlic, parsley and lemon zest. Simmer for 1½ hours, then press through a fine sieve. Return the puréed sauce to the pan. Season generously with salt and freshly ground pepper, and simmer until thick. Just before using, stir in the olive oil and butter.

To Prepare the Lasagne: Preheat the oven to 190°C/375°F, and butter a large rectangular baking dish.

Cook the lasagne sheets, a few at a time, in boiling salted water, for 6 minutes only. Drain carefully.

To Assemble the Dish: Line the baking dish with a layer of lasagne sheets. Add a layer of diced mozzarella cheese, a layer of chopped mortadella, and a layer of sliced hard-boiled eggs. Sprinkle generously with freshly grated Parmesan cheese and dollops of ricotta cheese. Season to taste with salt, freshly ground pepper and crushed dried chiles, and moisten with the well-seasoned tomato sauce. Repeat, using the same quantities, until you have several layers and all the ingredients are used up, finishing with tomato sauce. Dot with butter and bake in the preheated oven for about 30 minutes. Serve immediately.

Serves 4

Vegetarian Lasagne

I have been experimenting with vegetables – particularly eggplants and portobello mushrooms – to replace meat in lighter, 'vegetarian' versions of favourite international dinner-party dishes. If you want to make lighter, meat-less versions of two of my favourite pasta dishes, just substitute chopped or diced eggplant and portobello mushrooms for the minced beef and pancetta in the ragù for spaghetti Bolognese, and follow this recipe for vegetarian lasagne.

450g/1lb lasagne
salt
225g/8oz mozzarella cheese, diced
2 hard-boiled eggs, sliced
50g/2oz Parmesan cheese, freshly grated
225g/8oz ricotta cheese
tomato sauce (page 248)
butter

For the Vegetables
225g/8oz eggplant, cut into 6mm/¼in slices and coarsely chopped
2–3 tablespoons olive oil
salt and freshly ground pepper
crushed dried chiles
2 small green zucchini, finely sliced

To Prepare the Vegetables: In a large frying pan, sauté the chopped eggplant in 2 tablespoons of olive oil, stirring constantly, until well browned on all sides. Season to taste with salt, freshly ground pepper and crushed dried chiles. Remove from the pan and reserve. In the same pan, adding a little more oil if needed, sauté the sliced zucchini until they are soft but not golden. Season as above, remove from the heat and reserve.

To Prepare the Lasagne: Preheat the oven to 190°C/375°F, and butter a large rectangular baking dish.

Cook the lasagne sheets, a few at a time, in boiling salted water for 6 minutes only. Drain carefully.

To Assemble the Dish: Line the baking dish with a layer of half the lasagne sheets. Make a layer of half the diced mozzarella cheese, then add half the eggplant, half the zucchini and finally half the sliced hard-boiled egg. Sprinkle generously with freshly grated Parmesan cheese and dollops of ricotta cheese. Moisten with the well-seasoned tomato sauce. Repeat, using the same quantities, finishing with tomato sauce. Dot with butter and bake in the preheated oven for 30 minutes. Serve immediately.

Serves 4

Spaghetti with Tuscan Herbs

Italian country-style pasta at its best, this simple recipe includes finely chopped garlic and, surprisingly enough, anchovy filets (in oil, of course) with a hint of puréed tomato to achieve its sumptuous sauce. Finely chopped fresh herbs – thyme, rosemary and marjoram – complete the rustic flavours. If you are tempted to use dried herbs, halve the quantities.

450g/1lb spaghetti
salt
a little warm olive oil, if
desired
freshly grated Parmesan
cheese

For the Sauce
4 tablespoons olive oil
2 cloves garlic, finely chopped
8 anchovy filets in oil, drained
and chopped
2 tablespoons canned tomato
purée
2–3 tablespoons finely
chopped fresh flat-leaf
parsley
1 tablespoon each finely
chopped fresh thyme,
rosemary and marjoram
crushed dried chiles

To Cook the Pasta: Bring a large saucepan of salted water to the boil, add the spaghetti and cook for 7 to 11 minutes until *al dente*: just tender, but not overcooked.

To Prepare the Sauce: Heat the olive oil in a small saucepan. Sauté the finely chopped garlic gently until it just begins to change colour. Strain the olive oil into a frying pan (reserving the garlic), then add the chopped anchovies and cook over the lowest possible heat, stirring, until they have dissolved into a smooth paste. Stir in the canned tomato purée and continue to cook for 1 minute. Then add the finely chopped fresh herbs and stir over a low heat for a few minutes. Add the reserved garlic and remove the pan from the heat.

To Serve: Drain the spaghetti thoroughly in a colander and pile it in a deep, heated serving dish. Pour the sauce over, toss well and season with a little crushed dried chiles. Add a little salt and warm olive oil, too, if desired. Serve at once, with an accompanying bowl of freshly grated Parmesan.

Serves 4

Franco Taruschio's Bigoli with Chicken Liver Sauce

Franco Taruschio, born in the Marche region of Italy, chef-proprietor, with his wife Anne, of the Walnut Tree Inn, a lovely old-time pub a few miles from Abergavenny, loves homemade pasta. But with a difference. His sauces are rich and exuberant, a perfect blend of simplicity and sophistication: spaghetti with truffle paste and zucchini flowers, wholewheat fettuccine with a chopped eggplant, onion, garlic and tomato sauce, enlivened by a hot green chile pepper, and wide-noodle pappardelle with a rich hare sauce. But the one he chose to make for me on television when we filmed at the Walnut Tree is bigoli, Franco's special homemade wheat pasta, served with an incredibly rich chicken liver, sage and Marsala sauce.

For the Bigoli
250g/9oz wholewheat flour
75g/3oz flour
salt
6 large eggs, beaten

For the Chicken Liver Sauce
4 tablespoons olive oil
75g/3oz butter
2 cloves garlic, finely chopped
4 teaspoons finely chopped
   fresh sage leaves
350g/12oz chicken livers,
   cleaned and cut into small
   pieces
4 tablespoons Marsala
4 tablespoons dry white wine
salt and freshly ground pepper

To Serve
freshly grated Parmesan
   cheese

To Prepare the Bigoli: In a large mixing bowl, combine the dry ingredients. Make a well in the center and pour in the beaten eggs. Mix the flour into the eggs until a dough is formed, then knead the dough for 10 minutes. Pass the dough through a spaghetti-cutting machine, or through the tagliatelle blades of a pasta machine, following the manufacturer's instructions.

Cover the pasta with a clean dish towel and leave it to rest for an hour before cooking. When ready, cook in abundant salted water until *al dente*.

To Make the Chicken Liver Sauce: Heat the olive oil and butter in a frying pan. When the butter is foaming, add the finely chopped garlic and sage and sauté until the garlic is golden. Add the chicken livers and sauté briskly for 1 to 2 minutes, stirring constantly. Pour the Marsala and wine over the livers and cook briskly until the liquid is reduced to a glaze. Season to taste with salt and freshly ground pepper.

To Serve: Pour the chicken liver sauce over the bigoli, sprinkle with freshly grated Parmesan and serve immediately with extra freshly grated Parmesan.

Serves 4 to 6

Note: This sauce is also delicious with wholewheat spaghetti.

Spaghetti Bolognese

My version of the world's most famous tomato sauce for pasta.

450g/1lb spaghetti, or pasta of
   your choice
salt
freshly grated Parmesan
   cheese

For the Bolognese sauce
25g/1oz butter
4 tablespoons olive oil
100g/4oz pancetta, finely
   chopped
1 onion, finely chopped
2 carrots, finely chopped
1 stick celery, finely chopped
225g/8oz sirloin of beef,
   minced
1 strip of lemon zest
1 bay leaf
4 tablespoons tomato paste
300ml/10fl oz rich beef stock
150ml/5fl oz dry white wine
salt and freshly ground pepper
crushed dried chiles
freshly grated nutmeg
4 tablespoons heavy cream

To Prepare the Sauce: Heat the butter and olive oil in a thick-bottomed saucepan. Add the finely chopped pancetta, onion, carrot and celery and sauté over a medium heat, stirring occasionally, until the pancetta browns. Then stir in the minced beef and brown evenly, stirring continuously.

Add the lemon zest, bay leaf, tomato paste, beef stock and dry white wine. Season to taste with salt, freshly ground pepper, crushed dried chiles and freshly grated nutmeg. Cover and simmer very gently for 30 minutes, stirring occasionally. Check the seasonings.

Remove the lemon zest and bay leaf from the sauce and simmer, uncovered, for a further 30 minutes, or until the sauce has slightly thickened. Meanwhile, prepare the pasta.

To Cook the Pasta: Bring a large saucepan of salted water to the boil, add the spaghetti or other pasta and cook for 7 to 11 minutes (3 to 5 minutes for fresh pasta), until *al dente*: just tender, but not overcooked.

To Serve: Stir the heavy cream into the sauce and simmer for 2 to 3 minutes more. Drain the freshly cooked pasta and transfer to a warmed bowl. Pour the sauce over and toss well. Sprinkle with a little freshly grated Parmesan and serve immediately, with an accompanying bowl of freshly grated Parmesan.

Great Vegetarian

Indian Vegetable Bhajee

A southern Indian vegetarian dish of high flavour, mixed vegetable bhajee (vegetables and spices simmered in ghee with no other liquid than what the vegetables themselves provide) makes a superb vegetarian main course. This recipe stars carrots, cabbage, young okra and tomatoes as its main ingredients, but you can substitute or add other vegetables of your choice: eggplant, cauliflower, zucchini, green beans, potatoes and scallions are just a few that come to mind.

100g/4oz ghee or clarified butter
1 small onion, finely chopped
4 cloves garlic, finely chopped
1 teaspoon cumin seeds
1 teaspoon ground turmeric
4 small carrots cut into 1cm/½in segments
4–6 young okra, cut into 1cm/½in segments
½ small cabbage, coarsely chopped
salt
4 plum tomatoes, cut into wedges
1–2 fresh chiles, seeded and finely chopped
1½ tablespoons fresh ginger, peeled and finely chopped
sprigs of fresh coriander

To Prepare the Bhajee: Melt the ghee or clarified butter in a heatproof casserole, add the chopped onion and cook over a medium heat for 5 to 7 minutes, stirring from time to time, until the onion is brown. Add the garlic and cook for a further 2 minutes. Stir in the cumin seeds and turmeric and cook for 1 to 2 minutes more.

Add the segments of carrot, okra and the chopped cabbage and cook over a low heat for 5 minutes, stirring occasionally. Season with salt, cover the pan and leave to cook over a very low heat for 10 minutes.

Stir in the tomato wedges and finely chopped chiles and ginger. Cover the pan and simmer for a further 10 to 15 minutes, or until the vegetables are tender.

To Serve: Garnish with fresh coriander sprigs and serve immediately.

Serves 4

Vegetable Hot Pot

Every once in a while I am asked to create a dish for a special personality. I recently created this delicate vegetarian dish in honour of one of Britain's top stand-up comics, Victoria Wood. Cubes of butternut squash, turnips, carrots and leeks are simmered in a pale pink sauce thickened only with a tablespoon or two of pearl barley. Delicious.

1 medium-sized butternut
    squash
2 medium-sized turnips
3 large carrots
3 leeks
4 tablespoons flour,
    seasoned with 1 teaspoon
    each salt and freshly ground
    pepper and ½ teaspoon each
    paprika and crushed dried
    chiles
25g/1oz butter
4 tablespoons olive oil

For the Aromatics and Sauce
2 tablespoons olive oil
1 medium-sized onion, finely
    chopped
2–3 extra-large cloves garlic,
    finely chopped
2 carrots, finely chopped
2 sticks celery, finely chopped
2 bay leaves
2 sprigs of fresh thyme
1 sprig of fresh rosemary
8–10 peppercorns
450ml/15fl oz vegetable stock
    (or 1 vegetable stock cube
    and 450ml/15fl oz water)
2 tablespoons tomato paste
1–2 tablespoons pearl barley
salt and crushed dried chiles

For the Garnish
4–6 lightly poached leaves of
    a small savoy cabbage
    (optional)
2–3 tablespoons finely
chopped fresh flat-leaf parsley

To Prepare the Root Vegetables: Peel the butternut squash and the turnips. Cut the squash in half lengthways and scoop out the seeds. Then cut the squash and turnips into 2.5cm/1in cubes. Peel the carrots. Wash and trim the leeks, and cut the carrots and leeks into 2.5cm/1in lengths. You will need 8 to 12 pieces of each of these four vegetables.

Toss the cubed vegetables in the seasoned flour. Melt the butter and olive oil in a large frying pan. Add the vegetables and sauté until lightly browned on all sides. With a slotted spoon, transfer the vegetables to a casserole. Reserve.

To Prepare the Aromatics: Heat the olive oil in a frying pan and add the chopped onion, garlic, carrots and celery. Sauté, stirring constantly, until the vegetables begin to change colour. Add the herbs and peppercorns and cook for 5 to 8 minutes more.

In a medium-sized saucepan, bring the vegetable stock to the boil. Add the tomato paste and stir until well blended. Add the pearl barley and the aromatics, bring back to the boil and season to taste with salt and crushed dried chiles. Pour over the vegetables in the casserole.

To Cook the Hot Pot: Preheat the oven to 160°C/325°F. Place the casserole in the preheated oven and cook for 1 to 1¼ hours, or until the vegetables are tender but not mushy.

Just before serving, remove the casserole from the oven. Taste the sauce and correct the seasoning if necessary. Tuck the lightly poached cabbage leaves around the edge of the casserole, sprinkle with finely chopped parsley and leave for a moment for the cabbage leaves to heat through.

To Serve: Serve the vegetable hot pot directly from the casserole in the traditional way. Or arrange a savoy cabbage leaf on each heated dinner plate and, with a ladle, spoon the vegetables, aromatics, pearl barley and a little sauce over each serving.

Serves 4 to 6

Wild Mushrooms in Filo Pastry

Sliced porcini, enoki and yellow oyster mushrooms in a Madeira sauce fill these crisp golden parcels of filo pastry, shaped like beggar's purses. Serve 2 or 3 to each guest.

225g/8oz fresh porcini
    mushrooms (ceps)
225g/8oz fresh yellow oyster
    mushrooms
1 packet of fresh enoki
    mushrooms
1 Spanish onion, finely
    chopped
2 cloves garlic, finely chopped
25g/1oz butter
3 tablespoons olive oil
salt and freshly ground pepper
150ml/5fl oz vegetable stock
150ml/5fl oz Madeira
24 sheets fresh filo pastry
melted butter
1 leek, cut into 12 thin threads
2 egg yolks, beaten with a
    little milk

For the Madeira Sauce
40g/1½ oz butter
2 tablespoons flour
150ml/5fl oz Madeira
300ml/10fl oz vegetable stock
6-8 tablespoons crème fraîche
salt and freshly ground pepper

To Prepare the Wild Mushroom Filling: Trim the stems from the mushrooms. Wash them or brush them dry to conserve flavour. With a large kitchen knife or cleaver, chop the mushrooms coarsely.

In a large frying pan, sauté the chopped onion and garlic in the butter and olive oil until the vegetables are translucent. Add the coarsely chopped mushrooms to the pan and continue to cook, stirring, until the mushrooms are golden-brown. Season to taste with salt and freshly ground pepper.

Skim off excess fat from the pan, then add the stock and the Madeira. Cover and simmer for 10 minutes. Remove the pan from the heat and allow the mushrooms to cool completely.

To Make the Sauce: Melt the butter in a thick-bottomed saucepan. Add the flour and stir over a moderate heat until it is a deep golden colour. Remove the pan from the heat and beat in the Madeira, the vegetable stock and the pan juices from the cooked mushrooms. Return the pan to the heat and stir in the crème fraîche. Bring to the boil, stirring constantly, and simmer the sauce until it is reduced to the desired consistency. Season to taste with salt and freshly ground pepper, then remove from the heat and allow to cool.

To Make and Bake the Filo Pastry Parcels: Preheat the oven to 220°C/425°F. Lay 4 sheets of filo pastry on a clean working surface. Brush each piece with melted butter, then cover with another piece, placed crossways, and brush again with melted butter. Place 2 to 3 tablespoons of the Madeira mushroom filling in the center of each pastry cross. Moisten the filling with a little of the cooled Madeira sauce and gather the pastry up over the filling to make a beggar's purse, pressing the pastry together at the top with your fingers and tying it securely in place with a thin strip of raw leek. Repeat twice more with the remaining pastry and filling to make 12 parcels in all.

Arrange the parcels on a buttered baking sheet. Glaze the pastry with the beaten egg yolks and bake for 20 minutes, or until the parcels are crisp and golden brown. Reheat the remaining Madeira sauce and serve with the mushroom parcels.

Serves 4 to 6

Apple and Onion Fritters in Fresh Sage Batter

An easy English vegetarian fritter that makes an excellent light dish suitable for breakfast, brunch or a light supper, or, combined with deep-fried okra, a delicious and colourful dinner.

2 eating apples, McIntosh or Empire
1 Spanish onion, finely chopped
salt and freshly ground pepper
crushed dried chiles
vegetable oil for deep-frying

For the Fresh Sage Batter
100g/4oz flour
½ teaspoon salt
1 tablespoon finely chopped fresh sage
1 large egg, separated
1 tablespoon vegetable oil
150ml/5fl oz apple juice or cider

For the Garnish
watercress sprigs
lemon quarters

To Prepare the Fresh Sage Batter: Sift the flour with the salt into a large bowl, then stir in the sage. Make a well in the center and add the egg yolk, vegetable oil and half the apple juice or cider. Using a wire whisk, gradually stir the dry ingredients into the liquid. When the flour is completely incorporated, gradually whisk in the remaining juice or cider to form a smooth batter. Cover the batter and allow to stand for 30 minutes.

To Make the Fritters: Peel, core and finely chop the apples, then stir into the batter. Add the chopped onion and season to taste with salt, freshly ground pepper and crushed dried chiles.

Just before deep-frying, whisk the egg white in a clean, dry bowl until stiff, then lightly fold into the batter.

To Deep-fry: Preheat the oven to 100°C/225°F (to keep fried fritters hot). Heat vegetable oil in a deep-fryer. When the oil is sizzling, drop a few tablespoons of the batter mixture into the pan, forming them into neat, even rounds with a fish slice. Deep-fry the fritters until they are puffed and golden brown.

Drain the fritters on paper towel, transfer to a serving platter and keep hot in the oven. Continue to fry batches of fritters in the same manner.

To Serve: Garnish the fritters with watercress sprigs and lemon quarters and serve immediately with, if you like, apple sauce (page 250) or homemade tomato chutney (page 165).

Serves 4 to 6

Fricassee of Mushrooms, Eggplants and Sun-Dried Tomatoes

Strips of portobello mushrooms and purple eggplant are pan-seared and then fricasseed with aromatics and sun-dried tomatoes. The colourful vegetable fricassee is served with rice garnished with thin lemon slices and flat-leaf parsley.

4 portobello mushrooms
1 large eggplant or 2 smaller
   ones
4 tablespoons olive oil
1 large Spanish onion, finely
   chopped
2 cloves garlic, finely chopped
1–1½ teaspoon(s) each chopped
   fresh oregano and thyme
salt and freshly ground pepper
crushed dried chiles
4 ripe plum tomatoes, peeled,
   seeded and chopped

For the Garnish
4–6 sun-dried tomatoes (in oil),
   thinly sliced lengthways
freshly boiled rice
thin lemon slices
sprigs of fresh flat-leaf parsley

To Prepare the Vegetables: Wash the mushrooms and cut off the stems. Cut the caps into 6mm/¼in thick slices. Trim the eggplants and cut into 6mm/¼in thick rounds. Then cut each round into 6mm/¼in strips.

To Cook the Vegetables: In a large nonstick frying pan or shallow heatproof casserole, sear the eggplant strips in 1 tablespoon olive oil until well coloured on all sides. Remove from the pan and reserve. Add 1 more tablespoon of olive oil to the pan and sear the mushroom slices, stirring constantly, until well coloured on all sides. Remove from the pan and reserve.

Add the remaining olive oil to the pan and sauté the finely chopped onion and garlic in the oil until the onion is translucent. Add the chopped fresh herbs and salt, freshly ground pepper and crushed dried chiles to taste. Then add the chopped tomatoes and continue to cook until the excess moisture has evaporated.

Note: All the above preparation can be done in advance.

When Ready to Serve: Add the reserved eggplant strips and mushroom slices to the tomato mixture and heat through, stirring from time to time. Add the strips of sun-dried tomato and transfer to a heated serving dish. Surround the fricassee of vegetables with freshly boiled rice. Garnish the rice with lemon slices and sprigs of flat-leaf parsley and serve immediately.

Serves 4

Vegetables in Coconut Cream

This Malaysian-inspired recipe dresses up vegetables – Chinese cabbage, tomatoes, snow peas – with a subtly flavoured coconut cream to create a light vegetarian dish of distinction. Or serve it as a zesty accompaniment to skewers of poultry or seafood. Serve with freshly boiled fragrant rice from a Chinese or Asian store, if you can get it.

For the Vegetables
100g/4oz snow peas
225g/8oz Chinese cabbage
4 plum tomatoes, cut into thin
  wedges
100g/4oz shelled or frozen
  peas
4-6 baby carrots, peeled and
  quartered

For the Aromatics
2 tablespoons vegetable oil
½ Spanish onion, chopped
1 clove garlic, finely chopped
¼ teaspoon ground turmeric
1/8 teaspoon chile powder
salt
300ml/10fl oz canned coconut
  milk

To Prepare the Vegetables: Trim the snow peas. Cut the cabbage into thin slices, as you would for coleslaw. Cut the plum tomatoes into thin wedges and then cut in half crossways. Shell the peas, if fresh, and peel and quarter the carrots. Set aside.

To Stir-fry: Heat the vegetable oil in a wok or large frying pan and stir-fry the chopped onion and garlic for 2 to 3 minutes, until slightly softened. Add the snow peas, peas and carrots along with the turmeric, chile powder, salt to taste and half of the coconut milk. Cook for 3 minutes, stirring constantly.

   Add the sliced cabbage and the tomato wedges and cook for a further 3 minutes. Pour in the remaining coconut milk and simmer for 1 to 2 minutes, so that the vegetables are hot but still crunchy. Taste and correct the seasoning, and serve immediately.

Serves 4

Frédy Girardet's Vegetable Charlottes

Frédy Girardet's restaurant at Crissier near Lausanne was one of the 'musts' for any gastronomic tour of Europe. His charlottes of eggplant and zucchini – pretty parcels of lightly poached vegetables – are a worthy tribute to this great chef.

2 large eggplants
3 tablespoons olive oil
15g/½oz butter
4 medium-sized zucchini
4 small onions, finely chopped
4 cloves garlic, finely chopped
salt and freshly ground pepper
4 sun-dried tomatoes (in oil),
    chopped
2 teaspoons finely chopped
    flat-leaf parsley

To Prepare the Eggplants: Using a sharp knife, peel off the purple skins of the eggplants (reserve the flesh). Cut most of the skin into long thin strips, about 2.5cm/1in wide. Cut the remaining skin into 4 squares of about 5cm/2in. Blanch the skin in boiling water for 30 seconds, then drain and sauté quickly in 1 tablespoon of olive oil and the butter.

To Prepare the Soufflé Molds: Butter 4 soufflé molds, about 7.5cm/3in across the top and 4cm/1½in high. Line each mold with blanched eggplant strips, with the purple side of the skins facing out (each strip to be placed from the center of the mold so the strips hang over the edge). Cover the bottom of each mold with a square of eggplant skin.

If desired, you could line the molds instead with long thin strips of zucchini skin prepared in the same manner. (In this case you will need extra zucchini.)

To Prepare the Stuffing: Preheat the oven to 130°C/250°F. Trim the zucchini and dice them and the eggplant flesh.

In a thick-bottomed frying pan, heat the remaining olive oil and sauté the finely chopped onions and garlic until soft. Add equal quantities of diced zucchini and eggplant (you'll find you have extra eggplant flesh for another use). Season to taste with salt and freshly ground pepper, and sauté for a further 3 minutes. Using a slotted spoon, transfer the sautéed vegetables to a bowl.

Season the chopped sun-dried tomatoes generously with salt and freshly ground pepper and sauté for a few minutes in the remaining pan juices. Using a slotted spoon, transfer to the bowl of cooked vegetables. Add the finely chopped parsley and mix well.

To Finish the Dish: Fill the molds with the stuffing of cooked vegetables, pressing well down with a wooden spoon. Fold over the eggplant strips, pressing down with the palm of your hand. Place in a roasting tin and pour in boiling water to come a third of the way up the sides of the molds. Set the tin over a high heat until the water comes to the boil again, then cook in the preheated oven for 20 minutes. Unmold and serve immediately.

Serves 4

Jansson's Vegetarian Temptation

A Swedish dish of layered potatoes and onions with, in its vegetarian version, chopped sun-dried tomatoes instead of the usual anchovies. Believe me, it is even more delicious made in the vegetarian way.

675g/1½ lb new potatoes, peeled and thinly sliced
10–12 sun-dried tomatoes (in oil), cut into strips
1 Spanish onion, finely chopped
5 tablespoons melted butter
1½ tablespoons flour
salt and freshly ground pepper
5 tablespoons heavy cream
150ml/5fl oz milk

To Prepare the Baking dish: Preheat the oven to 190°C/375°F. Butter a round 22cm/9in shallow heatproof baking dish and arrange a layer of potato slices in the bottom. Sprinkle with a few strips of sun-dried tomatoes, a little finely chopped onion, melted butter and flour, and season with salt and freshly ground pepper to taste. Continue in this manner until all the ingredients are used up, ending with a neat layer of sliced potatoes.

To Make the Sauce: In a bowl combine the heavy cream with the milk. Pour over the top of the potatoes, add a sprinkling of freshly ground pepper and cover the baking dish with a lid. Bake for 1 hour in the preheated oven. Remove the lid and continue to cook for 25 to 30 minutes, or until golden brown on top. Serve hot.

Serves 4

Chris Jackman's Twice-Cooked Eggs in Chile and Palm Sugar Bouillon

Chris Jackman is an unusual young cook who has achieved great status in his native Tasmania. Self-trained, imaginative, and incredibly hard-working, he creates staggeringly different dishes unaided in a kitchen the size of a teacloth. His restaurant, Mit Zitrone, three small rooms, is not much bigger. This recipe for soft-poached eggs, deep-fried for only seconds and served in a light Thai bouillon, is one of the most creative dishes I met on my recent judging tour of Australia.

8–12 eggs
vegetable oil, for deep-frying

For the Chile and Palm Sugar Bouillon
100g/4oz chopped palm sugar
2 tablespoons fish sauce
120ml/4fl oz cold water
1–2 small fresh hot red chiles
8 fresh coriander roots and stems
juice of 1 large lime

For the Egg-poaching Medium
1 litre/35fl oz water
4–6 tablespoons rice wine vinegar

For the Garnish
2–3 large cloves garlic, thinly sliced
8–12 young spinach leaves
8 sprigs of fresh coriander
2 small fresh hot chiles, thinly sliced

Note: Wash hands thoroughly with soap and water after touching chile peppers. Do not touch your eyes until all traces of the hot chiles are removed from your fingers.

To Prepare the Chile and Palm Sugar Bouillon: In a medium-sized saucepan, melt the palm sugar with the fish sauce and water. Remove the pan from the heat and allow to cool.

Break the red chile pepper(s) in half, squeeze to remove the seeds and dry-roast in a frying pan over a high heat until aromatic. When cool, crush the chile halves between your fingertips and add to the palm sugar sauce. (See note, left, about preparing chile.)

Wash and chop the coriander roots and stems and add them to the sauce with the lime juice. Taste the sauce: it should taste sweet, a little salt and slightly sour. Add a little more palm sugar, fish sauce or lime juice, if desired, and a little more water, if necessary. Reserve.

To Poach the Eggs: Pour the water and rice wine vinegar into a large saucepan and bring to the boil. Poach a few eggs at a time until soft, then transfer with a slotted spoon to a bowl of cold water. Cook the remaining eggs in the same way and reserve in cold water.

To Finish the Dish: Heat the bouillon and keep hot. Then, heat a small wok or saucepan two-thirds filled with vegetable oil until a 2.5cm/1in piece of bread sizzles in the hot oil and turns golden brown within 1 minute. Deep-fry the eggs in the hot oil, 3 or 4 at a time, for 20 to 30 seconds until crisp and golden. With a slotted spoon, transfer the lightly fried eggs to folded paper towel to remove excess oil. Repeat with the remaining eggs and keep warm.

Toss the thinly sliced garlic into the hot oil, standing well back from the pan as the oil will spatter when the garlic hits it. Use a slotted spoon to remove the garlic after a second or two, when it is golden, then add the spinach leaves to the hot oil, standing well back again from the pan. Remove with a slotted spoon after a second or two.

To Serve: Arrange 2 or 3 twice-cooked eggs in each of 4 heated shallow soup plates. Top each egg with a fried spinach leaf, scatter garlic slices around the plate, and garnish with 2 coriander sprigs and a few chile slices. Pour over the hot bouillon and serve immediately.

Serves 4

Great Vegetarian

Creole Saffron Rice with Roasted Red Peppers

This Creole version of saffron rice (made with long-grain rice), enriched with colourful diced and sliced vegetables, is served as an attractive golden dome garnished with roasted red pepper quarters and plump black olives or sprigs of watercress. I sometimes substitute couscous for the rice, using less stock to moisten the couscous. It is a delicious variation.

1 large Spanish onion, chopped
4 tablespoons olive oil
1½ green peppers, diced
4 sticks celery, thinly sliced
2 cloves garlic, finely chopped
350g/12oz long-grain rice
1 large pinch saffron threads
1 teaspoon ground turmeric
salt and freshly ground pepper
crushed dried chiles
hot vegetable stock
6 scallions, green parts
    only, cut into 6mm/¼ in
    segments, or 6 tablespoons
    frozen peas

For the Garnish
2 red peppers, roasted (page
    12) and cut into thick strips
black olives or sprigs of
    watercress

To Prepare the Rice: In a large heatproof casserole, sauté the chopped onion in the olive oil until the onion is translucent. Add the diced green peppers, sliced celery and finely chopped garlic and continue to cook, stirring, for 3 minutes more.

Add the rice and continue to cook, stirring from time to time, until the rice is translucent. Add the saffron threads, turmeric, and salt, freshly ground pepper and crushed dried chiles to taste. Stir well to distribute the flavours.

Add a ladle or two of hot vegetable stock. Mix well and continue to cook, adding more hot stock as necessary, until the rice is tender, but not mushy. Then stir in the chopped scallions or peas, and taste and correct the seasoning. Transfer the hot rice to a large heated mixing bowl (to form a rounded shape on the serving dish).

To Serve: Place a heated serving dish over the bowl of rice and carefully invert the dish and bowl so that you can lift off the bowl to leave a mound of rice in the center of the dish.

Garnish the mound of rice with strips of roasted red pepper and place a small mound of black olives, or sprigs of fresh watercress, on top. You can also serve the rice unmolded, and garnish loosely with the red pepper and olives or watercress. Either way, serve immediately.

Serves 6

Eggplants Imam Bayeldi

Eggplants – like portobello mushrooms – are an integral part of vegetarian cooking. Their meaty texture and rich, full flavour make them wonderful bases for a thousand fillings. Here we use the eggplant as the Turks, the Greeks and the Arabs do, as a supremely edible base for a rich cargo of chopped eggplant, tomatoes, onion and garlic, flavoured in the eastern way with sugar, cinnamon, saffron and crushed dried chiles.

4 medium-sized eggplants, stems trimmed

salt

3–4 tablespoons olive oil

4 tomatoes

sugar

freshly ground pepper

sprigs of fresh coriander and flat-leaf parsley

For the Stuffing

2 Spanish onions, sliced

2 tablespoons olive oil

2 cloves garlic, finely chopped

2 tablespoons finely chopped fresh flat-leaf parsley

½ teaspoon ground cinnamon

1 large pinch saffron threads

crushed dried chiles

6 ripe tomatoes, seeded and chopped

To Prepare the Eggplants: Cut the eggplants in half lengthways and scoop out and reserve some of the flesh, leaving shells about 6mm/¼ in thick. Make 4 incisions lengthways in each half, being careful not to cut through the skin. Salt the eggplant halves, making sure the salt goes into the incisions, and leave for 20 minutes. Rinse the eggplants and squeeze them dry, then sauté in the olive oil in a frying pan until soft and pliable. Set the eggplants aside, and reserve the oil.

To Prepare the Stuffing: In another frying pan, sauté the sliced onions in the olive oil until translucent. Add the finely chopped garlic and parsley, the cinnamon, saffron threads, crushed dried chiles to taste, the seeded and chopped tomatoes and the reserved chopped eggplant flesh. Sauté for a few minutes more, stirring from time to time. Remove from the heat and allow to cool.

To Bake the Eggplants: Preheat the oven to 170°C/325°F. Place the sautéed eggplant shells, cut-side up, in a fairly deep baking dish or shallow casserole. Stuff with the onion and tomato mixture, spooning any that is left over around the eggplants.

Slice the whole tomatoes and place the slices on top of the stuffing. Sprinkle with a little sugar, salt and freshly ground pepper to taste. Pour over the reserved oil. Add a little water to the dish and cook in the preheated oven for 1 hour.

To Serve: Transfer the stuffed eggplants to a heated serving dish and surround with sprigs of coriander and flat-leaf parsley.

Serves 4

Great
Lunches

Sally Clarke's Grilled Eggplant with Black Olives, Mozzarella and Bitter Leaves

Sally Clarke's restaurant in Kensington is one of my favourites, as is Sally, herself. Her intriguing recipe calls for a thick slice of grilled eggplant topped with a mountain of black olives, capers and Italian mozzarella balls. A great appetizer and an even better luncheon dish.

1 large eggplant
olive oil
sea salt and freshly ground
  pepper
1 teaspoon chopped fresh
  thyme
selection of salad leaves, such
  as arugula, escarole, mâche
  and radicchio
4 small balls of mozzarella –
  buffalo if possible

*For the Olive and Herb
Dressing*
2 cloves garlic
4 tablespoons extra virgin
  olive oil
4 teaspoons small capers
8–12 tablespoons pitted and
  roughly chopped black
  olives
4 tablespoons chopped fresh
  flat-leaf parsley
4 tablespoons chopped fresh
  coriander
sea salt

To Make the Olive and Herb Dressing: Crush the garlic to a cream and marinate in the extra virgin olive oil. In a bowl combine the capers, chopped olives and chopped flat-leaf parsley and coriander with the garlic and oil mixture. Season with sea salt and mix together.

To Prepare the Eggplant: Slice the eggplant crossways into 4 thick rounds. Drizzle some olive oil over both sides of the eggplant and season with sea salt and freshly ground pepper.

Grill the eggplant slices on both sides on a very hot ridged cast-iron char-grill pan (or you can use a barbecue). Using tongs, remove the slices from the pan and sprinkle with chopped thyme.

To Prepare the Leaves and Mozzarella: Mix the salad leaves together in a bowl and toss with a little olive oil. Season with sea salt and freshly ground pepper.

Cut the mozzarella balls into quarters, sprinkle with any remaining thyme and season with salt and pepper.

To Serve: Pile the olive and herb dressing on top of the eggplant slices and surround with the salad leaves. Top with the quartered mozzarella.

Give a final drizzle of olive oil and serve, immediately, with breadsticks or crusty bread.

Serves 4

Moroccan Kefta with Poached Eggs

The combination of eggs poached on a bed of highly spiced meats or vegetables (see Tunisian adja with poached eggs on page 33) is a North African speciality. The comforting blandness of the soft cooked eggs is the perfect foil for the spicy sauce.

450g/1lb boneless lamb, taken from the leg
100g/4oz lamb fat, or make up this amount with beef suet
½ Spanish onion, finely chopped
6–8 sprigs of fresh flat-leaf parsley or coriander, finely chopped
½ teaspoon dried marjoram
salt and freshly ground pepper
¼ teaspoon each ground cumin, cayenne pepper and paprika
1 generous pinch of 2 or more of the following: freshly grated nutmeg and ground cinnamon, cloves, ginger and cardamom
40g/1½oz butter
3 tablespoons olive oil

For the Kefta Sauce
450g/1lb tomatoes, peeled, seeded and coarsely chopped
½ Spanish onion, finely chopped
2 tablespoons finely chopped fresh flat-leaf parsley or coriander
1 clove garlic, finely chopped
4 tablespoons olive oil
paprika, cayenne pepper and salt

For the Garnish
6 medium eggs

To Prepare the Kefta Sauce: Combine all the ingredients in a large, shallow, thick-bottomed pan and simmer for 1 hour, uncovered (the sauce should be very highly flavoured).

To Prepare the Kefta Balls: Meanwhile, put the lamb, lamb fat and chopped onion through the finest blade of your mincer 3 times or grind in a food processor.

Combine the lamb mixture with the chopped parsley or coriander and the dried marjoram. Season to taste with salt, freshly ground pepper and all the spices. Mix well. The kefta mixture should be very highly flavoured.

Form the mixture into little balls the size of a marble and poach gently in water for 10 minutes. Then sauté gently in butter and olive oil until lightly browned.

To Finish and Serve: Add the lamb balls to the kefta sauce and simmer for at least 10 minutes before poaching the eggs. Make six depressions in the mixture using the back of a spoon, and carefully break an egg into each one. Cover the pan and poach the eggs for 10 minutes, until set. Serve on a bed of boiled rice.

Serves 6

Chile Mussels

South Sea aromatics – coriander, turmeric, hot red chiles and ginger – partner finely chopped garlic, onion and slivers of orange zest to make this one of the greatest mussel dishes you have ever tasted. Go easy on the chiles on your first try … and then go chile wild.

For the Chile Mussels
1kg/2¼lb mussels
4 tablespoons olive oil
1 clove garlic, finely chopped
½ Spanish onion, finely chopped
grated zest of 1 orange
6–8 thin slices fresh ginger
1-2 fresh red chiles, thinly sliced
5–6 tablespoons dry white wine
¼–½ teaspoon ground turmeric

For the Garnish
12 fresh coriander leaves
12 basil leaves
2-4 fresh red chiles

To Prepare the Mussels: Place the mussels in a large colander and rinse well under running water. Scrape each shell with a knife, removing all traces of mud, seaweed and barnacles. Discard any mussels with cracked, broken or open shells: they are unfit to eat. Rinse again under running water and remove the 'beards'.

When Ready to Cook the Mussels: In a large, flat, heatproof casserole, heat the olive oil. Add the finely chopped garlic and onion and sauté, stirring constantly, until the onion is translucent. Add the orange zest, sliced ginger and chile, and continue to cook, stirring, for 30 seconds.

Drain the mussels of any water and add to the casserole with the wine and the turmeric. Cover and simmer for 2 to 3 minutes, or until the mussels have opened.

To Serve: Discard any mussels that have not opened. Add the fresh coriander, basil and whole chiles to the mussels, pour into a heated serving bowl or individual bowls, and serve immediately.

Serves 4

Seared Salmon with Greek Garlic Potato Purée

A light luncheon dish of pan-seared salmon filet over a Greek garlic-flavoured potato purée is another, lighter version of the chicken and garlic theme so beloved by cooks since the time of the early Greeks and Mediterraneans.

**4 filets of fresh salmon,
    175–225g/6–8oz each**
4 tablespoons olive oil
sea salt
crushed dried chiles
juice of ½ lemon

For the Greek Garlic Potato Purée
4 baking potatoes
sea salt
6 large cloves garlic, sliced
**4 slices white bread, crusts
    removed**
150ml/5fl oz olive oil
juice of 1 lemon
freshly ground pepper

For the Garnish
**4 ripe plum tomatoes, seeded
    and diced**
**½ cucumber (unpeeled), seeded
    and diced**
½ red onion, diced

To Prepare the Greek Garlic Potato Purée: Peel the potatoes and cut into quarters. Put into a medium-sized saucepan, pour in enough water to cover, add a good pinch of salt and bring to the boil over a high heat. Reduce the heat to medium and cook until the potatoes are tender. Drain, saving a little of the potato water for further use.

Pound the sliced garlic and 2 teaspoons sea salt in a mortar until smooth. Soak the bread in a little potato water then squeeze dry and add to the pounded garlic. Pound again. Add this mixture to the potatoes and mash until smooth, then gradually add the olive oil and lemon juice, continuing to mash, until you have a smooth purée. Season to taste with sea salt and freshly ground pepper. Keep the potato purée warm.

You can also make the purée in a food processor using start-stop start-stop bursts until smooth.

To Pan-sear the Salmon Filets: In a large frying pan, or two smaller ones, heat the olive oil until sizzling. Add the salmon filets, season each one generously with sea salt and a pinch of crushed dried chiles and cook for 4 minutes. With a metal spatula, carefully turn the filets over in the pan(s) and cook for 3 more minutes until done. The salmon, when done, should be well seared on both sides and meltingly tender in the middle.

Two minutes before the salmon filets are done, add the garnish of diced plum tomatoes, cucumber and red onion to the pan(s) and warm through.

To Serve: Place a helping of purée on each of 4 heated plates and arrange a salmon filet on top. Spoon over the diced vegetable garnish, drizzle with pan juices and sprinkle with lemon juice. Serve immediately.

Serves 4

Joyce Molyneux's Dart Salmon with Samphire

Rock samphire is one of the 'new' garnishes that the more sophisticated restaurants are using to lend flavour and substance to imaginative fish dishes. Lucky if you live near the seashore (Joyce Molyneux's restaurant, the Carved Angel, is indeed by the sea, in Dartmouth, Devon), where samphire grows wild at the water's edge, but not so easy if you are looking for it in your local supermarket. I use sprigs of fresh young rosemary from the garden, perfect with the Champagne that adds sparkle to this great dish. But you could use marsh samphire or purslane (from the herb garden), or even sprigs of fresh watercress with thin strips of lemon grass (now found in most supermarkets) for the lemony taste.

4 x 150g/5oz portions of salmon filet, cleaned and stray bones removed
sea salt
handful of rock samphire, well washed
120ml/4fl oz dry white wine or Champagne

For the Sauce
the pan juices
150ml/5fl oz heavy cream, or a few pats of butter

To Prepare the Salmon: Preheat the oven to 140°C/275°F.

Lay the salmon in a buttered shallow heatproof dish. Season with a little sea salt and arrange the samphire on top, then pour the wine or Champagne over. Cover with a sheet of aluminium foil and cook in the preheated oven for 10 minutes.

To Prepare the Sauce: Transfer the salmon and samphire to a warm place and strain their pan juices into a saucepan. Bubble the juices over a high heat until reduced by half, then add the cream and reduce again, or finish the sauce by beating in a few pats of butter. Remove the skin from the salmon before serving.

To Serve: Arrange the salmon and samphire on heated plates and pour the sauce around them. Serve immediately.

Serves 4

Tagine of Monkfish with Mussels and Saffron Potatoes

Monkfish, often surreptitiously substituted for more expensive lobster or prawns in the old days, is now a highly prized, highly priced ingredient in its own right. I love its firm, tight texture when simmered with mussels and saffron potatoes in bouillon.

1kg/2¼ lb fresh mussels
4–6 small monkfish tails, skinned and each cut into 3-4 pieces

For the 'Dry' Marinade
½ Spanish onion, finely chopped
2 cloves garlic, finely chopped
4–6 tablespoons fresh coriander, finely chopped
4–6 tablespoons fresh flat-leaf parsley, finely chopped
6 tablespoons olive oil
1 fish stock cube, crumbled
½ teaspoon each salt, powdered cumin and paprika
¼ teaspoon each powdered ginger and cayenne pepper

For the Saffron Potatoes
675g/1½ lb medium-sized new potatoes
1 large pinch saffron threads
1 vegetable stock cube, crumbled
salt and crushed dried chiles

To Prepare the Mussels: Place the mussels in a large colander and rinse well under running water. Scrape each shell with a knife, removing all traces of mud, seaweed and barnacles. Discard any mussels with cracked, broken or open shells: they are unfit to eat. Rinse again under running water and remove the 'beards'.

To Flavour the Monkfish and the Mussels: Combine all the ingredients for the dry marinade. Dip each piece of monkfish into this flavourful mixture, rubbing the aromatics and spices well into the flesh. Place the monkfish in a heatproof Moroccan tagine, a shallow casserole with a lid or even a covered roasting pan. Set aside.

Preheat the oven to 180°C/350°F.

Spoon the remaining marinade into a saucepan and add the prepared mussels. Add 6 tablespoons of water and cover the pan, then steam the mussels for 3 to 5 minutes. Remove the opened mussels from the pan – discarding any that did not open – and reserve, with their juices.

Cover the tagine and cook the monkfish in the preheated oven for 10 to 15 minutes or until the fish is cooked through. Remove the tagine from the oven and reserve.

To Prepare the Saffron Potatoes: While the fish is cooking, peel and slice the potatoes thickly. Put in a medium-sized saucepan and cover with water, adding the vegetable stock cube and the saffron threads and seasoning to taste with salt and crushed dried chiles. Cook gently until tender.

To Serve the Tagine: Add the mussels and their juices to the tagine. (If you have more mussels than you need, the remainder can be refrigerated and served in another meal the following day, such as with vinaigrette or mayonnaise.) Use a slotted spoon to remove the potato slices from their saffron bouillon. Scatter the potato over the seafood, spoon over the saffron bouillon, and warm through. Serve immediately.

Serves 4

Redfish Saltimbocca with Rosemary and Citrus Zest

Little 'jump-in-the-mouth' segments of pan-seared red mullet or red snapper (instead of milk-fed veal), garnished with sprigs of fresh rosemary and threads of citrus zest (instead of traditional sage leaves), provide a new slant on the classic Italian saltimbocca. You will love the difference. Serve with boiled new potatoes and wilted salad greens (page 17).

4-8 filets of rouget (red mullet) or red snapper, depending on size of fish
olive oil
thinly pared zest and juice of ½ lime
thinly pared zest and juice of ½ lemon or orange
salt and freshly ground pepper
¼ crumbled fish stock cube
12 small sprigs of fresh rosemary
crushed dried chiles

To Prepare the Saltimbocca Packets: With a sharp knife, cut each fish filet into 3 diagonal segments. Brush the fish filets with olive oil, sprinkle with lime or lemon juice, season with salt and freshly ground pepper and reserve.

Reserve the remaining citrus juice. Cut the thinly pared zests lengthways into threads. Blanch, then drain and reserve.

When Ready to Cook: In 1 large frying pan or 2 smaller ones (enough to take all the saltimbocca in a single layer), heat 2 to 4 tablespoons of olive oil. Add the crumbled fish stock cube and stir until well blended. Then add the fish segments, sprinkle with the citrus threads and cook for 3 minutes on one side, adding a little more olive oil if necessary.

With a metal spatula, turn the fish segments over. Top each with a small sprig of fresh rosemary, cover the pan(s) and cook for 3 minutes more. Season to taste with crushed dried chiles and sprinkle with the reserved lime and lemon or orange juices.

To Serve: With a metal spatula, transfer the saltimbocca, topped with rosemary sprigs, to 4 heated plates: 3-4 saltimbocca per serving. Spoon over the citrus threads and pan juices and serve immediately.

Serves 4

Wolfgang Puck's Salmon in Fresh Basil Sauce

Looking for a fresh salmon dish that literally takes minutes to prepare but is elegant enough for a special lunch or dinner party? Look no further: famous Californian chef Wolfgang Puck's salmon in fresh basil sauce is made in minutes. Once the basil sauce is done (before your guests arrive), the last-minute preparation of the raw salmon and cooked sauce takes literally one minute under the broiler. Now that's quick cooking!

1kg/2¼ lb filet of fresh salmon, cut into 2mm thick slices (you may have to pick out small pin-sized central bones with tweezers)

For the Sauce
8 tablespoons chopped fresh basil
50g/2oz butter
3 large shallots, sliced
2 medium-sized mushrooms, sliced
450ml/15fl oz dry white wine
450ml/15fl oz fish stock
450ml/15fl oz heavy cream
100g/4oz butter in 4 equal-sized pieces
salt (optional)

For the Garnish
fresh basil leaves

To Prepare the Basil Sauce: In a heavy saucepan, melt the butter over a low heat. Add the sliced shallots and mushrooms and cook for 10 minutes. Add the dry white wine and half the chopped basil and continue to cook until the liquid is reduced to half its original quantity.

Add the fish stock to the pan and continue to cook until the liquid is reduced to half its original quantity.

Reserving 1 to 2 tablespoons heavy cream, add the remaining cream to the pan and continue to cook until the sauce is reduced and thick enough to coat the back of a spoon.

Strain the sauce through a fine sieve into a clean pan. Measure about 120ml/4fl oz into a blender or food processor, add the remaining basil and purée until smooth. Whisk the purée back into the sauce. Set the pan over a low heat and whisk in the butter, 1 piece at a time. Season with salt, if necessary. Strain through a fine sieve into a bowl.

To Prepare the Salmon: Preheat the broiler to high. Stir the reserved cream into the sauce and pour it over the bottom of a heatproof serving dish. Arrange the salmon slices on top and broil 7.5cm/3in from the heat for about 1 minute, or until the salmon changes colour and is slightly underdone.

Serve immediately, garnished with basil leaves.

Serves 4 to 6

Gordon Ramsay's Filets of John Dory and Crushed New Potatoes

Very 'new cooking' is Gordon Ramsay's way with potatoes and olive oil – not a purée, more of a chunky mash. Flavoured with extra virgin olive oil, tomato concassé, chopped fresh herbs and a spark of lemon juice, the potatoes are then shaped with a large pastry cutter to give an architectural look to the dish. Use this splendid idea to lend distinction to grilled lamb cutlets, pan-seared chicken or just plain bangers, as well as to fish, as here.

4 x 200g/7oz filets of John Dory or halibut, skinned
600g/1lb 5oz Jersey Royals (or other fine baby new potatoes), scrubbed
2 tablespoons extra virgin olive oil
100g/4oz very finely diced peeled tomato (concassé) plus 4 teaspoons for sauce
1 tablespoon finely diced and sautéed shallots (confit)
50g/2oz fresh chives, snipped
1 tablespoon chopped fresh basil
1 tablespoon chopped fresh tarragon
1 tablespoon chopped fresh coriander
juice of 1 lemon
salt and freshly ground pepper
3 tablespoons olive oil

For the Sauce
200ml/7fl oz vegetable stock
4 teaspoons tomato concassé
3 tablespoons olive oil
1 tablespoon balsamic vinegar
1 tablespoon chopped fresh basil

To Prepare the Fish: Cut each filet into 3 long strips, then cut these into 5cm/2in diamond shapes. Set aside.

To Prepare the Potatoes: Boil the potatoes, still in their skins, until just tender: about 12 minutes. Drain and leave for a few minutes until just cool enough to handle. Peel while warm and place in a large bowl.

Gently heat the extra virgin olive oil in a small saucepan, then pour it over the potatoes. Lightly crush the potatoes with a fork into a chunky purée.

Mix in the tomato concassé, confit of shallots, chopped fresh herbs and the lemon juice. Season lightly, cover and keep warm.

To Prepare the Sauce: Put all the sauce ingredients into a small saucepan and set aside until ready to serve.

To Finish and Serve: Heat the olive oil in a large nonstick or well-seasoned frying pan and fry the John Dory (or halibut) 'diamonds' for 2 or 3 minutes, turning once, until golden brown.

Using a pastry cutter, about 6cm/2½in across, press the potato into rounds and transfer to 4 warm dinner plates. Stack the fish on top, overlapping attractively.

Bring the sauce ingredients to the boil, spoon around each fish and potato mould and serve immediately.

Serves 4

Risotto with Arugula, Asparagus and Parmesan Shavings

Fresh green asparagus spears, cut into bite-sized pieces, and bitter green arugula leaves, very coarsely chopped, lend colour and a very special flavour to this vegetable risotto. Use a vegetable peeler to shave off thin curls from a piece of fresh Parmesan cheese. Don't use the pre-packed variety – it just will not work. And remember: the bigger the piece of fresh Parmesan, the easier to cut the shavings.

18 fresh asparagus spears, trimmed
salt
75g/3oz salted butter
½ crumbled vegetable stock cube
1 Spanish onion, finely chopped
275g/10oz arborio rice
150ml/5fl oz dry white wine (and/or dry white vermouth)
1 litre/35fl oz hot light stock
6–8 tablespoons arugula leaves, very coarsely chopped
freshly ground pepper
crushed dried chiles
4–6 tablespoons freshly grated Parmesan cheese

For the Garnish
thin shavings of fresh Parmesan cheese

To Prepare the Asparagus: Cut the asparagus into 4cm/1½in segments (discard the ends of the trimmed stems if woody). Place in a saucepan, cover with water and add salt. Bring to the boil and cook for 5 minutes. Remove from the liquid with a slotted spoon and reserve. Add the cooking liquid to the hot light stock.

To Make the Risotto: In a heavy saucepan, melt two-thirds of the butter with the ½ stock cube. Add the chopped onion and sauté over a medium heat, stirring constantly, for about 5 minutes, or until the onion is translucent. Add the arborio rice and stir over the heat for a further 2 to 3 minutes.

Pour in the wine and cook, stirring, until it has been absorbed, then add a third of the hot stock and cook until the stock has been absorbed, stirring often. Add the blanched asparagus segments and half the remaining stock. Continue cooking, gradually adding the remaining stock, until all the liquid has been absorbed and the rice is tender: about 15 to 20 minutes.

Stir in the chopped arugula leaves. Season to taste with salt, freshly ground pepper and crushed dried chiles, and fork in the remaining butter and the freshly grated Parmesan cheese. Garnish with Parmesan shavings and serve immediately.

Serves 4 to 6

Red Snapper in Saffron Sauce

This is one of the most colourful luncheon dishes I know, and one of the quickest to prepare. Just simmer snapper filets (or substitute filets of sole or red mullet) for minutes only in the highly flavoured court bouillon. Then serve them in a saffron cream heavily spiked with a reduction of the fish's own bouillon. Garnish the dish with a painter's palette of shiny black olives, cooked green vegetables and thinly sliced sun-dried tomatoes.

4 filets of red snapper

For the Marinade
2 tablespoons olive oil
juice of 1 lime
2 teaspoons Thai fish sauce
sea salt
crushed dried chiles

For the Court Bouillon
1 fish stock cube (or chicken or vegetable)
600ml/20fl oz water
crushed dried chiles
fennel seeds
coriander seeds

For the Saffron Cream Sauce
1 x 400ml/14fl oz tub crème fraîche
2–4 generous pinches of saffron threads

For the Garnish
12 black olives (the wrinkled Greek type)
12 cooked sugarsnap peas
12 cooked small broccoli florets
12 cooked small snow peas
12 thinly sliced sun-dried tomatoes (in oil)

To Make the Marinade: Combine the olive oil, lime juice and Thai fish sauce in a dish large enough to contain the fish. Add sea salt and crushed dried chiles to taste. Rub the fish filets with this marinade and allow them to 'marinate' in the flavoursome mixture for at least 20 minutes.

To Cook the Fish in the Court Bouillon: In a shallow stainless steel sauté pan (or stainless steel frying pan) large enough to contain the snapper filets comfortably, combine the fish stock cube and water. Add a pinch or two each of crushed dried chiles and fennel and coriander seeds and bring to the boil.

Add the snapper filets, gently flattening each one with a wooden spoon or spatula. Bring back to the boil over a medium heat, then allow the fish to cook for 1 minute longer. Remove the pan from the heat; the fish will continue to cook in the hot court bouillon.

To Prepare the Sauce: Transfer 150ml/¼ pint of the court bouillon to a small saucepan. Cook over a high heat until it reduces to about 2 tablespoons. Add the crème fraîche and saffron threads, to taste, and stir until the mixture is a creamy golden colour and coats the back of a spoon.

Return the pan containing the fish filets to the heat. Heat through and, when hot, transfer the filets (using a fish slice) to a heated serving dish.

To Serve: Strain the sauce over the fish and garnish with black olives, cooked sugarsnap peas, broccoli and snow peas, and thinly sliced sun-dried tomatoes.

Serves 4

Chris Jackman's Rare Beef and Red Pepper 'Sandwich' with Parmesan Shavings

When judging Australia's most exciting restaurants, I travelled to Hobart to find a laid-back young chef–proprietor whose creative dishes were among the freshest-tasting, most imaginative in the Pacific Rim. Simple to execute, but wonderfully different in flavour and texture. His rare beef and red pepper 'sandwich' is a case in point. Chris peels his peppers rather than roasting them to give a crisper texture to this great dish. Ask a butcher for what New Yorkers call 'strip' steaks: the boneless strip of loin left once the filet is removed from the sirloin.

2 medium-sized red peppers
200ml/6½ fl oz olive oil
2 cloves garlic, thinly sliced
2 bay leaves
1 sprig of thyme
2 sirloin 'strip' steaks,
   2.5cm/1in thick
freshly ground pepper
4 tablespoons fresh flat-leaf
   parsley, leaves only, chopped
16 anchovy filets, in oil, each
   sliced lengthways into 3

For the Garnish
thin shavings of Parmesan
   cheese

To Prepare the Peppers: Peel the red peppers with a vegetable peeler and remove stems and seeds. Cut each pepper into quarters. Place the quarters in a saucepan and add the olive oil, sliced garlic, bay leaves and thyme. Simmer gently until the peppers are soft. Cool, and then refrigerate the peppers, garlic, herbs and oil.

To Prepare the Beef, Parsley and Anchovy Salad: In a very hot nonstick frying pan, sear the beef on all sides, including the edges. The steaks should remain very rare inside the crusty seared edges. Season to taste with freshly ground pepper.

Chop the parsley leaves.

Cut the beef, lengthways, into 3mm/⅛in-thick slices. In a shallow bowl, combine the rare beef strips with the chopped parsley and the anchovy. Season with freshly ground pepper and half of the oil from the peppers. Chill.

When Ready to Serve: Place 2 quarters of red pepper in the center of each of 4 salad plates. Arrange the marinated rare beef and anchovy strips on the bed of red peppers, allowing the bed of red peppers to show through. Garnish the salad with thin shavings of Parmesan cheese, and serve.

Serves 4

The Paramount's Eggplant, Goat Cheese and Pesto Sandwich

In the words of its creators, Christine Manfield and Marjie Harris, based in Melbourne and two of Australia's foremost restaurateurs: 'The success of this dish lies in its combination of flavours and its last-minute cooking and assembly. Its construction is a play on the concept of a sandwich, where the eggplant takes on the role of bread and simply transforms a classic idea into a more theatrical presentation.'

3 medium-sized eggplants
sea salt
vegetable oil, for deep-frying
2 tablespoons balsamic vinegar
6 tablespoons olive oil
freshly ground pepper
300g/10oz fresh goat cheese,
   at room temperature
2 red peppers, roasted
   (page 12) and cut into strips
   lengthways
3 tablespoons pesto sauce
3 tablespoons finely shredded
   arugula leaves

To Prepare the Eggplants: Trim the eggplants and cut each one crossways into 4 thick slices (about 2cm/¾in). Sprinkle with salt and leave to sweat for 1 hour. Pat dry with kitchen paper to remove any excess moisture and salt.

Heat vegetable oil in a deep-fat fryer or large saucepan to 180°C/350°F. Fry the eggplant slices until golden-brown on both sides. Drain, then pat dry with kitchen paper.

To Prepare a Vinaigrette: Whisk together the balsamic vinegar and the olive oil with a pinch of sea salt and freshly ground pepper.

To Assemble the Sandwiches: Cut the goat cheese into 6 slices of 2cm/¾in thick. Put a slice of eggplant on a plate and top with a slice of goat cheese. Cover the cheese with a few strips of roasted red pepper and then add a teaspoon of pesto. Drizzle over some vinaigrette and sprinkle on some finely shredded arugula leaves. Cover with another slice of eggplant, and top with a little extra pesto, vinaigrette and shredded arugula.

Repeat this process using the remaining ingredients to make 6 sandwiches. Serve immediately, while the arugula is hot.

Serves 6

Fresh Cod in Crisp Beer Batter

James Beard, famous American food guru, was one of the first chefs to use beer batter for frying fish. Now it is a commonplace in every professional chef's kitchen. If you are not already familiar with this great batter, get acquainted. You will never look back. And try the homemade tomato chutney, too, to bring simple fish-'n'-chips into gourmet terrain.

675g/1½lb filets of fresh cod
oil for deep-frying
lemon wedges

For the Beer Batter
125g/5oz flour
2 pinches of salt
2 tablespoons olive oil
150ml/5fl oz beer, preferably lager
1–4 tablespoons water
1 egg white

For the Flavouring Bath
6 tablespoons lemon juice
½ Spanish onion, very finely chopped
1–2 pinches each of salt and cayenne pepper

For the Tomato Chutney
1.2kg/2½lb fresh tomatoes, quartered and seeded
225g/8oz Spanish onions, sliced
450g/1lb cooking apples, peeled, cored and sliced
225g/8oz light brown sugar
1 teaspoon salt
1 teaspoon allspice
1½ teaspoons mustard seeds
150ml/5fl oz water
4 cloves
1 short cinnamon stick
100-150ml/4-5fl oz malt vinegar
crushed dried chiles

To Prepare the Beer Batter: Sift the flour and salt into a mixing bowl and make a well in the center. Pour in the olive oil and gradually add the beer, stirring with a wooden spoon to incorporate the flour from the sides until the batter is completely smooth. It should be slightly thicker than a crêpe batter: add a little water if necessary. Allow to rest for 2 hours. (Reserve the egg white.)

To Prepare the Cod: Cut the cod into serving pieces, 2 or 3 per person. Place in a flat porcelain bowl and sprinkle with the ingredients of the flavouring bath. Allow the fish to marinate in its bath for at least 1 hour, turning it once or twice.

When Ready to Fry: Heat the oil in a deep-fat fryer or a large saucepan to 190°C/375°F. Whisk the egg white until stiff but not dry, then fold gently into the batter. Use immediately.

With a slotted spoon or fish slice, remove the fish from the flavouring bath and pat it dry on both sides with paper towel. Dip the fish, piece by piece, into the batter, then deep-fry in the hot oil until golden brown and crisp. Place the fried fish in a dish lined with paper towel (to absorb excess fat) and keep warm while you fry the remaining fish pieces.

Serve immediately on a heated serving dish. Garnish with lemon wedges and serve with the tomato chutney or a bowl of homemade pesto (page 13) or one of the salsas on pages 14-16.

To Make the Tomato Chutney: In a large enamelled or stainless-steel pan (or a preserving pan), combine the tomatoes, onions, apples, sugar, salt, allspice and mustard seeds. Cook over a moderate heat, stirring occasionally to keep the ingredients from sticking, until thickened. Then add the water, cloves and cinnamon stick, along with malt vinegar and crushed dried chiles to taste, and stir well. Use a large baking dish to almost cover the pan and to keep the juices from evaporating, and then simmer for 1½-2 hours, stirring occasionally and adding a little water from time to time if the chutney shows signs of sticking or scorching.

While the chutney is still hot, pour it into sterilized, warm, dry preserving jars. Allow to cool then chill until ready to serve.

Serves 4

Barry Wine's Marinated Chicken with Sweet Potato Chips

Grilled chicken with an Asian flavour makes this New York grill special. Serve it with crisp, golden sweet potato chips, and with blanched broccoli florets, tiny button mushrooms and the sweetest smallest cherry tomatoes you can find.

4 tablespoons olive oil
4 tablespoons sesame oil
4 fat cloves garlic, finely
    chopped
4 thick slices fresh ginger,
    peeled and finely chopped
1 x 1.4kg/3lb chicken
salt and freshly ground pepper

For the Aïoli
1 teaspoon lemon juice
1 egg yolk
2 tablespoons olive oil
2 tablespoons sesame oil
2 tablespoons peanut oil
2 tablespoons heavy cream
2 cloves garlic, finely chopped
salt and freshly ground pepper

For the Sweet Potato Chips
900g/2lb sweet potatoes
salt
oil, for deep-frying

To Prepare the Chicken: In a heavy frying pan, combine the olive oil, sesame oil and finely chopped garlic and ginger and cook over a low heat for 10 minutes, stirring occasionally.

Pour the garlic and ginger marinade into a porcelain or earthenware (not metal) dish.

Using a sharp knife, cut the chicken into 6 serving pieces: 2 drumsticks, 2 thighs, and 2 breasts. (Save carcasses and wings for another use.) Season the chicken pieces generously with salt and freshly ground pepper, then place in the marinade, spooning it over. Leave in a refrigerator for at least 3 hours, turning several times.

To Prepare the Aïoli: Beat together the lemon juice and egg yolk. Gradually beat in the olive oil, sesame oil and peanut oil. Add the heavy cream and garlic, season with salt and freshly ground pepper and beat until smooth.

To Prepare the Chips: Scrub the sweet potatoes and cook in boiling salted water for 10 minutes. Drain, then cut into strips 5cm/2in long and 6mm/¼in wide. Dry with paper towel.

To Cook: Preheat the grill to high. Drain the chicken pieces, reserving the marinade. Brush the rack of a grill pan with olive oil and lay the chicken drumsticks and thighs, fleshy side up, on the rack. Place 12cm/5in from the heat and grill for 5 minutes.

Place the chicken breasts, fleshy side up, on the rack with the drumsticks and thighs, brush all the pieces with marinade and continue to grill for a further 15 minutes, or until cooked through, turning and brushing with marinade once more.

Meanwhile, heat the oil in a deep-fat fryer to 180°C/350°F.

Deep-fry a small quantity of chips at a time in the hot oil for 3 minutes, or until crisp and golden brown with a soft center. Drain on paper towel.

To Serve: Slice each chicken breast crossways into 4 to 6 thick slices. Sprinkle the chips with salt. Divide the chicken and the sweet potato chips among 4 heated plates. Drizzle a little aïoli over the chicken and serve the remainder separately.

Jamaican Jerk Chicken

On a recent trip to Jamaica to film *Carrier's Caribbean* I discovered a wonderful seasoning mix called 'jerk' which vies in excellence with the other great international 'dry' marinade for grilled meats, fish and poultry: Morocco's famed chermoula (chopped onion, garlic and coriander seasoned with saffron, cumin, cinnamon, ginger, paprika and cayenne – page 16); Make sure you make one or both of these wonderful seasoning mixes your own when grilling, pan-grilling or cooking over the open fire – they add stupendous flavour.

1 x 1.4kg/3lb chicken, cut into quarters, or 4 chicken thighs and 4 drumsticks

For the Jerk Seasoning
8–10 allspice berries
2 scallions, green parts only, thinly sliced
2 tablespoons finely chopped garlic
pinch of finely chopped fresh ginger
pinch of freshly grated nutmeg
2 pinches of ground cinnamon
2 Scotch Bonnet, Habañero or other hot chiles, chopped
leaves from 2–3 sprigs of fresh thyme
2 tablespoons soy sauce
4 tablespoons vegetable oil
3–6 tablespoons lime juice
½ teaspoon salt
freshly ground pepper

To Make the Jerk Seasoning: Crush the allspice berries in a mortar, or process in short bursts in a food processor. Add the scallions and pound (or process) with the berries until well mixed.

Add the finely chopped garlic and ginger, grated nutmeg and ground cinnamon, and then the chiles and thyme leaves. (Jamaicans like their jerk seasoning really hot; try using just one chopped chile at first and then, if desired, add the second one before seasoning the chicken.)

Mix the aromatic seasoning well and add the soy sauce, vegetable oil, lime juice and salt, with freshly ground pepper to taste.

To Grill the Chicken and Serve: Preheat the grill to very hot, or prepare a charcoal fire in a barbecue. In the meantime, with a sharp knife, score the chicken pieces on all sides and rub the jerk seasoning in well.

When ready to cook, grill the chicken until crusty on the outside, and moist and tender on the inside. Serve immediately.

Note: Jamaican grill chefs often add green branches from the pimento tree (which gives us Jamaican pimento or allspice berries) to the fire to give the added savour of scented smoke. For a similar effect, if barbecuing, soak some allspice berries for half an hour in boiling water, then drain and throw on to the coals before grilling.

Serves 4

Pan-Seared Monkfish and Lobster with Truffle Oil

This is 'instant' cooking at its best – tried and tested on a 3-minute 20-second slot in front of 2 million people on the *This Morning* programme. Expensive ingredients, perhaps, but well worth it: just ask Richard and Judy.

2 tablespoons olive oil
2 small monkfish tails, cut into 12-16 rounds altogether
salt and freshly ground pepper
crushed dried chiles
1-2 teaspoons truffle oil (or, if unavailable, light sesame oil)
8 thin slices cooked lobster
juice of ½ lemon

For the Garnish
8 scallions, cut into 10cm/4in segments
12 thin strips of red pepper
¼ vegetable stock cube, crumbled
25g/1oz butter
2 tablespoons water
100g/4oz fresh spinach leaves (or arugula leaves)

To Prepare the Garnish: In a small frying pan (nonstick preferably), combine the scallions, red pepper strips, crumbled vegetable stock cube, butter and water.

Simmer gently over a low heat for a minute or two, until the spring onions and pepper strips are crisp-tender. Add the spinach leaves and remove the pan from the heat. The spinach will 'melt' (soften) in the heated pan.

To Prepare the Monkfish Rounds: Place a large nonstick frying pan over a high heat, pour in the olive oil and add the monkfish rounds in a single layer. Season with salt, freshly ground pepper and a pinch or two of crushed dried chiles. After about 1 minute, sprinkle with 1 teaspoon of truffle oil (or sesame oil) and turn the monkfish over to cook on the other side: it should cook no longer than 3 minutes in all. Before it's ready, add the lobster slices to warm through.

Remove the pan from the heat and, with a metal spatula, transfer 3-4 monkfish rounds and 2 lobster slices to each heated plate. Garnish with spinach leaves, scallions and red pepper strips, and sprinkle with a little more truffle oil and a squeeze of lemon juice. Serve immediately.

Serves 4

Great Dinners

Raymond Blanc's Filet of Lamb Baked in a Salt Crust with Rosemary

Raymond Blanc's hotel-restaurant, Le Manoir aux Quat' Saisons, near Oxford, is one of Britain's finest and most attractive eating places, and his method of baking in salt-pastry parcels is a wonderful way of presenting tender rosemary-scented lamb. It can also be used for filets of pork, chicken and even whole fish.

2 racks (best end of neck) of
    lamb
2 tablespoons olive oil
4 sprigs of fresh rosemary
1 egg yolk, beaten
coarse sea salt

For the Pastry
350g/12oz flour
175g/6oz salt
8–10 tablespoons water
2 egg whites
3 sprigs of fresh rosemary,
    finely chopped

For the Lamb Sauce
2 tablespoons olive oil
1 medium-sized onion, thinly
    sliced
1 clove garlic, halved
2 sprigs of fresh thyme
1 sprig of fresh rosemary
450ml/15fl oz water
150ml/5fl oz well-flavoured
    beef or veal stock, reduced
    to 4–5 tablespoons
salt and freshly ground pepper

To Prepare the Lamb: Cut the meat from the lamb bones to make 2 'filets'. Coarsely chop the bones and reserve with meat trimmings.

To Prepare the Salt Pastry: In a food processor, combine the flour and salt and mix at low speed. Gradually add the water, then the egg whites and rosemary. The dough should be firm: add a little more flour if it is wet. Wrap the dough in plastic wrap and chill for 1 hour.

To Make the Lamb Sauce: In a heavy saucepan, heat the olive oil and sauté the reserved bones and trimmings, stirring, until lightly coloured. Add the onion, garlic, thyme and rosemary and cook, stirring constantly, for 5 minutes. Add the water and bring to the boil, skimming to remove impurities. Lower the heat and simmer for 20 minutes, then strain the stock into a clean pan and set aside.

To Make the Parcels: Preheat the oven to 230°C/450°F. Divide the salt pastry into 4 equal pieces and roll out each into a rectangle 20cm/8in long, 17.5cm/7in wide and 6mm/¼in thick.
    Cut each 'filet' of lamb lengthways in half and sauté in olive oil for 2 minutes, or until golden-brown on all sides. Leave to cool.
    Wrap each lamb piece, plus 1 sprig of rosemary, in the pastry, brushing the outer edge with water to seal. Brush a baking tray with olive oil and place the salt-pastry parcels, seam-side down, on it.
    Brush the salt-pastry parcels with beaten egg yolk and sprinkle over a little coarse sea salt. (It is important that there is no hole in the pastry through which heat can escape.) Bake in the preheated oven for 8 minutes. Leave to 'relax' in a warm place for 5 minutes.

To Finish the Sauce: Set the pan over a high heat and reduce the lamb stock to a third of its original quantity. Add the reduced beef or veal stock, and season to taste with salt and freshly ground pepper.

To Serve: Cut through the salt crust. Remove the lamb, thinly slice and arrange in an overlapping circle on warmed dinner plates. Discard the salt crust. Garnish each serving with lamb sauce.

Serves 4

Tagine of Lamb with Prunes, Hard-Boiled Eggs and Almonds

Melt-in-the-mouth lamb, cooked with Moroccan spices and dried fruit, is the perfect dinner-party dish. A tagine is Morocco's age-old cooking pot: a shallow, heatproof clay dish with a pointed conical lid, whose almost magical qualities are at their best during long, slow cooking.

1.2–1.4kg/1½–2lb shoulder of lamb, in 4cm/1½in cubes
24 extra large dried prunes
2 tablespoons honey
1 strip orange peel
2 short cinnamon sticks
1 bunch of fresh coriander, chopped

For the 'Dry' Moroccan Marinade
2 large Spanish onions, coarsely grated
2 cloves garlic, finely chopped
4 tablespoons olive oil
½ teaspoon coarse sea salt
½ teaspoon each coarsely ground black pepper and ground cumin, ginger and paprika
1 large pinch saffron threads

For the Honey Tomato Sauce
25g/1oz butter
2x400g/14oz cans peeled whole Italian tomatoes, seeds removed, juice reserved
2 tablespoons honey
crushed dried chiles

For the Garnish
100g/4oz blanched almonds, sautéed in butter and seasoned to taste with salt
4–6 hard-boiled eggs, halved
sprigs of fresh mint or watercress

To Prepare the Meat: In a large earthenware tagine (or enamelled iron baking dish), combine the Moroccan marinade ingredients, then add the meat cubes. Mix well, rubbing the aromatics into each piece of meat. Leave the meat to marinate in this aromatic mixture for at least 2 hours at room temperature, or in the refrigerator overnight.

To Make the Honey Tomato Sauce: In a saucepan, combine the butter, tomatoes, juice and honey. Season with a pinch or 2 of crushed dried chiles and simmer for 10 minutes. Reserve.

When Ready to Cook: Preheat the oven to 140°C/275°F.

Heat a large frying pan, then add the meat and aromatics. Cook over a high heat, stirring constantly, until the meat is well browned on all sides. Transfer the meat and aromatics to a tagine (or casserole), spoon the honey tomato sauce over and mix well. Cover and place in the preheated oven to cook for 45 to 60 minutes or until the meat is meltingly tender. Meanwhile, prepare the prunes. They will be added 10 minutes before the end of cooking time.

Place the dried prunes in a bowl and cover with boiling water. Allow to infuse for 10 minutes, then drain. Transfer 2 to 3 ladles (about 200ml/6½fl oz) of the sauce from the tagine or casserole to a medium-sized saucepan. Skim the fat, then add the honey, orange peel, cinnamon and prunes, and simmer for 15 minutes or until the prunes are soft, adding a little water to the sauce if necessary.

Ten minutes before the end of cooking time, add the prunes, their sauce and the coriander to the tagine and continue cooking.

To Serve: If serving directly from a tagine, remove the cover, skim excess fat from the surface of the sauce and correct the seasoning, adding more sea salt, spices or crushed dried chiles if desired. Sprinkle with sautéed salted almonds and garnish with halved hard-boiled eggs and sprigs of mint or watercress. Serve immediately.

If you used an enamelled iron casserole to prepare the dish, transfer the lamb, prunes and sauce to a heated serving dish and garnish as above.

Serves 4 to 6

Chorizo and Prawn Risotto with Red Beans

An elegant risotto garnished with slices of chorizo and whole prawns makes a light but interesting main course for a special dinner. Precede it by a fresh-tasting vine-ripened tomato salad with sprigs of watercress and slices of red onion, and follow with a chilled chocolate pudding and the day is won.

24–36 raw tiger prawns with shells (defrosted)
8 tablespoons olive oil
1 large Spanish onion, finely chopped
1 clove garlic, finely chopped
1 fish stock cube, crumbled
1 pinch saffron threads
350g/12oz arborio rice
salt and freshly ground pepper
crushed dried chiles
6 tablespoons dry white wine
1.2 litres/40fl oz boiling water
1 or 2 chorizo sausages, ends trimmed, thinly sliced
1 x 400g/14oz can red kidney beans, drained and rinsed
2 tablespoons snipped fresh chives or chopped fresh coriander

To Prepare the Tiger Prawns: Peel the shells from the prawns (leaving the tails intact). Reserve the prawn shells in a small bowl. Then, with a small sharp kitchen knife, cut down the back of each prawn and remove the black thread. Reserve the prawns.

In a large, shallow, heatproof casserole or saucepan, heat 6 tablespoons of the olive oil. Add the prawn shells and cook, stirring constantly, until the shells are pink. With a metal spatula, transfer the shells to a flat plate to drain briefly. Return the excess oil to the pan and discard the shells. Add the prepared prawns to the flavoured oil and sauté until they are pink. Remove and reserve.

Add the onion and garlic and sauté, stirring, until the vegetables have changed colour. Then stir in the crumbled fish stock cube and saffron threads and continue to cook, stirring, for 1 minute more.

When Ready to Prepare the Risotto: Add the rice to the casserole or shallow saucepan, and season to taste with salt, freshly ground pepper and crushed dried chiles. Cook over a moderate heat for 2 to 3 minutes, stirring with a wooden spoon so that every grain of rice is individually coated with the flavoured oil.

Moisten with the white wine and let it sizzle away. Then add enough of the boiling water just to cover the rice and simmer until the rice is tender, adding a little more water from time to time, as needed. This takes 20 to 25 minutes in all.

To Prepare the Chorizo, Prawn and Red Bean Garnish: In a large frying pan, sauté the chorizo slices in the remaining 2 tablespoons of olive oil until lightly coloured. Add the prawns and cook for 1 minute more. Then add the drained red kidney beans and heat through. Season generously with salt, freshly ground pepper and crushed dried chiles. Keep warm.

To Serve: Transfer the risotto to a heated serving dish or individual dishes. Garnish with the chorizo, prawns and red beans. Sprinkle with snipped chives or chopped coriander and serve immediately.

Serves 4 to 6

Frédy Girardet's Pan-Seared Filets of Red Mullet

Filets of red mullet, pan-seared for only 30 seconds on each side, are the quick and easy side of this recipe. The delicious rosemary-infused, reduced fish sauce created by the greatest Swiss chef, Frédy Girardet, takes a little longer to accomplish. But most of the advance preparations can be finished long before your guests arrive. A dish to remember.

4 x 150–200g/5–7oz red mullets
50g/2oz butter
2 medium-sized shallots, finely chopped
1 sprig of fresh rosemary, cut into 4 pieces
7 tablespoons dry white wine
7 tablespoons water
240ml/8fl oz crème fraîche
juice of ½ lemon
salt and freshly ground pepper
2 tablespoons olive oil

To Prepare the Fish and Make the Stock: Ask your fishmonger to scale and filet the red mullets, and remove the pin-sized bones along the center of the filet. Ask him to reserve the livers and fish heads, bones and trimmings for you..

Finely chop the fish livers and reserve.

Chop the fish heads, bones and trimmings. In a heavy saucepan, melt 25g/1oz of the butter and add the chopped fish parts. Simmer for 2 to 3 minutes, pressing the bones and trimmings into the butter with a wooden spoon to extract all the juices.

Add the finely chopped shallots to the pan and continue to simmer for a further 2 minutes, stirring constantly. Add the rosemary, dry white wine and water and simmer for a further 7 minutes. Remove the rosemary from the pan and reserve.

Pass the stock through a fine sieve into a clean pan, pressing down with a wooden spoon to extract all the juices. Set the pan over a high heat and reduce the stock to half its original quantity.

To Finish the Sauce: Put the crème fraîche into a bowl, pour the reduced stock into it and stir well. Return the mixture to the pan. Reduce the sauce until thick enough to coat the back of a wooden spoon.

Remove the pan from the heat and gradually beat in the remaining butter, a little at a time. Add the finely chopped fish livers and lemon juice and season to taste with salt and freshly ground pepper. Keep warm.

To Cook the Fish Filets: Heat 2 heavy frying pans. Pour 1 tablespoon of olive oil into each pan and arrange 4 filets, red-skin-side down, in each pan. Season generously with salt and freshly ground pepper. Cook for 30 seconds. Turn the filets over and season again. Cook for another 30 seconds.

To Serve: Cover the bottom of 4 heated plates with sauce, place 2 filets on each plate with the rosy skin uppermost and garnish with the reserved rosemary pieces.

Serves 4

Poulet au Blanc

Corn-fed free-range chickens are readily available now. Here is a delicious way of dealing with this superior bird, first poached in a light stock and then served in a light velouté sauce with mushroom caps simmered in butter and fresh-tasting lemon. Accompany with steamed white rice and green vegetables.

1 x 1.4kg/3lb corn-fed
   free-range chicken
1 bouquet garni (2 sprigs of
   fresh parsley, 1 sprig of fresh
   thyme and 1 bay leaf, tied
   into a neat packet with
   2 short segments of celery)
1 litre/35fl oz white stock
   (chicken or vegetable)
salt and freshly ground pepper
12 medium-sized mushroom
   caps
50g/2oz butter
juice of 1 lemon
2 tablespoons flour
2 egg yolks, whisked with
   6 tablespoons crème fraîche
crushed dried chiles (optional)

For the Garnish
chopped fresh flat-leaf parsley,
   or watercress leaves

To Prepare and Cook the Chicken: Preheat the oven to 110°C/225°F. Cut the chicken into 8 serving pieces: 2 drumsticks, 2 thighs and 4 breast pieces, saving the neck and backbone to enrich the stock.

Place the chicken pieces (including the neck and backbone) and bouquet garni in a casserole. Add enough stock just to cover the chicken. Season to taste with salt and freshly ground pepper. Cover the exposed parts of the chicken (if any) with a piece of buttered aluminum foil.

Place the lid on the casserole and simmer in the preheated oven for about 1 hour, or until the chicken is tender. Remove the bouquet garni and the chicken neck and backbone. Remove the chicken pieces from the casserole; keep warm. Reserve the cooking liquid.

To Prepare the Mushroom Caps: Simmer the caps in 25g/1oz of the butter and the lemon juice in a small pan until tender. Keep warm.

To Make the Chicken Velouté Sauce: Make a white roux with the remaining butter and the flour. Strain 600ml/1 pint of the liquid in which the chicken was cooked into the roux to make a velouté sauce. (See page 248 for details.)

Just before serving, remove the sauce from the heat and whisk it into the egg yolks and crème fraîche in a bowl. Correct the seasoning, adding a little more lemon juice, salt, freshly ground pepper or crushed dried chiles to the sauce if desired.

To Serve: Return the chicken pieces to a clean casserole, add the prepared mushroom caps and strain over the creamy chicken velouté sauce. Place the casserole in the lowest of ovens to warm through while you are enjoying your first course. Serve in the casserole, sprinkled with a garnish of chopped flat-leaf parsley or a scattering of watercress leaves.

Serves 4

The Hotel Crillon's 'Hearts' of Squab with Chicory

The Hotel Crillon – bastion of French nineteenth-century elegance, located in the Place de la Concorde in Paris – boasts one of the most gracious dining rooms in Europe. Chef Jean-Paul Biffi's elegant way with fat-breasted French squabs is to pan-fry the breasts for minutes only (the legs are simmered in sauce just until tender) and cut them open to form two decorative pink-cooked 'hearts'. Crisp chicory and wilted spinach leaves complete the picture, with the sauce, a light glaze really, poured around.

4 plump squabs
salt and freshly ground pepper
65g/2½oz butter
2 tablespoons olive oil
½ medium onion, coarsely chopped
1 medium carrot, coarsely chopped
150ml/5fl oz red wine
12 young spinach leaves
squeeze of lemon juice
20 small chicory leaves

To Prepare the Squabs: Ask your supplier to remove the breasts and legs from the squabs and to chop the carcasses and giblets coarsely. Season the breasts and legs lightly with salt and pepper.

To Make the Squab Sauce: In a heavy frying pan, melt 25g/1oz butter with 1 tablespoon of olive oil. Sauté the chopped squab carcasses and giblets with the coarsely chopped onion and carrot, stirring occasionally, until the vegetables are soft.

Add the squab legs to the pan and cook until they just begin to turn colour. Add the red wine, then lower the heat and simmer for 5 minutes, or until the squab is tender. Using a slotted spoon, transfer the squab legs to a heated dish and keep warm.

Strain the sauce into a clean saucepan, pressing the squab trimmings and vegetables in the sieve to extract the maximum juices. Simmer the sauce until reduced to about 120ml/4fl oz. Keep warm.

To Cook the Squab Breasts: Preheat the oven to 250°C/500°F. In a heavy frying pan with an ovenproof handle, melt 15g/½oz butter with the remaining olive oil and sauté the squab breasts for a few minutes until lightly browned on each side. Place the pan in the preheated oven and cook for 5 minutes.

To Prepare the Spinach: Sauté the spinach in the remaining butter for 1 minute, or until just beginning to wilt. Season to taste with lemon juice, salt and freshly ground pepper.

To Finish and Serve: Remove the squab breasts from the oven and cut in half lengthways, opening each one up to form a 'heart' shape.

Have ready 4 heated plates. Arrange 2 squab 'hearts' overlapping on the right of each plate; crumple up 3 spinach leaves and place between the 'hearts'. Place 2 squab legs overlapping on the left of each plate and arrange 5 chicory leaves in a fan shape about the legs. Strain 2 tablespoons of squab sauce on to each plate. Serve at once.

Serves 4

Chamonix Peppered Loin of Venison

Perhaps one of the best game dishes I've had on the Cape: a wonderfully flavoured Springbok in a cracked black pepper crust. Richard Carstens, creative young master chef at the Auberge de Chamonix, prepares his delicious red wine *jus* first (stock with a reduction of red wine and port) to dress his peppered, pan-seared 'minute' roast of rare venison. Accompany it, as Richard does, with crunchy cinnamon-sweet red cabbage and buttery grilled pears.

4 x 200g/7oz pieces of loin
    of venison
cracked black pepper
25g/1oz butter
1 tablespoon olive oil

For the Red Wine Jus
240ml/8fl oz red wine
1 sprig of fresh thyme
1½ tablespoons port
500ml/16fl oz venison stock
120ml/4fl oz veal or chicken
    stock
15g/½oz butter

For the Red Cabbage Garnish
25g/1oz butter
2 tablespoons olive oil
½ red cabbage, finely sliced
120ml/4fl oz red wine
finely grated zest of ½ orange
1–2 pinches of ground
    cinnamon
2–3 tablespoons sugar
salt and freshly ground pepper

For the Buttery Grilled Pears
25g/1oz butter
2 small pears, peeled, halved
    and cored
granulated sugar

To Make the Red Wine Jus: In a medium-sized saucepan, combine the red wine, thyme and port, and bring to the boil. Skim, then lower the heat and cook, uncovered, until the liquid is reduced by two-thirds. Remove the thyme, add the venison and veal (or chicken) stock and bring back to the boil. Skim, lower the heat and continue cooking, uncovered, until reduced by half. Strain into a clean saucepan, stir in the butter and keep warm.

To Prepare the Red Cabbage: In a medium-sized saucepan, melt the butter with the olive oil over a medium heat. Add the red cabbage and cook for 2 minutes, stirring constantly, until it begins to soften and is coated with butter and oil. Add the red wine, orange zest, cinnamon and just enough sugar to 'caramelize' the cabbage. Mix well and continue to cook until the cabbage is crisp-tender (still a little crunchy to the bite). Season to taste with salt and freshly ground pepper, and a little more cinnamon if desired. Keep warm.

To Grill the Pears: Preheat the grill to hot. In a small frying pan, melt the butter over a moderate heat and add the halved pears, round-side up. Sprinkle with enough sugar to cover the pears and cook for 1 minute, shaking the pan from time to time. Turn the pears over with a spatula, sprinkle with a little more sugar and cook for 1 minute more. Transfer the pan to the hot grill and brown the pears until golden: about 2 minutes. Keep warm.

To Cook the Venison: Preheat the oven to 230°C/450°F. Roll the 4 venison pieces in cracked black pepper. In a large frying pan with an ovenproof handle, heat the butter with the olive oil until sizzling hot. Add the peppered venison and cook over a high heat until is seared on all sides. Transfer immediately to the very hot oven and cook for 2 to 3 minutes more. Venison should be very rare.

To Assemble the Dish: Slice each piece of venison and fan out on 4 warm dinner plates. Place a small mound of red cabbage on each plate and top with a pear half. Spoon red wine *jus* over the venison and serve immediately.

Serves 4

Broiled Marinated Lamb Chops with Green Butter

Tender baby lamb chops deserve tender, loving care. And when they are not so young and tender, they benefit even more from a well-flavoured marinade. These are two of my favourite recipes, guaranteed to bring out the best in your lamb. (Illustrated on page 170.)

For Lamb Chops I
8–12 baby loin lamb chops
sea salt and freshly ground
    pepper
crushed dried chiles
2 dried bay leaves, crumbled
2 tablespoons finely chopped
    onion
6 tablespoons olive oil
6 tablespoons dry white wine

For Lamb Chops II
6–12 medium-sized lamb chops
salt and freshly ground pepper
crushed dried chiles
6–8 tablespoons olive oil
3–6 tablespoons lemon juice
4 tablespoons finely chopped
    fresh mint
1 teaspoon finely grated
    lemon zest
1 clove garlic, finely chopped

For the Green Butter
100g/4oz butter, softened
1–2 cloves garlic, crushed
4 tablespoons finely chopped
    watercress
1–2 tablespoons lemon juice
salt and freshly ground pepper
4-6 tablespoons finely
    chopped fresh parsley

To Prepare Lamb Chops I: Arrange the chops in a large, flat dish and season to taste with sea salt, freshly ground pepper and a pinch of crushed dried chiles. Add the crumbled bay leaves (finely chop the leaves if they are fresh), finely chopped onion, olive oil and dry white wine. Marinate the chops in this mixture, turning them once or twice, for at least 2 hours.

To Broil Lamb Chops I: Preheat the broiler for 15 to 20 minutes until very hot. Place the chops on the hot broiler rack and broil for 3 to 4 minutes on each side for rare, a little longer for medium pink. Serve immediately, with balls of green butter.

To Prepare Lamb Chops II: Season the chops generously with salt and freshly ground pepper and lightly with crushed dried chiles. Combine the remaining ingredients in a small bowl. Place the chops in a large flat dish and pour the marinade mixture over them. Leave to marinate, turning them once or twice, for 2 to 4 hours.

To Broil Lamb Chops II: Broil over charcoal or under a preheated gas or electric broiler for 5 minutes. Turn and broil for 5 minutes longer, or until the chops are cooked through. Brush with the marinade mixture during cooking. Serve with balls of green butter.

To Make the Green Butter: Cream the butter with the crushed garlic and chopped watercress. Season to taste with lemon juice, salt and freshly ground pepper. Roll into balls about the size of a marble. Chill in the refrigerator until firm, then re-roll into more perfect shapes before coating them in finely chopped parsley. Each ball should be completely covered with parsley. Chill until ready to serve.

Lamb Chops I serves 4 to 6
Lamb Chops II serves 6

Alain Fabrègues' Tournedos of Beef with Potato Barigoule Béarnaise

Alain Fabrègues, French-born chef-proprietor of one of Australia's top restaurants, the Loose Box in Mundaring, Western Australia, has been awarded more prestigious awards than almost any chef I know. His tournedos barigoule, which I chose as one of the six best recipes in Australia on my last award-giving tour, is brilliant in appearance and wonderful in flavour. It is, I'm afraid, not easy to prepare for it requires two classic French sauces: Béarnaise and Madeira. But once these sauces are ready for serving, and the brilliant potato barigoule is shaped and cooked in its saffron bouillon, preparation at serving time is very easy.

6–8 tablespoons Béarnaise or Choron sauce (pages 249-50)
225ml/8fl oz Madeira sauce (page 250)
4 x 100–150g/4–6oz tournedos steaks, 3cm/1¼in thick, cut from the eye of the filet: tie into a perfect round with string around the circumference to help the meat hold its shape while cooking

For the Potato Barigoule
225ml/8fl oz chicken stock
pinch of saffron threads, soaked in a little water
2 sprigs of dried herb fennel, with some seeds
3 black peppercorns
1 tablespoon olive oil
4 medium-sized red potatoes

For the Parsnips
4 young parsnips
15g/½oz butter
1 tablespoon olive oil
salt and freshly ground pepper

To Prepare Ahead: Make Béarnaise (or Choron) and Madeira sauces as described on pages 249-50.

To Prepare the Potato Barigoule: Bring the chicken stock to the boil. Remove the pan from the heat and add the saffron threads and their soaking water, the dried fennel and seeds, peppercorns and olive oil. Cover the pan and allow to steep for 10 minutes.

With a small paring knife, peel the potatoes and trim to a uniform round or oval shape. Poach in the steeped bouillon until almost cooked, then remove the pan from the heat and let the potatoes absorb the flavour and colour of the bouillon as they finish cooking in the hot liquid. Then, using a slotted spoon, transfer the potatoes to a chopping board and, with a teaspoon, scoop out the centers, leaving a 6mm/¼in shell around the sides. Reserve.

To Prepare the Parsnips: Preheat the oven to 180°C/350°F. With a small paring knife, peel the parsnips and give them a uniform conical shape. (If they are large, quarter them: see picture.) Melt the butter with the olive oil in a small heatproof roasting pan over direct heat. Add the parsnips and sear on all sides, then transfer the pan to the preheated oven and roast the parsnips for 7 to 10 minutes or until just tender. Season with salt and pepper and keep warm.

When Ready to Serve: Preheat the broiler (or ridged grill pan). Season the tournedos and char-broil (or pan-grill) on each side for 3 minutes for rare; 3 to 4 minutes for medium rare; 4 to 5 minutes for well done. Snip off the strings and keep the tournedos warm.

To Serve: Place a broiled tournedos in the center of each of 4 warm dinner plates and spoon hot Madeira sauce around. Fill the potatoes with hot béarnaise (or choron) sauce and carefully place on each tournedos along with a roasted parsnip. Serve immediately.

Serves 4

Simon Hopkinson's Lemon Roast Chicken

Simon Hopkinson is a man passionately in love with cooking. His uncomplicated but delicious dishes linger on in our taste memories long after the meal is over.

1 x 1.8kg/4lb free-range chicken
100g/4oz butter, at room temperature
salt and freshly ground pepper
1 lemon
several sprigs of fresh thyme or tarragon, or a mixture of both
1 clove garlic, chopped

To Prepare the Chicken: Preheat the oven to 230°C/450°F.

Using your hands, smear the butter all over the bird. Put the chicken in a roasting pan that will accommodate it with room to spare. Season liberally with salt and freshly ground pepper and squeeze over the juice of the lemon. Put the herbs and garlic inside the cavity, together with the squeezed-out lemon halves – this will add a fragrant lemony flavour to the finished dish.

To Roast the Chicken: Roast the chicken in the preheated oven for 10 to 15 minutes. Baste, then turn the oven temperature down to 190°C/375°F and roast for a further 30 to 45 minutes with further occasional basting. The bird should be golden brown all over with a crisp skin and quite gorgeous buttery, lemony juices of a nut-brown colour in the bottom of the pan.

Turn off the oven, leaving the door ajar, and allow the chicken to rest for at least 15 minutes before carving. This enables the flesh to relax, retaining the juices in the meat and ensuring easy, trouble-free carving and a moist bird.

To Make the Gravy: With this roasting method, what you end up with in the pan is an amalgamation of butter, lemon juice and chicken juices, a perfect homogenization of fats and liquids. All it needs is a light whisk or a stir, and you have the most wonderful 'gravy' imaginable.

Serves 4

No-Roast Roast Beef

This is one of my classics: a roast of beef that you roast for only 5 minutes per pound in a very hot oven, then turn off the heat and leave, unattended, in the oven for exactly 2 hours. And it's perfect every time.

Remember: small joints of beef do not make good roasts, they shrink away to nothing. Two or three ribs of beef, or at least 2.5kg/5lb of boned and rolled meat, are the minimum you should go for when making this recipe. If this amount of beef is too much for your needs, don't forget there is nothing like cold rare beef for another meal.

1 x 2.5kg/5lb (or more) boned and rolled beef joint or joint of 2 or 3 ribs of beef
salt and freshly ground pepper
4 tablespoons dripping or butter at room temperature

To Prepare the Beef: At least 2 hours before you intend to roast the beef, remove the joint from the refrigerator. Preheat the oven to 250°C/500°F at least 20 minutes ahead of time.

Rub the joint all over with salt and freshly ground pepper, and spread it with the dripping or butter. Place it on a rack over a roasting pan.

To Roast the Beef: Place the meat in the oven. Roast for 5 minutes per 450g/1lb, then, without opening the oven door, switch off the heat and leave for a further 2 hours. Do not, under any circumstances, open the oven door during this time.

When the 2 hours are up, open the door and, without removing the pan from the oven, touch the beef with your finger. If it feels hot, go ahead and serve it. However, as some ovens do not retain their heat as well as others (electricity is often rather better than gas in this instance), you may find the beef on the lukewarm side. If so, close the door, put the oven back on, still set at 250°C/500°F, and give it a further 10 minutes or so. This will raise the temperature of the beef without affecting its rareness.

To Serve: Serve as usual, on a hot platter, accompanied by gravy made with the pan juices.

Tetsuya's Poached Corn-Fed Chicken with Bread Sauce

Tetsuya Wakuda, a young Franco-Japanese chef, now working and living in Sydney, Australia, was the grand prize-winner of the prestigious 1996 Australian Restaurant of the Year award.

Every dish he presented in his little restaurant in Sydney on the day we dropped in to sample his cooking was outstanding. But this dish – in essence, a simple poached chicken served with a bread sauce and a port-flavoured *jus* – was the greatest of them all: one of the most interesting dishes I have tasted in my many, many visits over the years to the world's greatest restaurants.

Tetsuya's way of dealing with chicken is inspired. He treats the chicken breasts and legs in a totally new way, making a fine fat chicken 'leg' out of the breast, thigh and drumstick by boning the thigh and tucking it back into the breast. And as if this is not enough, follow Tetsuya as he pops the newly created 'leg' into a freezer bag, anoints it with goose fat subtly flavoured with a hint of sugar and salt and then poaches the bagged 'leg' in simmering water for 35 minutes at a low temperature. Tetsuya's chicken is, in fact, a masterpiece of flavour, texture and imagination. Well worth the effort involved. (Illustrated on page 171, at the top.)

2 corn-fed free-range chickens, about 1.4kg/3lb each
120ml/4fl oz goose fat
½ teaspoon table salt
sea salt
½ teaspoon white pepper
pinch of sugar

To Prepare the Plump Chicken 'Legs': With a sharp knife, cut from 1 chicken, in 1 piece, a breast and leg (complete with drumstick and thigh). Repeat with the other 3 breast-and-leg sections. You will be left with 2 carcasses with wings, which can be used to make a well-flavoured stock for this recipe, or to make a soup for another meal.

Lay 1 chicken section on the chopping board, skin-side down. With a sharp knife, cut out and remove the thigh bone of the chicken leg. You will be left with the breast, the boned thigh and the drumstick complete with its bone. Fold the drumstick back upon the inside of the breast and secure it with a piece of kitchen twine. You will have what looks like a fine, fat chicken 'leg' made from the breast and boned thigh section with its visible drumstick.

Note: To keep the skin from drawing back from the breast meat during the cooking process, it might be wise to stitch it down in two or three places to hold it firmly. These tiny stitches can be snipped off with a pair of scissors after cooking.

Place each chicken 'leg' in the corner of a small heavy-duty plastic bag (measuring about 22x35cm/9x13in) and spoon over the goose fat seasoned with the salt, a pinch of sea salt, the white pepper and sugar. Press any air from the bag and secure it well (using paper clips or string, for example).

To Cook the Chicken 'Legs': Bring a large saucepan or deep casserole of water to 71°C/160°F (tested with a thermometer), then lower the bags with the chicken 'legs' into the water to poach for 35 minutes. (While the chicken is cooking, prepare the *jus* and bread sauce as described on the following page.)

For the Chicken Jus
450ml/15fl oz well-flavoured
  chicken stock
150ml/5fl oz port
pinch of salt
2 teaspoons soy sauce
½ teaspoon walnut oil

For the Bread Sauce
6 slices white bread, crusts
  removed
1 clove garlic, smashed and
  chopped
pinch of sea salt
pinch of white pepper
pinch of sugar
180ml/6fl oz grapeseed oil

For the Garnish
100g/4oz young spinach
  leaves, blanched
4 small red-skinned potatoes,
  boiled
4 x 1cm/½in-thick slices of
  daikon radish
100g/4oz broad beans,
  blanched, skins removed
4 baby leeks, or large scallions,
poached

Preheat the broiler to hot. Remove the poached chicken pieces from the water and release them from the bags. Season with sea salt and place under the hot broiler for a few minutes until golden brown.

To Prepare the Jus: In a medium-sized saucepan, reduce the chicken stock over a high heat to two-thirds of its original quantity. Add the port and reduce to a syrup. Stir in the salt, soy sauce and walnut oil, remove from the heat and reserve.

To Prepare the Bread Sauce: Combine all the ingredients except the grapeseed oil in a food processor and process until crumbed. Slowly drizzle in the oil and process until a thick paste forms. Reserve.

To Serve: Divide the blanched spinach leaves among 4 heated individual plates. Top with the chicken 'legs' and *jus*. Garnish each plate with 1 boiled potato, 1 slice of daikon radish, 2 teaspoons of bread sauce and a scattering of broad beans, and top each leg with a poached baby leek or scallion. Serve immediately.

Serves 4

The White Tower's Roast Duckling Farci à la Grecque

A special Greek stuffing and a crisp, crisp skin were the twin secrets of my old friend John Stais's roast duckling, which he served at London's White Tower restaurant. The restaurant, once again in operation under the ownership of his niece Mary and her husband, still serves this wonderful dish.

1 duckling, about 2.3kg/5lb

2–3 tablespoons melted butter or dripping

flour

For the Stuffing

100g/4oz cracked wheat

chicken stock

1 Spanish onion, unpeeled

25g/1oz butter

the duckling's liver, heart and gizzard, chopped

2 tablespoons finely chopped shallots

4 tablespoons chopped, blanched almonds

3–6 fresh sage leaves, chopped

salt and freshly ground pepper

To Prepare the Stuffing: Simmer the cracked wheat with the unpeeled Spanish onion in chicken stock to cover until the cracked wheat is tender, then drain. Peel the onion and chop finely.

Melt the butter in a frying pan and sauté the chopped liver, heart and gizzard of the duck with the finely chopped shallots. Combine the chopped onion, giblets, shallots, almonds and fresh sage in a bowl, and mix well. Season to taste with salt and freshly ground pepper, and stir in the cracked wheat.

To Roast the Duck: Preheat the oven to 180°C/350°F. Stuff the duck with the cracked wheat mixture. Truss the duck with string and place, breast-side up, on a rack in a roasting pan. Cover the breast with buttered aluminum foil and roast in the preheated oven for 1½ to 1¾ hours, basting frequently with butter or dripping. Remove the foil 20 minutes before the duck has finished cooking.

Dredge the breast with flour and leave in the oven until well browned. Transfer to a hot serving dish, remove trussing strings and carve. Serve immediately.

Serves 4

Broiled Peppered Breast of Duck with Nutmeg Bread Sauce

Broiled marinated duck breasts make wonderful eating, especially when served with nutmeg bread sauce.

2 large duck breasts with skin (450g/1lb each) or
4 x 225g/8oz breasts
2 tablespoons crushed peppercorns

For the Marinade
6 tablespoons blackcurrant jam
150ml/5fl oz red wine
2 tablespoons crushed peppercorns

For the Nutmeg Bread Sauce
1 medium-sized onion, stuck with 2 cloves
1 small bay leaf
300ml/10fl oz milk
100g/4oz fresh white breadcrumbs
¼ teaspoon freshly grated nutmeg
salt and freshly ground pepper
cayenne pepper
15g/½oz butter
2 tablespoons heavy cream

To Prepare the Duck, the Day Before: In a small saucepan, combine the marinade ingredients. Bring to the boil and allow to cool. Place the duck breasts in a large shallow dish, pour the marinade over and leave to steep overnight in the refrigerator, turning the breasts once or twice if you get the chance.

To Prepare the Bread Sauce, the Next Day: In a small saucepan, combine the onion, bay leaf and milk. Cover and simmer over a low heat for about 10 minutes. Discard the bay leaf and reserve the onion.

Bring the milk to the boil and add the breadcrumbs. Reduce the heat and simmer, stirring, for 3 to 4 minutes, until the sauce is thick and creamy and the breadcrumbs have absorbed most of the liquid. Season with the nutmeg and with salt, freshly ground pepper and cayenne pepper to taste. Remove from the heat.

Remove the cloves from the onion and chop the onion finely. Stir the chopped onion into the bread sauce, and then add the butter and the heavy cream, mixing well.

Just before serving, reheat gently.

To Broil the Duck: Preheat the broiler to hot. Remove the duck breasts from the marinade, discard the marinade, and dry the breasts with paper towel. Press on the crushed peppercorns and broil the duck on an oiled rack for 7 to 9 minutes each side. The outer skin and flesh of the duck should blacken attractively, but the meat should remain pink and moist.

To Serve: Transfer the broiled duck breasts to a cutting board and carve lengthways into thin slices. Arrange the duck – 3 to 5 slices per person – in overlapping slices on heated dinner plates. Serve the hot bread sauce alongside.

Serves 4

Great Classics

Deep-Dish Chicken Pie with Forc'd Meat Balls

You will need a corn-fed, free-range chicken to bring out the best of this old English recipe, and it will help if you know how to bone it. If you do not yet have this skill, then cut the chicken into sections and cut the meat from the breast into pieces. You will love the herb- and sausage-flavoured 'forc'd meat balls', or little dumplings, that stud the deep dish pie. Excellent served with chicken velouté sauce (page 248).

1 x 1.4kg/3lb corn-fed free-range chicken
6 tablespoons flour
75g/3oz butter
salt and freshly ground pepper
2 hard-boiled eggs, quartered

For the White Forcemeat
100g/4oz stale bread, grated
finely grated zest of ½ lemon
1 teaspoon finely chopped fresh parsley
¼ teaspoon finely chopped fresh thyme
pinch of freshly grated nutmeg
½ teaspoon salt
freshly ground pepper
50g/2oz butter, diced
1 egg yolk

For the Sausage Forcemeat
liver and heart of the chicken
100g/4oz sausage
1 teaspoon finely chopped fresh parsley
1 teaspoon finely chopped fresh chives, or green parts of scallions

1 recipe-quantity fingertip pastry (page 251)

To Prepare the Chicken: Bone the chicken. Simmer the wings, neck, carcass and bones in a little seasoned water to make a light stock. Strain and reserve.

Roll the boned pieces of chicken lightly in the flour. Melt half the butter in a heavy saucepan and sauté the chicken pieces until they are a light golden on all sides. Season well, then cover the pan and cook over a low heat for 20 minutes, turning occasionally, until the chicken is cooked through. Set the pan aside.

To Prepare the White Forcemeat: Combine the breadcrumbs, lemon zest, parsley, thyme and nutmeg. Season to taste. Add the butter and egg yolk and work to a smooth paste with your fingers.

To Prepare the Sausage Forcemeat: Put the chicken liver and heart through a mincer together with the sausage. Combine this paste with the parsley and the chives or green parts of scallions.

To Assemble and Bake the Pie: Preheat the oven to 190°C/375°F. Form the two forcemeat mixtures into small balls the size of walnuts by rolling them between your hands, or on a board (there should be enough mixture for 12 to 16 balls). Brown lightly in the remaining butter.

Roll out the pastry to 6mm/¼in thickness. Transfer the chicken pieces from the saucepan to a deep, oval pie dish, and garnish with the forcemeat balls and quartered eggs. Pour 6 tablespoons of the chicken stock into the saucepan in which the chicken was cooked, blending well with the remaining butter and juices, then pour this sauce into the pie dish.

Cut an oval in the rolled out pastry, about 5cm/2in wider all the way around than the pie dish. Carefully place the pastry over the top of the dish. Moisten the edges of the pastry with water, pinch it down over the rim of the dish and cut one or two slits in the pastry center. Decorate as desired with pastry trimmings, and bake in the preheated oven for 30 minutes or until done.

Serves 4 to 6

Boeuf à la Ficelle

Tournedos steaks, wrapped in paper-thin strips of pork fat, cooked in a well-flavoured home-made beef stock, is my modern version of a nineteenth-century French classic. The tournedos are hung by a string from a wooden spoon or long skewer (hence the name in French: beef on a string) so that they can be removed easily from the bouillon after 8 minutes of simmering. The result: tender poached beef, beautifully cooked on the outside and wonderfully pink within, infused with the flavours of the bouillon. This recipe is delicious with breast of farm-raised squab as well.

450g/1lb carrots
450g/1lb small, sweet turnips
1.2 litres/40fl oz well-flavoured
  beef stock (not a cube)
225g/8oz small white button
  mushrooms
4 x 175g/6oz tournedos steaks,
  3cm/¼in thick, cut from the
  eye of the filet
4 thin strips of pork fat
freshly ground pepper
4 teaspoons brandy
finely chopped fresh parsley

To Prepare the Bouillon: Peel the carrots and cut them into strips 6mm/¼in wide and 4cm/1½in long. Peel the turnips and cut them into strips of the same size.

Select a wide pan that will take the tournedos steaks comfortably side by side. Pour in the well-flavoured beef stock and add the carrot strips. Bring to the boil and simmer for 4 minutes. Then add the turnips and simmer for 4 minutes longer.

Meanwhile, wipe or wash the mushrooms clean and trim the stems. Add them to the simmering bouillon and continue to cook gently for another 4 to 5 minutes, or until the vegetables are tender. Remove the vegetables with a slotted spoon and put them aside. Pour a little bouillon over them, leaving the remainder in the pan.

To Prepare the Tournedos: Wrap a thin piece of pork fat around the circumference of each tournedos. Cut 4 lengths of string long enough to tie around each circle of meat and hang over the side of the pan when submerged in bouillon. Tie one end of each string quite firmly round each tournedos to keep the pork fat in place.

When Ready to Serve: Bring the bouillon to the boil. If you like, wrap the free end of the tournedos strings firmly around the handle of a wooden spoon (whose length needs to be greater than the diameter of the pan) and lower them into the bouillon side by side. Or, holding the strings, lower the tournedos in together and then let the strings hang over the side of the pan. Simmer for 5 minutes for rare, 8 minutes for medium, and 12 minutes for well done.

When ready, fish them out. Drop the vegetables into the simmering bouillon to reheat. Remove the strings and strips of pork fat from the tournedos and arrange on a warmed serving dish.

To Serve: Season each steak liberally with freshly ground pepper and sprinkle with a teaspoon of brandy. Garnish with the reheated vegetables, moisten with a little bouillon, and sprinkle with finely chopped parsley. Serve immediately.

Serves 4

Old-Fashioned Irish Stew

One of the most satisfying dinners in the world is a simple Irish stew: shoulder or middle neck of lamb, or better yet, mutton, cooked, at its simple best, with a little sliced onion and mixed herbs for flavour, and sliced potato for thickening. The cooking medium is, of course, water, or at the most a light broth. A scattering of chopped flat-leaf parsley is enough to garnish this lovely dish. Or, if you want to ring the changes, pop in a few sticks of carrot and celery (see picture) to add colour and savour to this great dish, and a tablespoon of barley for thickening.

1.4kg/3lb boneless middle neck or shoulder of mutton or lamb
450g/1lb onions, thickly sliced
several pinches of dried mixed herbs, or ½ teaspoon each of finely chopped fresh thyme, marjoram and rosemary
salt and freshly ground pepper
crushed dried chiles (optional)
900g/2lb potatoes, thickly sliced or cut into strips
water or light stock

To Garnish
2–3 tablespoons finely chopped fresh flat-leaf parsley

For Optional Extras
See introduction, above

To Prepare the Stew: Cut the mutton or lamb into 6.5cm/2½in cubes. Place a layer of sliced onions in the bottom of a heatproof casserole and season with a pinch of dried mixed herbs or a little of the fresh herbs, salt, freshly ground pepper and, if using, a pinch of crushed dried chiles. Cover with a layer of meat and season again, then add a layer of potatoes and seasoning. Continue until the casserole is full and the ingredients are used up, finishing with a layer of potatoes.

To Cook and Serve the Stew: Add enough water or light stock to cover, then bring to the boil. Skim off the froth, then lower the heat and simmer, covered, until the meat is tender: almost 3 hours for mutton, about 2 hours for lamb. Just before serving, sprinkle with chopped fresh parsley.

If you prefer to oven-cook the stew: preheat the oven to 170°C/325°F. Bring the contents of the casserole to the boil on the top of the stove. Skim off the froth, cover the casserole and cook it in the preheated oven. Serve as above.

Serves 4 to 6

Lamb Cooked Like Game

Use this feisty marinade of spices and red wine to give game-like savour to delicious casseroles of lamb (as in the recipe) or for beef, pork … and even rabbit. This is low temperature cooking so cook gently for 1½ hours. Test a piece of the meat for tenderness and if it is still resistant to the bite, return it to the oven to cook a little more while you enjoy the first course.

**1.1kg/2½lb boned shoulder of
   lamb**
**120ml/4fl oz plus 3
   tablespoons olive oil**
2 Spanish onions, chopped
4 cloves garlic, chopped
**about 120ml/4fl oz red
   Burgundy**
4 tablespoons Cognac
finely grated zest of 1 orange
150ml/5fl oz chicken stock
40g/1½oz butter

For the Aromatic Spice Mixture
1 teaspoon salt
½ teaspoon grated nutmeg
¼ teaspoon ground cloves
2 bay leaves, crumbled
¼–½ teaspoon dried thyme
6 juniper berries, crushed
12 black peppercorns, crushed
1 tablespoon sugar

To Prepare the Lamb, 2 or 3 Days Ahead: Cut the shoulder of lamb into 2.5cm/1in cubes and place in a porcelain or earthenware bowl. Pour 120ml/4fl oz olive oil over the lamb.

Combine the ingredients of the aromatic spice mixture, add to the lamb and olive oil and toss well. Add the chopped onion and garlic, the red Burgundy and Cognac and toss again. Cover and keep in the refrigerator for 2 to 3 days, tossing the cubes of meat once or twice each day, to allow the rich flavours to permeate the lamb.

When Ready to Cook: Preheat the oven to 110°C/225°F. Remove the lamb from the refrigerator and bring it to room temperature. Add the orange zest and chicken stock.

To Cook and Serve the Lamb: Drain the lamb, reserving the marinade juices, and sauté in the butter and remaining 3 tablespoons of olive oil until lightly browned. Meanwhile, boil the marinade over a high heat until reduced by half. Strain into a heavy, heatproof casserole, add the lamb cubes and bring to the boil on top of the stove. Cover and cook in the preheated oven for about 1½ hours or until tender, adding more red wine, from time to time, if necessary.

Serves 4 to 6

Mexican Chile con Carne

If you like rich, rustic flavours, this is the perfect dish for informal entertaining, especially served in the Mexican manner with colourful bands of red beans and yellow rice. Mexican, or mild, chili powder is *not* pure ground chile or cayenne pepper; it is a combination of ground chiles, garlic, onion and even flour. You can buy a strong and a mild chili powder in the supermarkets now and I suggest you start out with the milder, sweeter version: you can always add a pinch or two of crushed dried chiles for a little more heat.

900g/2lb lean beef
450g/1lb fresh pork
1 Spanish onion, finely
    chopped
4 cloves garlic, chopped
2 tablespoons bacon fat
600ml/20fl oz boiling beef
    stock
3-4 tablespoons Mexican chili
    powder (make sure to use
    a level 15ml tablespoon)
1 tablespoon flour
2 bay leaves
½ teaspoon ground cumin
½ teaspoon dried oregano
salt and freshly ground pepper

For the Saffron Rice
½ teaspoon saffron threads
6 tablespoons dry white wine
850ml/30fl oz hot vegetable
    stock
350g/12oz basmati rice
salt and freshly ground pepper
1 ripe avocado pear
juice of 1 lemon

For the Quick Mexican Beans
½ Spanish onion, finely
    chopped
4 tablespoons olive oil
½ vegetable stock cube,
    crumbled
2 x 400g/14oz cans red kidney
    beans, drained
finely chopped fresh coriander
    or flat-leaf parsley

To Prepare the Meat: Chop the beef and pork into bite-sized cubes, trimming fat as you go. Brown the cubed meat and the chopped onion and garlic in hot bacon fat in a heavy casserole. Cover with boiling beef stock, bring back to the boil and then cover and simmer for about 1 hour.

To Make the Chile: Preheat the oven to 125°C/250°F. Blend the chili powder to taste with the flour in a small bowl, using a little of the hot pan juices. Add this mixture to the casserole together with the bay leaves, cumin and oregano. Season with salt and freshly ground pepper, and simmer in the low oven for 1 to 1¼ hours, or until the meat is tender. Check the seasoning and serve, with saffron rice and quick Mexican beans if desired.

To Make the Saffron Rice: Soak the saffron threads briefly in the dry white wine. Pour the hot vegetable stock into a large saucepan and add the wine and saffron threads. Add the rice to the stock, season to taste with salt and freshly ground pepper, then cover and simmer for about 30 minutes or until all the liquid is absorbed and the rice is tender.

Pit and peel the avocado, and dice the flesh into a small bowl containing lemon juice. When the rice is ready, transfer to a heated serving dish. Drain the diced avocado and scatter over the rice.

To Make the Quick Mexican Beans: In a medium-sized saucepan, combine the chopped onion and olive oil and cook, stirring constantly, until the onion begins to change colour. Add the crumbled vegetable stock cube and continue to cook for 1 minute. Then add the drained beans and cook until the beans are heated through. Transfer to a heated serving dish and sprinkle with finely chopped coriander or parsley.

Serves 4

Tagine of Chicken with Preserved Lemon

Living for many years in Morocco taught me a great deal about flavour – and presentation. This is a dish that brings chicken into a whole new realm. If you cannot find preserved lemons, make your own (page 10). You won't regret it. If there is no time, cut thinly pared lemon zest into thin slivers and cook them with the chicken. Different from the fabulous original, but rewarding *quand même*.

6 tablespoons peanut oil
75g/3oz butter
1 x 1.4kg/3lb chicken, cut into serving pieces
2 large Spanish onions, grated
2 cloves garlic, finely chopped
½ teaspoon powdered saffron
¼ teaspoon ground ginger
¼ teaspoon crushed dried chiles
240ml/8fl oz water
1 preserved lemon (see page 10), peel only, cut into eighths
36 green or purple olives, cracked
1–2 tablespoons lemon juice
1–2 tablespoons finely chopped fresh flat-leaf parsley or coriander

For the Garnish
Steamed white rice and/or sprigs of fresh watercress

To Prepare the Chicken: Heat the oil and butter until sizzling in a large frying pan. Add the chicken pieces and brown lightly on all sides.

To Cook the Tagine: Transfer the browned chicken and its pan juices to a tagine or a heatproof casserole and add the onion, garlic, spices and water. Cover and cook over a low heat, turning the chicken in the sauce from time to time, until the chicken is tender: 1 to 1¼ hours. Add a little more hot water from time to time during cooking if necessary. About 10–15 minutes before the end of cooking, add the preserved lemon peel and the olives. (If using fresh lemon peel, add it to the casserole after about 45 minutes.) Taste the sauce and correct the seasoning, adding lemon juice and chopped parsley or coriander.

To Serve: Place the chicken in the center of a heated serving dish, garnish with the preserved lemon peel and olives, and strain the sauce over. Finally, garnish with steamed white rice and/or sprigs of fresh watercress.

Serves 4

Turbot in Champagne

Louis Outhier was one of my great finds on the French Riviera. His restaurant, L'Oasis, located on a back street in La Napoule, a little seaside village on the outskirts of Cannes, was one of the great eating experiences of my young life. I first wrote about him when I was Food Editor of *Vogue*, long before he was awarded his three Michelin stars. This recipe for turbot cooked in Champagne still remains one of my all-time favourites.

100g/4oz butter
2 tablespoons olive oil
2 shallots, finely chopped
100g/4oz button mushrooms, thinly sliced
4 turbot filets about 225g/8oz each, skinned
6 tablespoons reduced fish court-bouillon (page 247)
½ of a quarter bottle of Champagne
salt and freshly ground pepper
150ml/5fl oz crème fraîche

To Prepare the Shallots and Mushrooms: Heat half the butter together with the olive oil in a heavy saucepan large enough to take the turbot filets in one layer, and sauté the finely chopped shallots until translucent. Add the sliced mushrooms and continue cooking until tender. Remove from the pan.

To Prepare the Fish: Add the remaining butter to the pan and sauté the turbot filets until lightly coloured on both sides. Return the sautéed mushrooms and shallots to the pan, together with the fish court-bouillon and half the Champagne, adding more Champagne, if necessary, to just cover the turbot filets. Season to taste with salt and freshly ground pepper, and simmer very gently for a few minutes until the filets are tender. Transfer the turbot filets and vegetables to a heated serving dish. Keep warm.

To Make the Sauce: Add the crème fraîche to the liquid in the pan and simmer, without boiling, until the sauce is smooth and rich.

When ready to serve, stir the remaining Champagne into the sauce and warm through. (For a thicker sauce, use less Champagne.) Strain the sauce over the turbot filets and mushrooms and serve immediately.

Serves 4

Le Grand Aïoli

It was Fifine, my grand old friend in St Tropez, one of the best cooks on the coast, who first introduced me to this great feast of sea and garden flavours in her little restaurant just behind the port. Fifine's aïoli was famous on the coast: great platters of poached salt cod, or fresh John Dory, hard-boiled eggs and cooked and raw vegetables, garnished with herbs, and accompanied by the most famous sauce in all Provence, the golden-yellow, garlic-infused mayonnaise from which the dish gets its name.

450g/1lb salt cod
6 white potatoes with skins
6 sweet potatoes with skins
6 zucchini
450g/1lb small carrots
450g/1lb French beans
6 hard-boiled eggs in shells
6 ripe tomatoes
lettuce leaves, arugula leaves
  and fresh herbs, such as flat-
  leaf parsley, basil, coriander
  and fennel, to decorate

For the Aïoli
16 large cloves garlic
salt
2 egg yolks
300ml/10fl oz olive oil
freshly ground pepper
lemon juice

To Prepare the Cod, the Day Before: Soak the salt cod overnight in cold water.

To Make the Aïoli: Crush the garlic to a smooth paste in a mortar with a little salt. Blend in the egg yolks until the mixture is a smooth homogenous mass. Now add the olive oil, drop by drop at first, a thin trickle later, whisking constantly as for a mayonnaise. The aïoli thickens gradually until it reaches its proper stiff, firm consistency.

Season to taste with additional salt, a little freshly ground pepper and lemon juice. Transfer to a serving bowl and put in the refrigerator to chill.

To Prepare the Ingredients, the Next Day: Boil the fish and the vegetables separately – white and sweet potatoes with skins, whole zucchini, carrots and French beans – until tender but still quite firm, and on no account overcooked. Drain very well.

To Serve: Serve hot vegetables, hard-boiled eggs, in their shells, and raw tomatoes on large serving dishes decorated with lettuce leaves, rocket leaves and sprigs of fresh herbs. Place the fish in the center. For best effect, group vegetables by colour. Serve with the bowl of aïoli sauce, from which guests will help themselves.

Serves 4 to 6

Pepper Pissaladière

Pissaladière, one of the great dishes of Provence, started life as an open onion tart, sprinkled with Provençal herbs and latticed with anchovies and black olives. Then the tomato jumped across the border from Italy and pissaladière moved up a gastronomic notch to the colourful version we know today. My favourite version adds strips of roasted red, yellow and orange peppers to the colourful garnish. As a variation, serve the pepper pissaladière as individual tartlets for a delightful first course or supper dish.

22cm/9in part-baked fingertip pastry crust (page 251)
1 egg white, beaten
2 tablespoons freshly grated Parmesan
1 pinch crushed dried chiles

For the Filling
4 tablespoons olive oil
2 tablespoons tomato purée
450g/1lb ripe tomatoes, skinned and chopped, or a 400g/14oz can chopped Italian tomatoes
1 teaspoon fresh oregano leaves, chopped
½ teaspoon sugar
salt and freshly ground pepper
crushed dried chiles
3 tablespoons freshly grated Parmesan
50g/2oz butter
3 Spanish onions, chopped
1 teaspoon fresh thyme leaves

For the Garnish
3 sweet peppers: 1 red, 1 yellow and 1 orange, roasted (page 12), seeded and cut into thick strips
12 Greek-style black olives
6 anchovies in oil, cut in half lengthways
sprigs of fresh thyme or oregano
olive oil

To Prepare the Pastry Crust: Brush the part-baked pastry crust with the beaten egg white and sprinkle with the freshly grated Parmesan and crushed dried chiles. Leave on its baking tray until you are ready to fill it.

To Prepare the Filling: In a large frying pan, heat the olive oil.

Add the tomato purée and chopped tomatoes, sprinkle with the oregano and sugar, and season with salt, freshly ground pepper and crushed dried chiles to taste. Cook over a low heat, stirring from time to time, for about 15 minutes or until the excess moisture has evaporated. Mash the tomatoes with a wooden spoon to reduce them to a thick purée. Stir in the freshly grated Parmesan cheese and allow to cool.

In another frying pan, melt the butter and sauté the onion with the thyme until the onions are transparent and very soft. Season to taste with salt and freshly ground pepper and allow to cool.

To Bake and Serve the Pissaladière: Preheat the oven to 180°C/350°F.

Mix together the prepared tomato and onion mixtures, correct the seasoning and fill the pastry crust with the combined mixture. Garnish the center of the pissaladière with two to three strips of each of the three roasted peppers (reserve the remaining strips, cut into thinner pieces, to use as a garnish for a salad of arugula and lettuce leaves). Scatter with the black olives and a few thin strips of anchovy. (Save any remaining anchovy, if desired, for a salad to serve alongside.) Brush with a little olive oil and bake in the preheated oven for about 30 minutes.

Serve hot or warm as a first or main course. Any leftovers can be cut into thin wedges and served cold as a canapé.

Serves 6

Osso Buco with Orange Gremolata

Veal shin, cut into rounds across the marrow-filled bone and simmered in a herb, wine and tomato-flavoured stock, is an Italian classic. Make sure your pieces of organically raised veal shin are all approximately the same size, with plenty of meat around the bone and enough marrow visible at the center of each to make rich eating. 'Simmer' is the operative word here, over the lowest of heats or in the lowest of ovens, to ensure that the veal is tender. Orange gremolata – finely grated orange zest, finely chopped garlic and flat-leaf parsley – is the modern touch.

4 x 5cm/2in equal-sized pieces of shin of veal
flour
salt and freshly ground pepper
2 tablespoons olive oil
25g/1oz butter
2 cloves garlic, finely chopped
½ Spanish onion, finely chopped
150ml/5fl oz light stock or boiling water
150ml/5fl oz dry white wine
2–4 tablespoons tomato purée
2 anchovy filets, finely chopped
4 tablespoons finely chopped fresh flat-leaf parsley
finely grated zest of ½-1 orange

To Prepare the Veal: Choose shin of veal with plenty of meat and have it sawn into pieces 5cm/2in thick. Dredge the pieces with flour and season to taste with salt and freshly ground pepper.

To Cook and Serve the Osso Buco: Heat the olive oil and butter in a heatproof casserole and brown the veal pieces. Add half the finely chopped garlic and all the onion, pour over the light stock or boiling water and dry white wine, and stir in the tomato purée. Cover and simmer for about 1½ hours.

Add the anchovy filet and stir well. Serve sprinkled with the gremolata: chopped parsley, orange zest and the remaining chopped garlic.

Serves 4

Broiled Chateaubriand

This method of preparing beef filet was invented by Montmireil, chef to Vicomte Chateaubriand. It is served with either Béarnaise sauce (page 249) or Chateaubriand sauce (see below), and is traditionally garnished with château potatoes, 'turned' potatoes sautéed in butter and oil. A Chateaubriand steak can be cooked completely under the broiler but, because of the thickness of the steak, it is usually better to start it under the broiler to seal the juices on both sides and then to finish cooking it in a low oven to retain a more even colour throughout the steak.

1 Chateaubriand steak,
    4cm/1½in thick, weighing
    450g/1lb
freshly ground pepper
salt
melted butter
olive oil

For the Chateaubriand Sauce
1 tablespoon *glace de viande*
3 tablespoons beef stock
100g/4oz unsalted butter,
    diced
1 tablespoon finely chopped
    fresh flat-leaf parsley
1 tablespoon lemon juice
salt and freshly ground pepper
cayenne pepper

To Prepare the Steak: Wipe the steak with paper towel and beat it once or twice on each side with a meat pounder. Season the steak generously with freshly ground pepper and leave to come to room temperature.

Preheat the broiler to high and the oven to 150°C/300°F.

To Cook the Steak: Season the steak with salt and brush it generously with melted butter and olive oil. Brush the broiler rack well with oil and place the steak on it. Broil the steak at a distance of 7.5cm/3in from the heat for 3 minutes on each side, to sear the surfaces.

If your broiler pan has ovenproof handles, transfer the whole pan to the preheated oven. If not, put the rack with the steak on it into a roasting pan and place in the oven. Cook for 10 minutes for steak *bleu* (very rare), 15 minutes for rare, 20 minutes for medium or 25 minutes for well done.

To Make the Sauce: In a small saucepan, stir together the *glace de viande* and beef stock until well blended. Bring to the boil and boil fast until reduced to 1 tablespoon. Reduce the heat to minimum and whisk in the diced butter a piece at a time, until the sauce thickens and emulsifies. The sauce should start to emulsify before the butter melts; if the sauce is too hot and melts the butter too quickly, remove the pan from the heat while you whisk. When all the butter is incorporated, add the chopped parsley and lemon juice and season to taste with salt, freshly ground pepper and cayenne pepper.

To Serve: Put the steak on a carving board and carve it downwards at a slight angle into 6 even slices. Transfer the slices to a heated serving dish and serve the sauce separately in a heated sauce boat.

Serves 2

Squab with 40 Cloves of Garlic

Large cloves of fresh young garlic – at long last available in supermarkets – play the role of deliciously sweet vegetables in this brilliant recipe. The secret is to blanch the peeled garlic cloves first and then to simmer them in butter and oil until they just begin to change colour, before removing them while you simmer thinly sliced leeks. Remove the leeks and then brown the birds in the leek and garlic-flavoured fats. The pale gold garlic cloves and leeks are then returned to the casserole with a little dry white wine and chicken stock and the casserole is simmered in the lowest of ovens until the pigeons are meltingly tender. Use this same cooking method, too, to create the more traditional casserole of chicken with 40 cloves of garlic, or a boned loin of pork for a large party of guests. I know that 40 cloves of garlic sounds a bit over the top, but just wait until you try it.

40 large cloves fresh, young garlic
2 large breasted squabs, ready for roasting
50g/2oz butter
4 tablespoons olive oil
2 leeks, trimmed and finely sliced
2–4 sprigs of fresh thyme
150ml/5fl oz dry white wine
150ml/5fl oz well-flavoured chicken stock
salt and freshly ground pepper
crushed dried chiles

To Prepare the Garlic and Leeks: Preheat the oven to 110°C/225°F. Remove the papery skins from the cloves of garlic but leave them whole. Put the garlic in a small pan, cover with cold water, bring to the boil, then drain thoroughly.

Place a large, oval, heatproof casserole (large enough to hold the 2 birds comfortably) over a medium heat. Add half the butter and olive oil to the casserole and, when the fats begin to sizzle, add the blanched garlic and cook over a low heat, stirring constantly, for 3 to 4 minutes, or until the garlic just begins to turn gold. Do not let the cloves brown, or they will be bitter instead of sweet. With a slotted spoon, transfer the garlic to a plate and reserve. Add the finely sliced leeks to the casserole and simmer in the garlic-flavoured fats, stirring constantly, until they are soft and just beginning to change colour. With a slotted spoon, transfer the softened leeks to the plate with the garlic. Reserve.

To Cook the Squabs: Add the remaining butter and olive oil to the casserole and brown the squabs gently on all sides. When the birds are a good colour, return the garlic and leeks to the casserole, and add the thyme, dry white wine and chicken stock. Season to taste with salt, freshly ground pepper and crushed dried chiles. Cover the casserole and cook in the preheated oven for 45 to 50 minutes or until the squabs are tender and the leeks have disintegrated to become part of the sauce.

To Serve: Remove the squabs from the casserole and place on a heated serving dish. Remove the trussing. Garnish with the garlic cloves. Skim the fat from the casserole juices, spoon some over the birds and serve the remainder in a heated serving boat.

Serves 2 to 4

Boeuf à la Bourguignonne

Boeuf à la bourguignonne and coq au vin are two of the truly great classics of the Burgundy region of France. Both are great dinner party dishes that I insist on making at least four times a year. I hope that you, too, will get into the Burgundian habit.

1.4kg/3lb topside or top rump of beef
flour
salt and freshly ground pepper
4 tablespoons olive oil
75g/3oz butter
100g/4oz fat salt pork or unsmoked bacon in one piece, cut into strips
4 tablespoons Cognac, warmed
2 carrots
1 leek
4 shallots
1 Spanish onion
1 clove garlic
1 calf's foot, split (optional)
1 fresh bouquet garni (2 sprigs of parsley, 1 sprig of thyme and 1 bay leaf, tied into a little packet with 2 short segments of celery)
½ bottle good red Burgundy
beef stock or hot water
18 boiling onions
sugar
12 button mushrooms
lemon juice
finely chopped fresh flat-leaf parsley

To Prepare the Beef and other Meats: Cut the beef into large cubes, removing the fat. Roll the cubes in flour seasoned generously with salt and freshly ground pepper, shaking off excess.

Heat 2 tablespoons of olive oil and 25g/1oz butter in a large heavy frying pan and sauté the fat salt pork or bacon until crisp and brown. Remove from the pan with a slotted spoon and transfer to a large heavy casserole.

Brown the beef well on all sides in the fats left in the frying pan. Season to taste with salt and freshly ground pepper, and moisten with warmed Cognac. Ignite the Cognac and let the flames die down. Add the meat to the casserole.

To Prepare the Vegetables: Coarsely chop the carrots, leek, shallots, onion and garlic and cook in the fat left in the frying pan, stirring occasionally until lightly browned, adding a little more butter and olive oil, if necessary. Transfer the vegetables to the casserole.

To Cook the Casserole: Preheat the oven to 140–150°C/275–300°F. Add the calf's foot, if available, and the bouquet garni. Pour over all but 4 tablespoons of the wine, and just enough good beef stock or hot water to cover the contents of the casserole. Cover and cook in the preheated oven for 1½ to 2 hours.

Remove the casserole, skim fat from the top and stir in a beurre manié (made by mashing 15g/½oz butter with 1 tablespoon flour to form a smooth paste) bit by bit to thicken the liquid. Cover and return to the oven to cook gently until the beef is tender.

To Glaze the Onions and Sauté the Mushrooms: Brown the boiling onions with a little sugar in 25g/1oz butter in a heavy saucepan. Add the remaining red wine, cover and cook over a low heat until the onions are almost tender. Keep warm.

Sauté the mushrooms in the remaining olive oil and butter, flavoured with a little lemon juice. Keep warm.

To Finish and Serve: When the meat is tender, remove the calf's foot and bouquet garni from the casserole. Correct the seasoning and add the glazed onions and sautéed mushrooms. Sprinkle generously with finely chopped flat-leaf parsley and serve directly from the casserole.

Serves 4 to 6

Coq au Vin de Chambertin

Top scorer in the Burgundy stakes – especially if you use a really good Burgundy and a rich homemade stock for its creation – is this recipe for coq au vin, with its classic garnish of fat lardons cut from a thick slice of bacon and glazed button mushrooms and baby onions. Delicious.

50g/2oz butter
2 tablespoons olive oil
100g/4oz unsmoked bacon in
   one piece, cut into cubes
12 boiling onions
12 button mushrooms
1 x 1.4kg/3lb chicken
salt and freshly ground pepper
flour
2 cloves garlic, finely chopped
sprig of fresh thyme
2 sprigs of fresh parsley
2 bay leaves
4 tablespoons Cognac, warmed
½ bottle good red Burgundy
1 sugar cube
finely chopped flat-leaf parsley

To Prepare the Bacon, Onions and Mushrooms: Heat 40g/1½oz butter and the olive oil in a heavy, heatproof casserole. Sauté the bacon cubes until they begin to turn golden, then add the onions and cook for 1 to 2 minutes. Add the mushrooms and sauté gently until the onions begin to turn translucent and the mushrooms brown. Remove the bacon, onions and mushrooms from the casserole using a slotted spoon and keep warm.

To Prepare the Chicken: Cut the chicken into serving pieces. Roll the chicken pieces in seasoned flour and sauté in the fat left in the casserole for about 5 minutes, or until they turn golden on one side. Then, without piercing the skin, turn the chicken pieces over to brown on the other side. As each of the chicken pieces begins to 'stiffen', transfer to a covered dish and keep warm.

To Cook the Casserole: Preheat the oven to 170°C/325°F. Return the bacon, onions, mushrooms and chicken pieces with their juices to the casserole. Add salt and freshly ground pepper to taste, the finely chopped garlic, sprigs of thyme and parsley, and the bay leaves. Cover the casserole and cook in the preheated oven for 35 to 45 minutes or until the chicken pieces are almost tender. Remove the chicken pieces, bacon and vegetables from the casserole and keep warm. Reduce the oven to 140–150°C/275–300°F.

To Make the Sauce: Skim off excess fat from the juices in the casserole. Set the casserole over a high heat, pour in the warmed Cognac and ignite it. Allow to burn for 1 to 2 minutes and then extinguish by pouring in the Burgundy. Add a lump of sugar. Bring to the boil and reduce the sauce over a high heat to half the original quantity. Thicken by whisking in a beurre manié (made by mashing the remaining butter with 1 tablespoon flour to form a smooth paste). Taste and correct the seasoning.

To Finish and Serve: Strain the sauce into a clean casserole and return the chicken pieces, bacon and vegetables. Cover and allow to simmer in the very low oven until ready to serve. Sprinkle generously with chopped flat-leaf parsley and serve directly from the casserole.

Serves 4

Racks of Lamb with Green Herb Crust

Racks of spring lamb are needed for this brilliant party dish. Roast the lamb for 20 minutes before patting on the buttery crust of breadcrumbs, watercress, parsley, green peppercorns and mustard powder. Then, 20 minutes before serving, just time to enjoy the first course, simply roast the crusted meat in a hot oven until the lamb is ready and the crust is crisp.

**2 racks (best end of neck) of
   baby lamb, each with
   6 cutlets: ask your butcher
   to skin and chine the racks
salt and freshly ground pepper
cayenne pepper**

For the Green Herb Crust
**1 tablespoon mustard powder
4 tablespoons softened butter
6 tablespoons fresh
   breadcrumbs
6 tablespoons finely chopped
   watercress
6 tablespoons finely chopped
   flat-leaf parsley
2 cloves garlic, finely chopped
1 tablespoon green
   peppercorns, crushed
2 tablespoons melted butter**

To Prepare the Lamb: Preheat the oven to 200°C/400°F. With a sharp knife, remove all but a very thin layer of fat from the meaty side of the racks of lamb. Score the remaining layer of fat diagonally in both directions to make a close-knit lattice pattern: this will hold the green herb crust during the final roasting.

Season the trimmed racks of lamb generously with salt and freshly ground pepper and add a hint of cayenne. Then roast them in a baking dish in the hot oven for 20 minutes. Remove from the oven and leave at room temperature to cool.

To Prepare the Green Herb Crust: Combine the mustard powder and softened butter to form a paste. Spread this over the meaty side of the lamb. Combine the breadcrumbs, finely chopped watercress, parsley and garlic and crushed green peppercorns, and pat this mixture over the buttery side of the lamb. Drizzle melted butter over the lamb, and keep at room temperature until ready for the final roasting.

To Finish and Serve: Preheat the oven to 200°C/400°F. Roast the buttery crusted lamb for 20 minutes in the hot oven.

To carve, hold the exposed end of the bones while cutting gently between them, releasing the 12 chops (cutlet frills, should you have them, prevent hands getting greasy during this task). Serve immediately, with 2 or 3 chops per person.

Serves 4 to 6

Navarin of Lamb

Spring lamb stew has been a welcome standby at my dinner parties here and abroad for as long as I can remember. This recipe for tender nuggets of lamb simmered in a tomato-flavoured sauce with spring vegetables is absolutely foolproof.

1.2kg/2½lb boned shoulder or breast of lamb

50g/2oz butter

2 tablespoons olive oil

1 Spanish onion, quartered

2 tablespoons flour

sugar

salt and freshly ground pepper

1 clove garlic, finely chopped

4 small turnips, quartered

1 fresh bouquet garni (2 sprigs of parsley, 1 sprig of thyme and 1 bay leaf, tied into a little packet with 2 short segments of celery)

450ml/15fl oz chicken stock

4 tablespoons tomato paste, diluted in a little water

12 small boiling onions

100g/4oz unsmoked bacon in one piece, diced

12 small potatoes, peeled

100g/4oz shelled fresh peas

2 tablespoons finely chopped fresh parsley

To Prepare the Meat: Cut the shoulder or breast of lamb into large cubes. Melt 25g/1oz butter with the olive oil in a heavy heatproof casserole and brown the lamb cubes with the onion.

Pour off some of the fat, then blend in the flour, stirring the meat and onions over a low heat until the pan juices thicken slightly. Sprinkle with a generous pinch of sugar to give a deeper colour to the sauce and season to taste with salt and freshly ground pepper.

To Cook the Casserole: Preheat the oven to 180°C/350°F. Add the finely chopped garlic, quartered turnips and bouquet garni to the casserole. Stir in 300ml/½ pint of the chicken stock and the diluted tomato paste. Cover and simmer in the preheated oven for 1 hour.

To Glaze the Onions and Sauté the Bacon: Meanwhile, melt the remaining butter in a heavy frying pan and add a generous pinch of sugar and the remaining chicken stock. Cook the boiling onions until tender and glazed. Blanch and sauté the diced bacon.

To Finish and Serve: Remove the lamb from the casserole and strain the sauce through a sieve. Allow the sauce to cool, then skim the fat from the surface and strain into a clean casserole. Add the lamb to the casserole with the glazed boiling onions, sautéed bacon, potatoes and fresh peas. Bring to the boil, then cover and return to the oven. Simmer for 20 to 30 minutes, or until the vegetables are cooked and the lamb is tender. Sprinkle with finely chopped parsley just before serving, straight from the casserole.

Serves 4 to 6

Beef Steak and Kidney Pie

An old English favourite, here enlivened by dry sherry and Worcestershire sauce just before serving. Try it … it really makes a difference.

350g/12oz calf's kidney
3 tablespoons flour
salt and freshly ground pepper
900g/2lb braising steak, cut
   into large cubes
4 tablespoons butter or suet
4 shallots, finely chopped
300ml/10fl oz beef stock
1 bay leaf
1 tablespoon chopped fresh
   parsley
pinch each of ground cloves
   and dried marjoram
1 x recipe quantity flaky pastry
   (page 251)
2 tablespoons dry sherry
1 teaspoon Worcestershire
   sauce

To Prepare the Kidney: Clean the kidney, split it, remove the fat and large tubes, and soak in salted water for 1 hour. Dry the kidney and cut into 6mm/¼in slices.

To Cook the Meat: Season 3 tablespoons of flour with 1 teaspoon salt and ½ teaspoon freshly ground pepper, and roll the beef and kidney in it, shaking off the excess.

Melt the butter, or suet, in a heavy saucepan and sauté the finely chopped shallots until golden. When the shallots have taken on a little colour, add the beef and kidney and brown them thoroughly, stirring almost constantly.

Moisten the steak and kidney with beef stock. Add ¼ teaspoon freshly ground pepper, the bay leaf, chopped parsley, ground cloves and marjoram, and stir well. Cover and simmer over a low heat for 1 to 1¼ hours, or until the meat is tender. If the liquid is too thin, thicken with a little flour mixed to a smooth paste with water.

To Finish and Bake the Pie: Preheat the oven to 230°C/450°F. Butter a 1-litre/2-pint deep pie dish. Place a pie bird (also known as a pie raiser) in the center of the dish. This will keep the top crust in place and allow the steam to escape. Add the meats and their liquid and allow to cool.

Roll out the flaky pastry and lay over the pie dish. Moisten the edges and press to the dish to seal. Make slits in the pastry to allow steam to escape, and bake in the preheated oven for 10 minutes. Lower the heat to 190°C/375°F and continue baking for 15 minutes, or until the pastry crust is golden brown.

Just before serving the pie, insert a small pie bird into the center slit and pour in a mixture of dry sherry and Worcestershire sauce.

Serves 4 to 6

Great
Desserts

South African Blueberry Pancakes with Vanilla Ice Cream

Hot blueberry pancakes (rather like griddle cakes) – three per serving – with homemade vanilla ice cream and a blueberry coulis (a purée of fresh blueberries with sugar and crème de cassis) are the simple ingredients of this delicious sweet from Cape Town's famous restaurant, the difficult-to-pronounce Buitenverwachting (it means land beyond all expectations). It was one of the great eating experiences of my last trip to South Africa.

For the Vanilla Ice Cream
240ml/8fl oz heavy cream
240ml/8fl oz milk
100g/4oz sugar
5 egg yolks
2 vanilla pods, split and seeds
   scraped out

For the Pancake Mixture
100g/4oz flour
3 tablespoons milk
2 eggs
1 egg yolk
½ teaspoon vanilla extract
pinch of salt
finely grated zest of ½ lemon
2–4 tablespoons rum
safflower oil, for frying
½ pint fresh blueberries
confectioners' sugar, for
   dusting

For the Garnish
blueberry coulis: ½ pint
   fresh blueberries puréed
   with 4 tablespoons each
   sugar and crème de cassis
crème fraîche

To Prepare the Vanilla Ice Cream: In a medium saucepan, bring the cream, milk and sugar to the boil. Remove from the heat.

Place the top of a double boiler over barely simmering water. Add the egg yolks and vanilla seeds and whisk until smooth. Then gradually whisk in the cream mixture until smooth. Cook gently, stirring constantly with a wooden spoon, until the custard thickens enough to coat the back of the spoon (71°C/160°F on an instant-read thermometer will indicate that any salmonella bacteria present have been killed). Do not allow the custard to come to the boil or it will curdle. Remove from the heat and allow to cool.

Transfer the mixture to an ice cream maker (you do need an ice cream maker to make a good job of this) and freeze according to the manufacturer's directions.

To Prepare the Pancakes: Sift the flour into a mixing bowl. Whisk in the milk, then the eggs and egg yolk. Add the vanilla, salt, freshly grated lemon zest and rum. Mix well.

Preheat the broiler to high. (You will use it to brown the pancakes.) Heat 2 large nonstick frying pans over a medium heat and brush with safflower oil. Wipe away excess oil with a piece of paper towel. Make 3 or 4 pancakes at a time in each pan, each one about 6cm/2½ in across, using 1 to 2 tablespoons of batter for each. While they are cooking (for about 1 minute, until light brown underneath), arrange fresh blueberries on top, allowing them to sink into the pancakes. As soon as the first batch of pancakes are light brown underneath, dust with confectioners' sugar and place under the preheated broiler. Gratinée (broil) until the pancakes are cooked through and slightly caramelized on top. Keep hot while the next batch is cooked and then goes under the broiler. Continue until you run out of batter: 12 is a good number of pancakes to have.

To Serve: Transfer the hot pancakes to dessert plates which you have decorated attractively with a little blueberry coulis and crème fraîche. Garnish with vanilla ice cream, and serve immediately.

Serves 4

Shepherd's Bread and Butter Pudding

Richard Shepherd's bread and butter pudding with apricots soaked in whisky is my favourite version of this comforting English pudding. Served at luncheon in his restaurant, Shepherd's, near the Houses of Parliament, it is a winner.

8–12 tablespoons chopped
    dried apricots
4 tablespoons golden raisins
whisky to cover dried fruit
300ml/10fl oz heavy cream
300ml/10fl oz milk
½ teaspoon pure vanilla essence
8 egg yolks
100g/4oz granulated sugar
butter
6 slices white bread

For the Apricot Glaze
6 tablespoons apricot jam
1–2 tablespoons whisky

To Prepare the Pudding: Place the chopped apricots and raisins in a shallow dish and cover with whisky. Set aside to soak.

In a heavy saucepan, combine the cream, milk and vanilla essence and bring to the boil. Remove from the heat. In a mixing bowl, whisk the egg yolks and sugar together, then stir this into the cream and milk mixture. Set aside.

Butter the bread, remove the crusts and cut the slices into quarters.

To Bake: Preheat the oven to 170°C/325°F. Take 6 ramekins or individual ovenproof dishes and put the whisky-soaked apricots and raisins in the bottom. Sprinkle any remaining whisky over them. Place the bread on top, cutting and patching it to fit. Pour in the cream mixture to cover the bread in each dish.

Place the dishes in a roasting pan and pour in hot water to come halfway up the sides. Bake in the preheated oven for 20–30 minutes.

To Prepare the Apricot Glaze and Serve: In a small saucepan, combine the apricot jam with the whisky. Heat through, stirring constantly, until the jam has melted. When the bread pudding is ready, glaze each serving with apricot jam, and serve immediately.

Serves 6

Strawberry Semifreddo with Orange and Pink Peppercorn Sauce

Semifreddo is an Italian custard-based iced dessert halfway between ice cream and a chilled *panna cotta*. Smooth, creamy and packed with delicious fruit, it makes a spectacular dinner-party or special-occasion sweet. You need to prepare it the day before serving.

For the Semifreddo Mixture
5 egg yolks
5 tablespoons sugar
225g/8oz mascarpone cheese
5 tablespoons Cognac
2 tablespoons orange juice

For the Strawberry Mixture
225g/8oz ripe strawberries,
     thinly sliced
4 tablespoons orange juice
2 tablespoons sugar

For the Chantilly Cream
300ml/10fl oz heavy cream
1–1½ teaspoons pure vanilla
     essence

For the Orange and Pink Peppercorn Syrup
finely grated zest of 1 orange
225g/8oz sugar
2 tablespoons Cognac
juice of 2 large oranges
juice of 1 large lemon
150ml/5fl oz water
1 tablespoon pink peppercorns

For the Garnish
20-24 small ripe strawberries
16–20 sprigs of fresh mint

To Prepare the Semifreddo Mixture: Place the egg yolks in the top of a double boiler set over 5cm/2in of barely simmering water and beat until light and lemon-coloured. Gradually beat in the sugar and continue to beat until the beater, lifted from the mixture, leaves a trail across the surface: about 5 minutes. Remove from the heat, pour into a large mixing bowl and allow to cool.

In a bowl, combine the mascarpone, Cognac and orange juice and beat until smooth. Fold into the egg yolks and sugar, and reserve.

To Prepare the Strawberries: In a medium-sized bowl, combine two-thirds of the strawberries with the orange juice and sugar and mash lightly with a fork. Fold into the semifreddo mixture.

To Prepare the Chantilly: Whip the cream until light peaks form. Beat in the vanilla, to taste. Fold the chantilly cream into the semifreddo mixture. Chill for at least 3 hours.

To Prepare the Orange and Pink Peppercorn Syrup: In a heavy saucepan, combine the orange zest and sugar. Set the pan over a medium heat and cook, stirring constantly, until the sugar is a light-brown caramel. Pour in the Cognac, remove from the heat and ignite. Carefully pour the orange and lemon juices and water into the pan, return to the heat and reduce the syrup to half the original quantity. Strain into a clean jug or bowl. Add the pink peppercorns and reserve.

When Ready to Freeze the Mixture: Add 6 tablespoons of syrup to the reserved sliced strawberries, and spoon down the insides of 4 small glass serving dishes. Fill the dishes with the strawberry semifreddo mixture, being careful not to dislodge the sliced strawberries and syrup on the inside of the glass bowls. Freeze overnight.

1½ Hours Before Serving: Remove the bowls of strawberry semifreddo from the freezer. Decorate each with 4 to 5 small strawberries and tiny sprigs of fresh mint. Place the desserts in the refrigerator to soften before serving.

Serves 4

Dark Chocolate Soufflé Glacé with Preserved Ginger Chantilly

Chocoholics beware: this richly flavoured cold chocolate soufflé with its distinctive notes of orange zest and dark rum is totally addictive. Highly flavoured, soft textured, with a secret 'well' piled high with chantilly cream studded with thin slices of stem ginger … fantastic.

450g/1lb very good quality dark chocolate (such as Valrhona)
4 tablespoons cocoa powder
100g/4oz unsalted butter, diced
6 tablespoons dark rum
zest and juice of 1 orange
6 large eggs, separated
3 extra egg whites
100g/4oz sugar
1x11.7g pack gelatin granules
6 tablespoons hot water
150ml/5fl oz heavy cream

For the Ginger Chantilly Cream
300ml/10fl oz heavy cream
2–3 tablespoons iced water
8 chunks of crystallized stem ginger, thinly sliced

To Serve
zest of ½ orange

To Prepare the Soufflé Mixture: Break the chocolate into the top of a double boiler. Add the cocoa powder and butter and heat over bubbling water, stirring occasionally, until smooth. Continue to cook, stirring from time to time, for 5 minutes more. Remove from the heat and stir in the orange juice and zest and the dark rum.

In a mixing bowl over barely simmering water, beat the egg yolks and sugar with an electric whisk until the mixture forms a ribbon when you lift the whisk. Add the warm chocolate-orange mixture, beating constantly until well blended, then strain into a clean bowl.

Soften the gelatin in the hot water. Add to the chocolate-orange mixture and stir until dissolved.

In a clean mixing bowl, using a clean whisk, whisk the egg whites until stiff.

Fold the whipped cream into the chocolate-orange mixture gently but thoroughly, using a spatula. Taste and add a little more rum if desired. Then, very gently, fold in the whisked egg whites.

To Chill the Soufflé: Wrap a collar of wax paper or foil tightly round a 1.2-litre/2½-pint soufflé dish to extend 5cm/2in above the rim. Fasten with paper clips top and bottom. Rinse a jam jar (you could use a 350g/12oz stem ginger in syrup jar) in cold water (you have already soaked off the label) and stand it in the center of the soufflé dish. Pour the chocolate mixture around it, making sure the jar stays in the middle. Chill until set.

To Prepare the Ginger Chantilly Cream: Whip the cream. Add the iced water and whip again until smooth and light. Then gently fold in three-quarters of the crystallized stem ginger slices, reserving the rest for decoration.

To Serve: Remove the soufflé from the refrigerator. Cut around the jar with a wet knife to loosen it. Pour a little warm water into the jar and gently remove it from the center of the chocolate mousse.

Carefully remove the paper collar. Fill the cavity left by the bottle with ginger chantilly cream, piling it high in the center. Decorate with the reserved ginger slices and orange zest, and serve.

Serves 6 to 8

Rich Ginger Ice Cream

The richest, most scrumptious ice-cream I know is this version of ginger ice cream, lavishly flavoured with ginger and topped with ginger syrup and thin slices of preserved ginger.

225g/8oz sugar
600ml/1 pint milk
300ml/10fl oz heavy cream
1 teaspoon ground ginger
finely grated zest of 1 large orange
8 medium egg yolks
1 x 350g/12oz jar crystallized stem ginger in syrup
½ teaspoon pure vanilla essence

To Make the Rich Ginger Custard: In a saucepan, combine the sugar, milk, heavy cream, ground ginger and most of the orange zest (reserving long threads as garnish), and bring to the boil. Remove the pan from the heat. Cover and leave to infuse for 5 to 10 minutes.

In a large bowl, lightly beat the egg yolks. Pour the ginger cream mixture into the lightly beaten egg yolks and mix until the custard is light and foamy. Pour the custard into the top of a double boiler over barely simmering water and cook, stirring with a wooden spoon, until the custard is thick enough to coat the back of the spoon (71°C/160°F on an instant-read thermometer will indicate that any salmonella bacteria present have been killed). Do not let the custard come to the boil or it will curdle.

Pour the custard into a bowl set in a larger one filled with ice cubes. Cover the smaller bowl with a plate and let the custard cool completely.

To Prepare the Crystallized Ginger: Drain the syrup from the ginger and reserve. Thinly slice 4 pieces of stem ginger, and finely chop the remainder. Stir the finely chopped stem ginger and the vanilla essence into the cooled custard. Cover and chill for at least 2 hours.

To Freeze: Cover the custard and freeze until it begins to harden about 2.5cm/1in around the sides of the container. Beat to break up the ice particles. Replace the cover and continue to freeze for 5 hours, or overnight.

To Serve: About 1 hour before serving, transfer the ice cream to the refrigerator to soften slightly.

Pile the ice cream into a glass serving dish. Scatter stem ginger and orange zest on top and dribble over a little reserved ginger syrup.

Serves 4 to 6

Chamonix Lemon Tart

The wine-growing village of Franschhoek is one of the most enchanting spots in South Africa. High on a hill overlooking their own vineyards is the Auberge de Chamonix, one of the Cape's finest restaurants. Here three fresh young talents are spearheading a new movement of inspired minimalist cooking based on the 'sunshine' ingredients of thè Cape. This classic lemon tart, which says lemon, lemon, lemon all the way, is a case in point. It is at its best eaten immediately – it does not keep well, but if your house is like my house you will not get the chance to find that out. Serve the tart at room temperature with crème fraîche, or a verbena or cardamom-scented sorbet, or both.

For the Pastry
1 egg, beaten
50g/2oz sugar
pinch of salt
3 tablespoons milk
300g/10oz flour, sifted
175g/6oz butter, slightly
   softened and diced

For the Lemon Filling
8 eggs, beaten
225g/8oz sugar
finely grated zest of 2 lemons
juice of 4 lemons

To Serve
sugar
300ml/10fl oz heavy cream,
   whipped
slices of strawberry or red
   plum

To Prepare the Pastry: In a mixing bowl, combine the beaten egg, sugar, salt and milk and mix well. Chill.

In another mixing bowl, combine the sifted flour and diced butter. Rub the mixture with your fingertips until it is like wet sand. Pour the chilled egg and milk mixture into the butter and flour mixture and knead quickly to a smooth dough. Wrap the dough in plastic wrap or aluminium foil and chill for 30 minutes.

To Make the Lemon Filling: In a mixing bowl, combine the beaten eggs and sugar and beat until light and lemon-coloured. Stir in the lemon zest and lemon juice and mix well.

To Bake the Pastry Blind: Preheat the oven to 180°C/350°F. Remove the pastry from the refrigerator and discard the plastic wrap or foil. Roll out the pastry carefully on a lightly floured surface to a round large enough to line a 27cm/10in loose-bottomed tart pan.

Place the pastry in the pan (lightly greased if necessary), gently pressing it into the corners, and prick the bottom with the tines of a fork. Cover with foil and fill with dried beans or rice.

Bake in the preheated oven for 10 minutes, or until the edge of the pastry is lightly browned. Remove from the oven, discard the foil and beans or rice, reduce the heat, and return to the oven. Continue baking the tart for another 10 minutes until the pastry base is lightly browned. Remove from the oven and cool. Turn the oven down to 170°C/325°F.

To Finish and Serve: Pour the rich lemon filling into the pastry. Bake the tart for about 30 minutes or until the filling is set. Sprinkle the top of the tart with granulated sugar and caramelize under a preheated broiler (or with a blowtorch). Serve at once with dollops of whipped cream and slices of strawberry or red plum.

Serves 4

Madée Trama's Salade de Fruits Glacées

Madée Trama is a self-taught French cook of enormous talent. Her enchanting little Paris restaurant, Tante Madée, was one of my favourites when I used to stay in the French capital. Her combination of fresh fruit sorbets and thinly sliced fresh fruits is one of the most delightfully easy desserts to produce that I know.

4–6 scoops of lemon sorbet
4–6 scoops of mango sorbet
2 oranges
2 pears
2 tablespoons lemon juice
450g/1lb raspberries
1 tablespoon confectioners'
sugar, sifted
2 tablespoons Cointreau

To Prepare the Sorbets: About 15 minutes before serving, transfer the sorbets from the freezer to the refrigerator to soften slightly. Chill 4 serving plates.

To Prepare the Fruit: With a vegetable peeler, pare the zest from the oranges; with a sharp knife remove any pith. Cut the zest into very fine threads. Simmer the threads in a small saucepan of boiling water for 5 to 6 minutes, then drain and refresh under cold running water. Segment the pith-free oranges into a small bowl.

Quarter the pears. Remove the center core and slice each quarter lengthways into 4 slices. Place in a bowl with the lemon juice and toss, to prevent discoloration.

In a blender, purée the raspberries with the confectioners' sugar. Sieve into a small bowl to remove the seeds, and stir in the Cointreau.

To Serve: Pour enough raspberry purée on each plate to cover the surface. Arrange 4 slices of pear overlapping on the outer edge of each plate, and arrange another 4 slices opposite. Repeat with 3 to 4 orange segments in between each pear decoration. Mould the lemon sorbet into 4 balls using an ice cream scoop or two tablespoons. Repeat with the mango sorbet, and place one ball of each sorbet in the center of the serving plates. Sprinkle with the threads of orange zest and serve.

Serves 4

Jo-Jo's Warm Chocolate Cake with Caramel Ice Cream

Top chef Jean-Georges Vongerichten, internationally known New York-based restaurateur, likes to play with his own rather difficult-to-remember name when it comes to his restaurants: fashionable Jo-Jo's on New York's Upper East Side, and his even more trendy Vong, in London and New York. Jo-Jo's cooking is just right for today: with a deep-down home-on-the-farm feeling that is completely sophisticated at Jo-Jo's, and the trendy Pacific Rim style at his two Thai- and French-inspired Vong restaurants. His chocolate cake, richly flavoured and meltingly soft on the inside, is a case in point. You have to try it. But remember: the key to making this superb chef's great dish is to use the best chocolate you can buy: Valrhona or Callebout.

100g/4oz very good quality dark chocolate, broken into pieces
100g/4oz unsalted butter, diced
4 egg yolks
4 whole eggs
100g/4oz sugar
1 tablespoon flour

To Serve
4–8 scoops caramel ice cream

To Prepare the Molds: Preheat the oven to 170°C/325°F. Grease (if necessary) four 12cm/5in fluted charlotte molds or other small round molds.

To Prepare the Cake Mixture: Combine the chocolate and the butter in the top of a double boiler and melt over simmering water. Remove the pan from the heat and set aside.

In a mixing bowl, whisk the egg yolks, whole eggs and sugar. Keep whisking until the mixture reaches the ribbon stage (when the whisk is lifted and leaves a ribbon trail on the surface), then beat in the flour gradually. Fold in the melted chocolate mixture.

To Cook and Serve: Pour the mixture into the molds up to the edges. Bake in the preheated oven for 4 minutes only. Serve at once, tipping the warm cakes out on to individual plates and garnishing with 1 or 2 scoops of caramel ice cream.

Serves 4

Orange, Raspberry and Blueberry Dessert with Crème Fraîche

Deceptively simple, this colourful fresh fruit dessert with Moroccan overtones – orange, lemon and orange-flower water – is like a breath of fresh air. Perfect after a rich tagine of lamb cooked with prunes and almonds … or monkfish cooked with saffron potatoes.

4–6 navel oranges
¾ pint fresh raspberries
¾ pint fresh blueberries

For the Orange-Flower Sauce
juice of 2 oranges
juice of ½ lemon
2–4 tablespoons orange-flower water
1–2 teaspoons pure vanilla essence
2 tablespoons confectioners' sugar

To Serve
crème fraîche (optional)

To Prepare the Oranges: Peel the oranges, removing all traces of skin or pith as you peel them. Then cut the oranges into 6mm/¼in slices. Metal cookie cutters, in 2 sizes, will make cutting attractive, even-sided slices of orange with no trace of pith or skin easy for you. Place the orange slices in a large flat bowl.

To Prepare the Orange-Flower Sauce: In a small bowl, combine the orange and lemon juices. Flavour with the orange-flower water and vanilla essence, to taste, and stir in the confectioners' sugar. Pour the sauce over the orange slices and chill.

To Assemble and Serve: With a slotted spoon, arrange the orange slices on 4 to 6 chilled dessert plates. Sprinkle with the raspberries and blueberries, spoon the orange-flower sauce over and garnish each plate, if desired, with a dollop of crème fraîche. Serve immediately.

Serves 4 to 6

Barry Wine's Hot Chocolate Soufflé with Espresso Ice Cream

Barry and Karen Wine's restaurant in New York, The Quilted Giraffe, was once the hottest ticket in town. And for me the most memorable treat there was the hot chocolate soufflé with cold coffee ice cream: what more surprising combination can there be? The icy-cold espresso ice cream was tossed, in front of the diner, into the chocolate soufflé, the rich, hot, sweet soufflé contrasting to perfection with the cold, bitter ice cream.

225g/8oz very good quality
    dark chocolate,
    broken into pieces
150g/5oz unsalted butter,
    diced
softened butter and sugar to
    prepare soufflé dishes
150ml/5fl oz lukewarm water
5 egg yolks
9 egg whites, at room
    temperature
100g/4oz sugar

To Serve
confectioners' sugar
4–6 scoops espresso ice cream
whipped cream

To Melt the Chocolate: Combine the chocolate and the butter in the top of a double boiler and melt over simmering water. Remove the pan from the heat and set aside.

To Prepare the Dishes: Brush the insides of 4 to 6 150–225g/6–8oz soufflé dishes with a thin coating of softened butter. Coat the dishes with sugar simply by filling the first one with sugar, turning it to coat the sides entirely, then pouring the sugar into the next dish, and so on. Preheat the oven to 220°C/425°F.

To Prepare the Soufflé: With an electric mixer, beat the lukewarm water and egg yolks together at high speed for 10 minutes.

In a clean bowl, and using a clean whisk, start whisking the egg whites with the sugar in an electric mixer at high speed. While they are whisking, fold the beaten egg yolks into the chocolate mixture. Beat the egg whites until quite glossy and moderately stiff. Fold the egg whites into the chocolate mixture, one third at a time. Ladle the soufflé mixture into the prepared soufflé dishes and bake in the preheated oven for 5 to 7 minutes, depending on their size.

To Serve: Immediately upon removing from the oven, sprinkle each soufflé with confectioners' sugar. At the table, drop a scoop of espresso ice cream into the center of each soufflé and cover with a dollop of whipped cream. Magic!

Serves 4 to 6

Old English Apple Pie

A richly flavoured deep-dish apple pie is hard to beat. This recipe uses dark brown sugar, nutmeg, cinnamon, orange, lemon zest and raisins to create a filling of incredible richness.

700g/1½lb cooking apples
juice of ½ lemon
fingertip pastry for shell and
    top (1½x recipe quantity,
    page 251)
100g/4oz sugar
50g/2oz dark soft brown sugar
1 tablespoon flour
several gratings of fresh
    nutmeg
¼ teaspoon ground cinnamon
finely grated zest of ½ orange
finely grated zest of ½ lemon
50g/2oz raisins chopped
2 tablespoons orange juice
15g/½oz butter

To Serve
heavy cream (optional)
Cheddar cheese (optional)

To Prepare the Apples: Peel and core the apples and slice thickly. Keep the slices in water to which you have added lemon juice to prevent them from going brown.

To Prepare the Pie Dish: Line a deep 22cm/9in pie dish (greased if necessary) with fingertip pastry.

Combine the sugar, dark brown sugar, flour, freshly grated nutmeg and ground cinnamon in a small bowl. Rub a little of this mixture into the pastry lining.

Add the orange and lemon zest to the remaining sugar mixture and reserve.

To Finish and Bake the Pie: Preheat the oven to 200°C/400°F. Drain the apple slices and spread a layer over the bottom of the pastry case. Sprinkle with a few of the chopped raisins and some of the sugar mixture. Repeat the layers until the pastry case is filled almost to overflowing. Sprinkle with the orange juice, dot with the butter and fit the pastry lid over, pressing the edges together or marking them with the tines of a fork.

Decorate the pastry lid with leaves and shapes cut from pastry trimmings. Cut slits in the lid so the steam can escape and bake in the preheated oven for 35 to 40 minutes or until the pastry is golden-brown. Serve warm with heavy cream or Cheddar cheese.

Makes a deep 22cm/9in pie

Moroccan Glazed Fruits in Filo Pastry

Filo pastry elegantly sets the scene for glazed fruits on a bed of Moroccan sugar, ground almonds and ground cinnamon. This is not easy to make – the filo cups are tricky – but well worth the effort involved, and once you learn to hold up the corners of the buttered filo-pastry leaves with marble-sized balls of crumpled aluminium foil, this spectacular dessert might well become your house speciality.

½ pint raspberries
12 small strawberries, hulled
    and halved
4 small slices canned pineapple
    (syrup reserved for glaze)
2 kiwi fruit, peeled and sliced
4 sprigs of fresh mint

For the Almond Filling
6 tablespoons ground toasted
    almonds
4 tablespoons sugar
½ teaspoon ground cinnamon

For the Pastry
6 sheets filo pastry, kept
    covered with a damp towel
4 tablespoons melted butter
confectioners' sugar

For the Glaze
syrup from a small can of
    pineapple
1 tablespoon lemon juice
1 tablespoon Kirsch

To Prepare the Almond Filling: In a small bowl, combine the ground almonds, sugar and cinnamon. Mix well.

To Prepare the Pastries: Preheat the oven to 190°C/375°F. Cut each sheet of filo pastry in half crossways and trim, if necessary, into 15cm/6in squares. Cover with the damp towel again. Brush 4 ramekins with melted butter. Line one ramekin with a filo square so that the corners extend over the side of the dish. Sprinkle the bottom with a little of the almond mixture, then cover with another square of filo, turned slightly so that the corners do not stand up in the same place as the existing corners. Sprinkle on more almond mixture, then top with a third filo square. Line the remaining ramekins in the same way. You can use little balls of crumpled aluminium foil to help keep the corners of filo pastry standing up. Bake the pastry-filled ramekins in the preheated oven for 5 minutes or until crisp and golden.

Remove the pastry cups from the ramekins and allow to cool on wire racks. Sprinkle with a little sieved confectioners' sugar.

To Prepare the Glaze: Boil the pineapple syrup until reduced by half. Add the lemon juice and Kirsch. Allow to cool.

To Serve: Decoratively arrange the raspberries, halved strawberries, canned pineapple, cut into chunks, and sliced kiwi, in the Moroccan pastries. Pour a little glaze over the fruit, decorate with a sprig of fresh mint and serve.

Serves 4

Moroccan Orange Tart

This is a fresh-tasting tart I created using the time-honoured ingredients of a Moroccan orange salad: sliced oranges, chopped dates, slivered almonds, orange-flower water and ground cinnamon, set on an almond filling. This dessert was a Marrakech favourite with my friends.

For the Pastry
300g/10oz butter, diced
10 tablespoons sugar
½ teaspoon salt
2 egg whites
1 teaspoon pure vanilla
essence, or the juice of
1 lemon
450g/1lb flour

For the Almond Filling
4 eggs
150g/5oz sugar
180ml/6fl oz heavy cream
225g/8oz ground almonds
juice of 1 large lemon
grated zest and juice of 1 large
orange

For the Orange Topping
6 small thin-skinned oranges
175g/6oz sugar cubes
300ml/10fl oz water
6 tablespoons sieved orange
marmalade

For the Garnish
50g/2oz flaked almonds
75g/3oz chopped dates

To Make the Pastry: Combine the diced butter, sugar and salt in a large bowl. Work together with a fork or pastry cutter until the mixture resembles coarse breadcrumbs. In a small bowl, beat the egg whites lightly with a fork or whisk. Add to the butter mixture, together with the vanilla or lemon juice, and continue to mix with a fork until thoroughly blended. Gradually sift the flour over the butter mixture, mixing it in with the fork to begin with, then using your fingertips as it becomes stiffer, to make a smooth dough. Roll the dough into a ball. Put in plastic wrap and chill for 30 minutes before using.

Turn the dough on to a floured board and roll out to just under 5mm/¼in thick. Line two 22cm/9in tart pans with the pastry and chill for 30 minutes. Preheat the oven to 220°C/425°F.

Line the pastry crusts with aluminum foil and fill with dried beans or rice. Bake for 15 minutes, then reduce the heat to 180°C/350°F and bake for 15 minutes more. If the edge of the pie crust browns more quickly than an ordinary pastry, cover with foil. Discard the foil and beans or rice and allow to cool.

To Prepare the Almond Filling: Preheat the oven to 180°C/350°F. Whisk the eggs with the sugar until thick and creamy. Add the remaining ingredients and beat vigorously with a wooden spoon until smooth. Spread the pie crusts with the almond mixture. Bake for 10 to 15 minutes until puffed and golden, and firm to the touch.

To Prepare the Orange Topping: Peel the oranges, taking off all the pith, and slice them thinly, removing pits as you come across them. In a large, deep frying pan, dissolve the sugar cubes in the water over a moderate heat. Bring to the boil. Place the orange slices in the syrup and simmer for 3 minutes. Remove with a slotted spoon.

Bubble the syrup over a moderate heat until reduced by half. Add the sieved marmalade and stir until melted to make a rich glaze.

To Serve: Arrange the orange slices on top of the tart in overlapping circles. Brush generously with the marmalade glaze and sprinkle with flaked almonds, chopped dates and ground cinnamon.

Makes 2 x 22cm/9in tarts

Caramelized Pears in Pastry and Cream

Thanks to ready-made fresh puff pastry, this very sophisticated sweet is surprisingly easy to make. And if you use ready-made fresh custard, jazzed up with a hint of the pure vanilla essence, to 'marble' your whipped cream, you are laughing all the way to the table.

450g/1lb sugar, plus extra
    sugar for dredging pears
600ml/20fl oz water
1 vanilla pod
2 pears
juice of ½ lemon
1 x 400g/14oz package of puff
    pastry
240ml/8fl oz heavy cream,
    whipped

For the Crème Patissière
150ml/5fl oz milk
4 tablespoons heavy cream
5cm/2in piece of vanilla pod,
    split
2 egg yolks
25g/1oz sugar
1 tablespoon flour
½ tablespoon cornflour
15g/½oz butter
1 tablespoon Kirsch

To Make the Crème Patissière: Pour the milk into a saucepan and add the cream and vanilla pod. Bring to boiling point over a low heat, then cover the pan and set aside to infuse until needed.

In a bowl, whisk the egg yolks with the sugar until thick and light. Gradually whisk in the flour and cornflour. Remove the vanilla pod from the milk. Slowly pour the milk into the egg yolk mixture, whisking until well blended. Return the mixture to the pan. Bring to the boil over a moderate heat, stirring constantly, then lower heat and continue to simmer, beating vigorously with wooden spoon until the mixture coats the back of the spoon.

Remove the pan from the heat. Beat in the butter, then continue to beat for 1 to 2 minutes longer to cool the cream before adding the Kirsch. Strain the cream through a sieve into a bowl and cover with a sheet of lightly buttered parchment paper to keep a skin from forming on top. Cool, then chill until needed.

To Poach the Pears: Pour the sugar and water into a saucepan. Add the vanilla pod and heat for 10 minutes to dissolve the sugar.

Peel the pears but leave them whole. Brush with the lemon juice, then add to the sugar syrup. Cover and poach gently for 5 minutes. Remove from the heat and leave the pears to cool in the syrup.

To Prepare the Pastry: Preheat the oven to 220°C/425°F. Roll out the pastry to a thickness of 3–6mm/⅛– ¼in, and cut out six 7.5cm/3in squares. Lightly score the top of each square to make sure the pastry rises evenly. Place the pastry squares on a baking sheet that has been sprinkled with water and bake for 12 to 15 minutes.

Cool the pastry squares on a wire rack, then cut each square in half horizontally making a top and bottom crust. With a teaspoon, scoop out any soft pastry from the centers of each half so you are left with only crisp layers.

To Finish and Serve: Swirl the whipped cream and the crème pâtissière together to create a marbled effect. Cover each bottom layer of pastry with the cream and top with the upper layer of pastry.

Preheat the broiler to hot. Quarter each poached pear lengthways, remove the core, then thinly slice each quarter lengthways into a fan shape. Using a palette knife, transfer the pear 'fans' to a baking sheet, dredge with sugar, then caramelize under the hot broiler. Place slices of caramelized pear on top of each pastry slice and serve.

Serves 6

233

Alain Senderens' Chilled Salad of Exotic Fruits with Vanilla, Ginger and Citrus-Flavoured Syrup

One of the first restaurateurs in France to highlight the exotic new fruits and flavours recently arrived from the Pacific was Alain Senderens, acknowledged 'chef of chefs'. Thin shreds of chile and orange and ginger and mint began to enliven his dishes, to be followed by combinations of lobster with mango, crayfish with peaches, turbot with raisins and curry of lamb with apple. But it is his way of serving chilled exotic fruits in a vanilla-, ginger- and citrus-flavoured syrup that I like best. I give you two fruit combinations to macerate in the great chef's truly brilliant syrup.

Fruit Salad I
1 small ripe papaya
16 lychees
20 strawberries
2 kiwi fruits
8 passion fruits
1–2 tablespoons finely slivered
   or chopped fresh mint

Fruit Salad II (see picture)
1 small ripe papaya
1 small ripe mango
20 ripe raspberries
20 ripe strawberries
2 kiwi fruits
1–2 tablespoons finely slivered
   or chopped fresh mint

For Alain Senderens' Syrup
6 tablespoons sugar
1 sprig of fresh mint
1 clove
¼ teaspoon Chinese fivespice
   powder (from good food
   shops and Chinese
   supermarkets)
thinly sliced zest of 1 lime
thinly sliced zest of ¼ lemon
1 vanilla pod, split lengthways
½ teaspoon finely chopped
   fresh ginger
2 coriander seeds
450ml/15fl oz water

To Prepare the Syrup: Combine all the ingredients for the syrup in a heavy saucepan. Bring to the boil, stirring to dissolve the sugar, then remove from the heat and leave to infuse until cool.

To Prepare Fruit Salad I: Peel the papaya over a bowl (to catch the juice) and cut the flesh into thin even-sized slices. Skin the lychees and remove the stones. Wash and hull the strawberries. Peel the kiwi fruits and slice thinly. Cut the passion fruits in half and squeeze the seeds and juice into the bowl with the papaya juice.

To Prepare Fruit Salad II: Peel the papaya and mango over a bowl (to catch the juices) and cut the flesh into thin even-sized slices. Wash the raspberries. Wash and hull the strawberries. Peel the kiwi fruits and slice thinly.

When the Syrup is Cool: Strain through a fine sieve into a shallow bowl. Add the prepared fruits and the reserved juices and chill for 2 to 3 hours.

To Serve: Divide the prepared fruits among 4 shallow dessert bowls. Spoon the syrup over, decorate with finely slivered or chopped mint and serve.

Serves 4

Tarte aux Poires Tatin

This is one of the truly great tarts of French bourgeois cookery. Created by the Tatin sisters before you and I were born, it is a favourite on many a French restaurant menu. Here the tart is made with pears, but try it too with sliced apples for the original tarte Tatin, or even with mango, for a tarte Tatin the sisters could never have eaten.

5 tablespoons softened butter
7 tablespoons sugar
4 firm ripe pears

For the Pâte Brisée Crust
225g/8oz flour
150g/5oz chilled butter, diced
1–2 tablespoons sugar
pinch of salt
1 egg yolk, beaten
1 tablespoon iced water

To Serve
Whipped cream or crème
fraîche

To Make the Pâte Brisée: Combine the flour, butter, sugar and salt in a bowl. Rub in the butter gradually with the tips of your fingers, lifting the flour and butter out of the bowl each time, until the mixture resembles coarse breadcrumbs.

Lightly beat together the beaten egg yolk and iced water and sprinkle over the flour mixture. Work in with a fork until a soft dough forms. Press the dough into a ball, put in plastic wrap and chill for at least 30 minutes.

On a floured surface, roll out the chilled dough to 3mm/⅛in thick. Carefully lift on to a sheet of wax paper and, using a pan lid as a guide, cut a circle to fit over the top of a 20cm/8in ovenproof frying pan with sloping sides. Discard the trimmings, and freeze the circle of pastry on the wax paper for at least 1 hour.

To Prepare the Pears: Preheat the oven to 190°C/375°F. Heat a baking sheet in the oven. Use 50g/2oz of the butter to grease an ovenproof frying pan. Sprinkle with 4 tablespoons of the sugar.

Peel, core and quarter the pears. Reserving 1 pear quarter, arrange as many quarters as will fit tightly, in one layer, with the wider ends at the outside edge. Balance the reserved quarter, round side down, in the center.

Sprinkle the pears with 2 tablespoons of the sugar. Cook over a moderately high heat, gently tilting the pan from time to time (without disturbing the pears), for about 15 minutes, or until the sugar has caramelized to a rich golden brown.

To Finish the Tart and Serve: Remove the pâte brisée circle from the freezer and invert it over the pears. Remove the wax paper. With the point of a sharp knife, make a small hole in the center of the pastry. Place the pan on the hot baking sheet and bake for 45 minutes, or until the crust is well browned.

Remove the pan from the oven and swirl and shake it over a high heat for 1 to 2 minutes to evaporate excess moisture and loosen any stuck caramel. Place a wire rack over the tart, place a baking tray over the wire rack (to catch any juices) and carefully turn over the pan, rack and tray, being careful not to burn yourself. Lift off the pan. Leave the tart to cool for about 45 minutes before sliding on to a dish and serving with whipped cream or crème fraîche.

Serves 4 to 6

Sally Clarke's Bitter Chocolate Mousse Tart

This is one of the best chocolate tarts I have ever tasted. If you like your chocolate filling super-rich and almost runny, bake the tart an hour or two before serving. The pie crust can, of course, be baked in advance.

325g/11oz good dark or bitter
  chocolate (such as Valrhona)
25g/1oz unsalted butter
2 eggs
4 egg yolks
a 18cm/7in pastry crust
  (use the fingertip pastry on
  page 251 or store-bought
  pre-baked pie crust),
50g/2oz sugar

To Prepare the Chocolate Mousse: Preheat the oven to 180°C/350°F.

Gently melt the dark chocolate with the butter in the top of a double boiler.

In a bowl, whisk the whole eggs with the egg yolks until white and creamy.

Gently fold the melted chocolate into the egg mixture. Pour the chocolate mousse into the pre-baked pie crust and bake in the preheated oven for 8 minutes.

To Serve: Sprinkle with sugar and allow to rest for a few minutes. Serve while still warm.

Serves 4

Tetsuya's Flourless Chocolate Cake

Tetsuya Wakuda is one of the world's most inventive chefs. His small, 50-seat, two-floored restaurant in Sydney, Australia, is one of the greatest eating places in the world. Everything this man touches turns to gastronomic gold. On a recent judging jaunt sponsored by Rémy Martin and the Australian *Gourmet Traveller* magazine, I judged Tetsuya Wakuda to be the best chef in Australia.

For the Chocolate Cake
50g/2oz very good quality
  chocolate (such as Valrhona),
  broken into pieces
20g/¾oz dark cocoa powder,
  plus extra for dusting
  the cake
20g/¾oz cornflour
50g/2oz butter
40g/1½oz sugar
4 eggs, separated
1 extra egg white
pinch of salt
¼ teaspoon cream of tartar

To Serve
1 x recipe quantity chocolate
  sorbet (page 240)
1 x recipe quantity orange
  ice cream (page 240)
whipped heavy cream
sprigs of fresh mint leaves
or
crème fraîche and strawberries

To Prepare the Chocolate Cake: Preheat the oven to 200°/400°F. Melt the chocolate in the top of a double boiler. Set aside to cool.

Sift the cocoa and cornflour together through a fine-meshed sieve three times (this is part of getting the right consistency).

In a medium-sized bowl, whisk the butter using a hand-held electric beater until light and creamy. Add half the sugar and continue to whisk for 3 to 4 minutes. Add the egg yolks, combine well, then whisk at top speed for a further 3 minutes. Add the melted chocolate and fold in gently.

In another bowl, whisk the egg whites with the remaining sugar, pinch of salt and cream of tartar until soft peaks form. Fold in one third of the cocoa and cornflour mixture, then the remainder. Then fold this mixture into the chocolate mixture, gently combining the two mixtures.

To Bake and Serve the Cake: Grease and flour a 10 x 25cm/4x10in loaf pan. Spoon the mixture into the loaf pan and place the pan in a baking dish half-filled with boiling water. Bake in the preheated oven for 30 minutes or until it is done when tested with a toothpick. Remove from the oven and cool the cake in the pan.

Remove the cooled cake from the pan, slice thinly and dust with cocoa powder (a tiny sieve or new tea-strainer is useful for this). Serve with a scoop each of chocolate sorbet and orange ice-cream, with whipped heavy cream and sprigs of fresh mint leaves to decorate. Or, more simply, with crème fraîche and strawberries.

Serves 6

Tetsuya's Chocolate Sorbet and Orange Ice-Cream

Two more of brilliant Tetsuya's brilliant recipes. Serve on their own or with Tetsuya's flourless chocolate cake (page 238). These are best made in an ice cream maker.

For the Chocolate Sorbet
1.2 litres/40fl oz cold water
100g/4oz dark cocoa powder
125g/5oz sugar
4 tablespoons dextrose (corn sugar)

For the Orange Ice Cream
1 litre/35fl oz fresh orange juice
100g/4oz sugar
10 egg yolks, beaten
finely grated zest of 1 orange
4 tablespoons dextrose (corn sugar)
120ml/4fl oz frozen concentrated orange juice, boiled down to 4 tablespoons, with grated zest of ½ orange, strained
300ml/10fl oz light cream

To Make the Chocolate Sorbet: In a medium-sized saucepan, bring the water to the boil and then slowly whisk in the cocoa powder until it dissolves thoroughly. Add the sugar and continue whisking until it, too, dissolves. Bring the liquid back to the boil, then lower the heat and simmer gently for 10 minutes or until its quantity is reduced by about a quarter. Add the dextrose (corn sugar) to the mixture and stir until dissolved.

Remove the pan from the heat, cover and allow to cool. Then refrigerate for at least 5 hours or overnight until completely chilled.

Churn in an ice cream maker for 10 to 15 minutes, or according to the manufacturer's instructions.

To Make the Orange Ice Cream: In a medium-sized saucepan, slowly bring the orange juice and grated orange zest to the boil.

In a large bowl, add the sugar to the beaten egg yolks and beat until light and creamy. Then add the boiled orange juice together with the orange zest and whisk together thoroughly. Return the mixture to the pan and heat gently, stirring with a wooden spoon, for 5 to 6 minutes or until it is slightly thickened and coats the back of the spoon (71°C/160°F on an instant-read thermometer will indicate that any salmonella bacteria present have been killed). Add the dextrose (corn sugar) to the mixture and stir until dissolved.

Remove the pan from the heat and strain the orange mixture through a fine sieve, removing all zest. Stir in the 4 tablespoons of strained, reduced orange concentrate for extra intensity of flavour. Cover the pan and set aside until cooled. Then refrigerate for at least 5 hours or overnight until completely chilled.

Stir the cream into the mixture, then churn in an ice cream maker for 10 to 15 minutes, or according to the manufacturer's instructions.

Each recipe makes approximately 1 litre/35fl oz

Burnt Honey Ice Cream

There are certain ice creams that I just have to make; others I am content to buy. Rich ginger ice cream (page 221), the vanilla ice cream on page 216, and Tetsuya's rich chocolate sorbet and super orange ice cream (page 240) are ones I must make. Burnt honey ice cream is a memorable addition to this list. A rich custard-based ice cream, marbled with burnt honey sauce and served with a final drizzle of the rich sauce, it makes a fabulous end to a meal.

For the Rich Custard
225g/8oz sugar
600ml/20fl oz milk
300ml/10fl oz heavy cream
8 egg yolks

For the Burnt Honey Sauce
225g/8oz sugar
8 tablespoons water
8 tablespoons honey

To Prepare the Rich Custard: In a saucepan, combine the sugar, milk and heavy cream and bring to the boil. Remove the pan from the heat, cover and leave to infuse for 5 to 10 minutes.

In a large bowl, beat the egg yolks lightly. Pour the cream mixture into the egg yolks and mix until light and foamy. Pour into the top of a double boiler over barely simmering water and cook, stirring with a wooden spoon, until the custard is thick enough to coat the back of the spoon (71°C/160°F on an instant-read thermometer will indicate that any salmonella bacteria present have been killed). Do not let the custard come to the boil or it will curdle. Pour the custard into a bowl set in a larger one filled with ice-cubes. Cover the smaller bowl with a plate and let the custard cool completely.

To Make the Burnt Honey Sauce: In a small saucepan, bring the sugar and 4 tablespoons of water to the boil. Boil, stirring constantly, for 5 minutes, or until the syrup turns to a deep brown caramel. Add another 4 tablespoons of water (covering your hand with a cloth to avoid being spattered), then stir with a wooden spoon. Cook for a further 1 to 2 minutes to 115°C/239°F (the soft ball stage). Stir in the honey, remove from the heat and allow to cool.

To Freeze the Ice Cream: Stir half the cooled burnt honey sauce into the cooled custard and chill, covered, for 2 hours (reserve the remaining sauce). Then freeze in an ice cream maker (according to manufacturer's instructions), or still-freeze in the following manner: pour the custard into a container that will fit in the freezer and freeze until the mixture begins to harden about 2.5cm/1in around the sides of the container. This takes 1 to 2 hours. At this point, beat the hardening mixture thoroughly with a whisk or fork to break up the ice particles, then leave until firmly frozen: 2 to 3 hours more.

About 1 hour before serving, transfer the ice cream to the refrigerator to soften.

To Serve: Pile the ice cream high in a glass serving dish and drizzle over a little burnt honey sauce. Serve immediately.

Serves 4

Basics

Potatoes

Super Potato Chips
500–700g/1–1½ lb potatoes
oil for deep frying
salt and freshly ground pepper

Peel the potatoes and cut them into sticks about 3mm/⅛in square and 7.5cm/3in long. Rinse in cold water to remove excess starch, drain thoroughly and dry on paper towels.

Heat the oil in a deep-fat fryer to 190°C/375°F.

Fill the frying basket half to two-thirds full of potatoes and immerse it gently in the hot oil. Shake the basket from time to time while frying to keep the potatoes from sticking together. Continue to fry until the potatoes are nearly tender. Drain them well and spread on a baking tray lined with paper towels. Leave to drain the excess oil while you fry the remaining potatoes in the same way.

Once all the potatoes have been cooked in this way, reheat the oil to 190°C/375°F and fry the potatoes a second time in small quantities until golden brown. Drain on paper towels.

Spoon into a heated serving dish, sprinkle with salt and freshly ground pepper, and serve immediately.

Serves 4

Pommes Soufflés
700g/1½ lb potatoes
oil for deep frying
salt and freshly ground pepper

Peel the potatoes and cut them into slices about a millimetre thick (paper thin – use a food processor or mandolin cutter if you have one).

Trim the slices to an even shape, about 5cm/2in long and 2cm/¾in wide. Don't rinse them, but pat the slices dry with paper towels.

Heat the oil in a deep-fat fryer to 140°C/275°F. When the oil is hot add a few of the potato slices. Fry for 4 to 5 minutes, until soft but not at all coloured. Remove from the oil, drain on paper towels and leave to cool. Repeat with the remaining potatoes in batches.

Raise the temperature of the oil to 190°C/375°F. Again working in small batches, put the part-cooked potatoes in the frying basket and lower it into the oil. Fry, turning the slices about gently with a slotted spoon, until they are puffed and golden.

Drain on paper towels and keep hot while you fry the remaining potatoes. Season to taste with salt and freshly ground pepper and serve immediately.

Note: I cannot pretend that these crisp, puffed little pillows are easy to make. The secret is in starting the cooking at a low temperature, so that the potatoes do not brown, leaving them to cool and then cooking at a higher temperature: it is the shock of the change in temperature that causes the puffing up. Console yourself that any pillows that have not puffed up will make excellent potato crisps.

Serves 4

Pommes de Terre Duchesse
1kg/2lb potatoes
salt
25–50g/1–2oz butter
2 eggs
2 egg yolks
freshly ground pepper
freshly grated nutmeg

Peel the potatoes and cut them into thick slices. Cook them, covered, in simmering salted water until they are soft but not mushy. Drain the potatoes well, then return them to the pan and remove all the moisture by shaking the pan over the heat until dry.

Rub the potatoes through a fine sieve. Add the butter, beating with a wooden spoon until the mixture is very smooth. Combine the eggs and egg yolks and beat gradually into the potato mixture. Season to taste with salt, freshly ground pepper and freshly grated nutmeg, and beat until the mixture is very fluffy.

If the potatoes are to be used as a garnish, form the potato mixture into individual shapes with a piping bag, brush with butter and brown under the grill.

Serves 4 to 6

Gratin Dauphinois

450g/1lb new potatoes
50g/2oz butter, plus extra for greasing
150ml/5fl oz heavy cream
8 tablespoons freshly grated Gruyère cheese
4 tablespoons freshly grated Parmesan cheese
salt and freshly ground pepper

Peel or scrape the potatoes and cut them into very thin slices of about 2mm/¹⁄₁₆in (use a mandolin cutter if you have one). Rinse thoroughly and leave to soak in a bowl of cold water for 15 minutes.

Select a shallow ovenproof dish about 22 x 12cm/9 x 5in and grease with butter. Preheat the oven to 150°C/300°F.

Drain the potato slices and dry them thoroughly with paper towels. Arrange a quarter of the potato slices in overlapping rows in the dish, pour over 2 tablespoons of cream, sprinkle with 2 tablespoons of Gruyère and 1 tablespoon of Parmesan, dot with 1 teaspoon butter and, finally, season to taste with salt and freshly ground black pepper.

Repeat the layers exactly as above, making 4 in all, and ending with grated cheese and butter. Bake for 1 hour 20 minutes, or until the

potatoes feel tender when pierced with a sharp skewer and are golden and bubbling on top. Allow to 'settle' for a few minutes before serving.

Note: If the top browns too quickly, cover with a sheet of foil. If you use old potatoes, the cooking time will be slightly shorter.

Serves 4

Pommes Fifine

3 large new potatoes (about 450g/1lb)
salt
1 medium-sized onion, finely chopped
15g/½oz butter
3 tablespoons olive oil
freshly ground pepper
2 tablespoons finely chopped fresh flat-leaf parsley

Scrub the potatoes clean and boil them with their skins in salted water for 15 minutes only, so that they remain undercooked. Cool them by plunging them into cold water.

Meanwhile, in a large heavy frying pan, sauté the finely chopped onion in the butter for 4 to 5 minutes until golden. With a slotted spoon, transfer the onion to a plate. Reserve.

Peel the potatoes and cut them into 6mm/¼ in dice.

Add the olive oil to the butter remaining in the frying pan. Add the diced potatoes and sauté over a high heat for 5 to 6 minutes until crisp and golden on all sides.

Season to taste with salt and freshly ground pepper. Return the sautéed onion to the pan. Toss lightly to mix it thoroughly with the potatoes and sauté for 1 minute longer.

Drain the potato and onion mixture well and serve immediately, garnished with finely chopped parsley.

Serves 3 to 4

Tessa Bramley's Pommes Anna

150g/5oz unsalted butter
1.8kg/4lb new potatoes (such as Jersey Royals, Pink Fir Apple or Charlottes)
12 scallions, trimmed and chopped
3 tablespoons finely chopped fresh chervil
2 tablespoons finely chopped fresh chives

Preheat the oven to 240°C/475°F.

Melt the butter and pour into a jug. Leave to settle. Peel the potatoes and cut them into very thin slices of about 2mm/1¹⁄₁₆in (use a mandolin cutter if you have one). Carefully pour the melted butter into a bowl, leaving behind the milky residue in the jug. Discard the milky residue. Put the potato slices into the clarified butter in the bowl and mix around to coat them.

Combine the scallions, chervil and chives in a small bowl.

To make 6 Annas, set 6 large ovenproof cookie cutters on a baking tray. Build up layers of potatoes within the rings, pushing the layers down firmly with the back of a spoon or with a ramekin slightly smaller than the cutter. After about 3 layers, lightly salt the potatoes and add a layer of mixed scallions and herbs. The idea is to build up layers of buttered potato interspersed with the herb flavourings. Continue until all the ingredients are used up.

Brush the Annas with any remaining butter. Bake in the preheated oven for 25 minutes until the potatoes are cooked through (test with a toothpick) and the tops golden brown.

Push the potatoes through the rings and invert on to a serving dish: the undersides are the smoothest and most attractive.

Serves 6

Vegetables

Crisp-Fried Zucchini

25g/1oz butter
2 tablespoons olive oil
½ vegetable stock cube, crumbled
8–12 zucchini, trimmed and
    thinly sliced
salt and freshly ground pepper

Heat the butter and olive oil in a large frying pan and stir in the crumbled vegetable stock cube. When the stock cube has dissolved in the hot fats, add the sliced zucchini and sauté over a medium heat until they are just tender, stirring from time to time to keep them from browning. Season generously with salt and freshly ground pepper, transfer to a warmed serving dish and serve immediately.

Serves 4 to 6

Buttered Peas Elysées

450g/1lb frozen peas, defrosted
50g/2oz butter
4 tablespoons vegetable stock
salt and freshly ground pepper
½ teaspoon sugar
4 lettuce leaves, cut into thin
    strips
1 egg yolk
4 tablespoons crème fraîche

In a medium-sized saucepan, combine the peas with the butter and vegetable stock, and season to taste with salt, freshly ground pepper and the sugar. Cover with the lettuce strips and simmer over a low heat for 10 minutes or until the peas have absorbed the liquid.

In a small bowl, blend the egg yolk and crème fraîche together with a whisk. Stir this mixture into the peas and lettuce and warm through. Correct the seasoning, transfer to a heated serving dish and serve immediately.

Serves 4

Green Pea Purée Saint-Germain

900g/2lb fresh shelled peas
1 lettuce heart, shredded
12 tiny scallions, trimmed
    and chopped
3 sprigs of fresh parsley
100g/4oz butter
4 tablespoons vegetable stock
sugar
salt
1 boiled baking potato, peeled
    and puréed (optional)
freshly ground pepper

Put the peas in a saucepan with the lettuce, scallions, parsley, half the butter, the vegetable stock, and sugar and salt to taste. Bring to the boil and cook slowly until the peas are tender. Discard the parsley. Drain the vegetables, reserving the juices.

Blend the vegetables to a fine purée in a blender or food processor (or press through a fine sieve), and reheat in the top of a double boiler, adding a little of the strained juice and the remaining butter. If the purée is too thin, add enough puréed potato to lend body. Season with freshly ground pepper, and serve.

Serves 4

Braised Lettuce

4–6 small romaine lettuces
50g/2oz butter
1 slice of bacon, diced
½ Spanish onion, thinly sliced
2 small carrots, thinly sliced
150ml/5fl oz chicken stock
salt and freshly ground pepper
finely chopped fresh parsley

Preheat the oven to 180°C/350°F. Wash the lettuces, leaving them whole. Pare the base of each lettuce to a point and drop them into a large saucepan filled with boiling water. Boil for 5 minutes, then drain and plunge into a bowl of cold water for a few minutes. Drain

the lettuces again and press out any excess moisture.

Heat half the butter in a frying pan over a medium heat and lightly sauté the bacon, onion and carrots.

Butter a heatproof dish large enough to take the lettuces in a single layer and place half the sautéed bacon and vegetables in the bottom. Put in the lettuces in a single layer and top with the remaining bacon and vegetables. Add the chicken stock and season to taste with salt and freshly ground pepper. Bring to the boil on top of the stove, then cover and transfer to the oven. Cook for 45 minutes or until tender. Transfer the lettuces to a heated serving dish.

Dice the remaining butter and whisk into the braising liquid. Pour this buttery liquid over the lettuces, garnish with finely chopped parsley and serve.

Serves 4 to 6

Brussels Sprouts au Gratin

450g/1lb small Brussels sprouts
salt and freshly ground pepper
crushed dried chiles
600ml/20fl oz hot rich cheese sauce
    (page 248)
50g/2oz butter
8 walnuts, finely chopped
4 tablespoons freshly grated
    breadcrumbs

Preheat the oven to 200°C/400°F. Butter an ovenproof dish.

Trim the Brussels sprouts. Put them into boiling salted water and simmer, uncovered, for 5 minutes. Cover the pan and continue to cook for 7 (if the sprouts are very young) to 15 minutes, or until just tender. Drain well and season generously with salt, freshly ground pepper and crushed dried chiles.

Place the hot, seasoned sprouts in the buttered dish and pour over the rich cheese sauce. Melt the butter in a small pan and add the nuts and breadcrumbs. Simmer for 1 or 2 minutes, then spoon over the cheese sauce. Bake the dish for 10 minutes, then serve.

Serves 4

Brussels Sprouts à la Polonaise

450g/1lb small Brussels sprouts
salt and freshly ground pepper
50–75g/2–3oz butter
grated zest and juice of 1 lemon
2 tablespoons finely chopped
   fresh flat-leaf parsley
whites of 2 hard-boiled eggs,
   finely chopped
thin lemon slices, to garnish

Trim the Brussels sprouts. Put them into boiling salted water and simmer, uncovered, for 5 minutes. Cover the pan and continue to cook for 7 (if the sprouts are very young) to 15 minutes, or until just tender. Drain well and season generously with salt and freshly ground pepper.

Place the hot seasoned Brussels sprouts in a heated serving dish. Brown the butter lightly in a frying pan, add lemon juice to taste, and pour over the sprouts. Sprinkle with grated lemon zest, finely chopped parsley and hard-boiled egg white, garnish with lemon slices and serve at once.

Serves 4

Leeks Vinaigrette

12 small leeks or 8 large ones,
   trimmed
6–8 tablespoons olive oil
2 tablespoons wine vinegar
salt and freshly ground pepper
mustard, such as Dijon
2–3 tablespoons finely chopped
   fresh flat-leaf parsley

Simmer the leeks in boiling salted water for 20 minutes or until tender, then drain well. Arrange them in a serving dish and allow to cool. Combine the olive oil and vinegar with salt, freshly ground pepper and mustard to taste, pour over the leeks, garnish with finely chopped parsley and serve.

Serves 4

Leeks Béchamel

12 small leeks or 8 large ones,
   trimmed
100g/4oz butter, cut into pieces
salt and freshly ground pepper
300-450ml/10-15fl oz hot rich
   cheese sauce (page 248)

Preheat the oven to 190°C/375°F. Simmer the leeks in boiling salted water for 5 minutes, then drain well and place in a shallow baking dish. Add the butter and season to taste with salt and freshly ground pepper. Cook in the preheated oven for 35 to 40 minutes or until tender. Drain the pan juices and add them to the hot rich cheese sauce. Pour over the leeks and serve immediately.

Serves 4

American Harvard Beets

2 teaspoons grated orange zest
150ml/5fl oz orange juice
2 tablespoons lemon juice
2 tablespoons sugar
1 tablespoon cornflour
2 large cooked beetroot, peeled
   and diced
15–25g/½–1oz butter
salt and freshly ground pepper

In a medium saucepan, heat the orange zest with the orange and lemon juices. Combine the sugar and cornflour, stir into the hot liquid and cook, stirring constantly, until the sauce is thickened and translucent. Add the diced beets and the butter. Season to taste with salt and freshly ground pepper, and serve at once.

Serves 4

Moroccan Carrots

450g/1lb carrots, peeled and
   cut into quarters lengthways
4 tablespoons olive oil
4 tablespoons cold water
2 cloves garlic, peeled
1–2 tablespoons vinegar
salt and freshly ground pepper
¼ teaspoon each paprika and
   ground cumin
pinch of cayenne
2 tablespoons finely chopped
   fresh coriander
lemon quarters

Blanch the carrot sticks in boiling water in a saucepan. Drain, then return the carrots to the pan and add the olive oil, water and garlic. Simmer until tender. Drain, discard the garlic if desired and transfer the carrots to a serving dish.

Flavour the carrots to taste with the vinegar, salt and freshly ground pepper, the paprika, cumin and cayenne. Toss well, and leave to cool. Serve cold, sprinkled with fresh coriander and with lemon quarters on the side.

Serves 4

Mediterranean Okra

450g/1lb okra
2 tablespoons olive oil
2 cloves garlic, finely chopped
2 shallots, finely chopped
450g/1lb tomatoes, peeled,
   seeded and chopped
1 teaspoon dried oregano
salt and freshly ground pepper
crushed dried chiles
1–2 tablespoons lemon juice
finely chopped fresh coriander

Remove the hard stems from the okra. Heat the olive oil in a saucepan, add the finely chopped garlic and shallots and cook for 5 minutes or until softened. Add the okra and cook for 5 minutes or until lightly golden.

Add the chopped tomatoes and oregano, season to taste with salt, freshly ground pepper and a pinch of crushed dried chiles, and cook for 15 to 20 minutes or until tender.

Transfer the mixture to a warm serving dish and sprinkle with lemon juice and finely chopped coriander. Serve immediately.

Serves 4

Stuffed Artichokes alla Romana

6 fresh artichokes
lemon juice
2–4 cloves garlic, finely chopped
2 tablespoons each finely chopped fresh flat-leaf parsley and mint
2–4 anchovy filets in oil, drained and mashed
4 tablespoons fresh breadcrumbs
150ml/5fl oz olive oil
300ml/10fl oz dry white wine
salt and freshly ground pepper

Cut off the stalks and tough outer leaves of 1 artichoke. Open up the artichoke by pressing it into the corner of a kitchen table or protruding work surface. Reach inside to remove the fuzzy 'choke', using a knife or sharp-edged teaspoon, and discard. Sprinkle inside the artichoke with lemon juice to prevent discoloration, then repeat the procedure with the remaining artichokes.

Preheat the oven to 170°C/325°F. Mix the finely chopped garlic, parsley and mint with the mashed anchovies, fresh breadcrumbs, a little of the olive oil or dry white wine to moisten, and salt and pepper to taste.

Stuff the artichokes and place in a casserole large enough to hold them snugly upright. Pour over the remaining olive oil and white wine and cover with oiled aluminum foil. Bake for 45 minutes or until tender. Serve cold in their own juices as an hors d'oeuvre, or hot as a vegetable.

Serves 6

Sautéed Cauliflower with Pine Nuts

1 cauliflower, trimmed and cut into florets
salt
50g/2oz butter
2 tablespoons olive oil
½ vegetable stock cube, crumbled
4 tablespoons pine nuts
2 teaspoons lemon juice
salt and freshly ground pepper
crushed dried chiles
2 tablespoons finely chopped fresh flat-leaf parsley

Cut each cauliflower floret into quarters. Bring a saucepan of salted water to the boil, add the cauliflower and blanch for 2 minutes. Drain thoroughly.

In a large frying pan, heat the butter with the olive oil. Add the drained cauliflower and the crumbled stock cube, and sauté over a moderate heat for 3 to 4 minutes or until tender, tossing the cauliflower florets with a slotted spoon.

Meanwhile, toast the pine nuts briefly under a hot grill, shaking the grill pan to toast them evenly. Scatter the toasted pine nuts over the sautéed cauliflower, then add the lemon juice and season to taste with salt, freshly ground pepper and crushed dried chiles. Sprinkle with finely chopped parsley and serve immediately.

Serves 4

Salad Dressings

French Dressing

To 2 tablespoons of red wine vinegar, add salt and freshly ground pepper to taste. Stir the mixture well, then add 6 to 8 tablespoons of olive oil and beat with a fork until the mixture thickens. For a creamier dressing, put an ice cube in the mixing bowl and stir the dressing for a minute or two longer. Remove the cube and serve.

Tarragon Dressing: Add 1 teaspoon finely chopped fresh tarragon leaves to the French dressing.

Curry Dressing: Add ½ teaspoon curry powder and 1 teaspoon finely chopped shallots to the French dressing.

Caper Dressing: Add 1 teaspoon chopped capers, ½ clove garlic, crushed, and anchovy paste to taste to the French dressing.

Roquefort Dressing: Add 2–4 tablespoons crumbled Roquefort cheese to the French dressing and blend well. Chill thoroughly before using.

Stocks

Classic Beef Stock

1kg/2lb beef shin (meat and bone)
1kg/2lb veal shin (meat and bone)
4 tablespoons beef, veal or pork dripping, melted
6 small carrots, chopped and browned in butter
1 Spanish onion, chopped and browned in butter
2 sticks celery, roughly chopped
1 bouquet garni (3 sprigs of fresh parsley, 1 sprig of fresh thyme and 1 bay leaf)
1 fat clove garlic
4–6 black peppercorns
100g/4oz lean raw ham

Preheat the oven to hot. Bone the meat, cut it into large pieces and tie the pieces together. Set aside. Break up the bones as finely as possible, place in a large roasting pan, sprinkle with 3 tablespoons of the dripping and brown in the hot oven for 40 to 45 minutes.

When the bones are slightly browned, add the chopped and browned carrots and onion, the celery, bouquet garni, garlic and black peppercorns, but no salt. Stir well and cook for 15 minutes, stirring from time to time.

Transfer the vegetables and bones to a large stockpot or saucepan, add 3 litres/110fl oz of cold water and bring slowly to the boil. Skim carefully, wipe the edge of the saucepan and put the lid half on. Leave the stock to cook gently for 4 hours. Then strain the liquid through a fine sieve into a large bowl and allow to cool. When cool, skim off the fat and reserve the stock for use in the next step.

Put the meat and ham in a saucepan just large enough to hold them. Brown in the remaining dripping, then pour off the excess fat. Add 300ml/½ pint of the prepared stock, cover and simmer very gently over a low heat until the stock is almost completely reduced, turning the meat from time to time so that it is bathed on all sides in the stock. Pour the remainder of the stock into the saucepan, bring to the boil and then simmer very gently and evenly with the lid off.

As soon as the meat is tender and the stock rich and well flavoured, strain into a large bowl. Cool, skim off the fat, then store in the refrigerator. Use the stock within 4 days. Serve the meat however you like.

Classic Chicken Stock

2.7kg/6lb boiling fowl
450g/1lb veal knuckle
2 chicken feet (optional)
salt
6 black peppercorns
2 leeks, white parts only, cut into 7.5cm/3in segments
6 small carrots
1 Spanish onion stuck with 2 cloves
2 sticks celery, cut into 7.5cm/3in segments
1 bouquet garni (3 sprigs of fresh parsley, 1 sprig of fresh thyme and 1 bay leaf)
1 clove garlic, peeled

Place the boiling fowl in a large stockpot with the veal knuckle and chicken feet (for their extra gelatine content) and cover with 3 litres/110fl oz of cold water. Add salt and black peppercorns and bring slowly to the boil. Skim, reduce the heat and simmer, with the water barely bubbling, for at least 1 hour, skimming from time to time.

Add the leeks, carrots, onion stuck with cloves, celery, bouquet garni and clove of garlic to the stockpot and continue to simmer for 1½ to 2 hours, or until the chicken is tender.

Transfer the chicken and vegetables to a serving dish and reserve for later use. Skim the fat from the surface, correct the seasoning and strain the stock into a large bowl. Cool, skim off the fat, then store in the refrigerator. Use the stock within 4 days.

Fish Stock from Trimmings

A well-flavoured fish stock can be made at little expense or effort from fish trimmings. If you have your fish fileted by the fishmonger, ask for the trimmings. Any white fish or the trimmings of white fish – haddock, cod, halibut or flounder – may be used; a cod's head makes a particularly economical foundation. And always ask your fishmonger for heads and bones of sole. I also like to add a lobster shell, or the heads and shells of prawns and shrimps, when available. Uncooked trimmings make a better stock than those which have already been cooked. Mackerel, herring and salmon are too oily and too strong in flavour to use.

Wash the trimmings, discarding any black-looking skin, and break the bones in pieces. Put in an enamelled saucepan with just enough water to cover, and add a sliced onion, a few parsley stalks and white peppercorns and a little salt. Simmer for at least ½ hour, then strain ready for use. White wine may be added with the water.

Fish Court-Bouillon

1 bottle dry white wine
450ml/15fl oz water
100g/4oz carrots, sliced
100g/4oz onions, sliced
1 handful of parsley stalks
1 bay leaf
1 sprig of fresh thyme
coarse salt
12 fennel seeds
12 peppercorns
pinch of cayenne pepper

Combine the ingredients in a large saucepan or fish kettle and bring to the boil. Skim, and boil gently for 45 minutes. Strain and cool.

For a simpler version, substitute water for the white wine and add a little wine, wine vinegar or lemon juice to taste.

Sauces

Classic Béchamel Sauce

75g/3oz butter
½ onion, finely chopped
2 tablespoons flour
900ml/30fl oz hot milk
1 chicken leg or thigh, bone and all, coarsely chopped
50g/2oz chopped lean veal or ham
1 stick celery, chopped
1 small sprig of fresh thyme
½ bay leaf
6 white peppercorns
freshly grated nutmeg

Melt 40g/1½oz butter in a heavy saucepan or the top of a double boiler, and cook the chopped onion over a low heat until soft and translucent but not coloured.

Stir in the flour and cook, stirring constantly with a wooden spoon, for 2 to 3 minutes, until the flour is cooked through. Add a quarter of the hot milk and cook, continuing to stir vigorously. As the sauce begins to thicken, gradually add the remaining hot milk, stirring constantly until the sauce begins to bubble.

In another saucepan, simmer the chopped chicken leg or thigh, the chopped lean veal or ham and the celery in 25g/1oz butter over a very low heat. Season with the thyme, bay leaf, peppercorns, and freshly grated nutmeg to taste. Cook for 5 minutes, stirring to keep the meat from browning. Add the meat and celery to the béchamel sauce, reduce the heat and simmer for 45 minutes to 1 hour, stirring occasionally.

When the sauce is reduced to the proper consistency (two-thirds of its original quantity), strain through a fine sieve and into a bowl, pressing meats and vegetables well to extract all the flavour. Dot the surface of the sauce with tiny pieces of the remaining butter to keep a skin from forming.

Makes about 600ml/1 pint

Cream Sauce: Add 4 tablespoons of heavy cream to the hot béchamel sauce and bring to boiling point. Add a few drops of freshly squeezed lemon juice. For fish, poultry, eggs and vegetables.

Onion Sauce: Roughly chop 1 Spanish onion, put it into a small pan and cover it with hot water. Parboil for 3 to 5 minutes. Drain and then cook the onion in a saucepan with a little butter until soft. Add the hot béchamel sauce and cook for 15 minutes.

Strain the sauce through a fine sieve, pressing the onion well to extract the juices, then return to the heat and gradually beat in 4 tablespoons of heavy cream. Correct the seasoning with salt and white pepper to taste. For fish, lamb or veal.

Aurore Sauce: Add 2 to 3 tablespoons of tomato purée to the hot béchamel sauce. Excellent with eggs, chicken or shellfish.

Chicken Velouté Sauce

40g/1½oz butter
2 tablespoons flour
900ml/30fl oz hot chicken stock
salt
white peppercorns
4 button mushrooms, finely chopped

Melt 25g/1oz of the butter in a heavy saucepan or in the top of a double boiler, add the flour and cook for 2 to 3 minutes, stirring constantly, until the flour is cooked through.

Add the boiling chicken stock with salt and white peppercorns to taste and cook, stirring vigorously. Add the chopped mushrooms, reduce the heat and simmer, stirring occasionally, and skimming from time to time, until the sauce is reduced by two-thirds and is thick but light and creamy.

Strain the sauce through a fine sieve, pressing the mushrooms against the sieve to extract their flavour. Dot the surface of the sauce with tiny pieces of butter to keep a skin from forming. Serve with poached chicken or hard-boiled eggs.

Makes about 600ml/1 pint

Rich Cheese Sauce

40g/1½oz butter
3 tablespoons flour
450ml/15fl oz hot chicken stock
300ml/10fl oz heavy cream
3 tablespoons freshly grated Gruyère cheese
3 tablespoons freshly grated Parmesan cheese
salt and freshly ground pepper
freshly grated nutmeg

Melt the butter in a heavy saucepan or in the top of a double boiler, stir in the flour and cook for 2 to 3 minutes, stirring constantly, until smooth. Blend in the hot chicken stock and then the heavy cream, stirring vigorously.

Stir in the grated Gruyère cheese and Parmesan cheese and season to taste with salt, freshly ground pepper and a little freshly grated nutmeg. Reduce the heat and simmer for about 20 minutes, stirring from time to time to keep a skin from forming. When the sauce is reduced to two-thirds of its original quantity, strain through a fine sieve. Good for poultry, fish, vegetables and eggs.

Makes about 300ml/½ pint

Tomato Sauce

1 Spanish onion, finely chopped
2 cloves garlic, finely chopped
25g/1oz butter
4 tablespoons olive oil
6 tablespoons tomato paste
800g/1lb 12oz can Italian peeled tomatoes
2 bay leaves
2 tablespoons finely chopped fresh flat-leaf parsley
¼ teaspoon dried oregano
1 small strip lemon zest
6 tablespoons each dry white wine and water
salt and freshly ground pepper
1 tablespoon Worcestershire sauce

Sauté the finely chopped onion and garlic in the butter and olive oil in a large, heavy frying pan until translucent and soft, but not coloured.

Stir in the tomato paste and cook for a minute or two longer, stirring constantly. Pour in the peeled tomatoes, and add the bay leaves, finely chopped parsley, dried oregano and the small strip of lemon zest. Add the dry white wine and water. Season to taste and simmer, stirring from time to time, for 1 to 2 hours. Strain.

Just before serving, stir in the Worcestershire sauce. Good for pasta, meat, poultry and veal.

Makes about 600ml/1 pint

Mayonnaise

2 egg yolks
½ teaspoon Dijon mustard
salt and freshly ground pepper
lemon juice
300ml/10fl oz olive oil

Place the egg yolks (make sure the gelatinous thread of the egg is removed), mustard and a little salt and freshly ground pepper in a bowl. Twist a cloth wrung out in icy-cold water round the bottom of the bowl to keep it steady and cool. Using a wire whisk, fork or wooden spoon, beat the yolks to a smooth paste.

Add a little lemon juice (the acid helps the emulsion), and beat in about a quarter of the oil, drop by drop. Add a little more lemon juice to the mixture and then, a little more quickly now, add more oil, beating all the time. Continue adding oil and beating until the sauce is of a good thick consistency. Correct the seasoning (more salt, freshly ground pepper and lemon juice) as desired.

If you are making the mayonnaise a day before using it, stir in 1 tablespoon of boiling water when it is of the desired consistency. This will keep it from turning or separating.

Makes 300ml/10fl oz

Safety note: The consumption of raw or partly cooked eggs can carry a risk of salmonella, particularly for pregnant women, very young children and the elderly.

Notes: If the mayonnaise should curdle, break another egg yolk into a clean bowl and gradually beat the curdled mayonnaise into it. Your mayonnaise will begin to 'take' immediately.

If mayonnaise is to be used for a salad, thin it down considerably with dry white wine, vinegar or lemon juice. If it is to be used for

coating meat, poultry or fish, add a little liquid aspic to stiffen it.

If the sauce is to be kept for several hours before serving, cover the bowl with a cloth wrung out in icy-cold water to keep a skin from forming on the top, and keep in the refrigerator.

Horseradish Mayonnaise: Add the juice of ½ small lemon and salt to taste. Just before serving, stir in 2 tablespoons freshly grated horseradish. For eggs, hard-boiled egg salads or seafood.

Russian Mayonnaise Dressing: Add 2 tablespoons ketchup, a dash of Worcestershire sauce or Tabasco and 1 level teaspoon each of chopped, canned pimientos and snipped chives. For eggs, cooked vegetable salads and seafood.

Coral Mayonnaise: Wash and dry lobster coral, pound it to a paste in a mortar and press it through a fine sieve. Add to the mayonnaise.

Tartare Sauce: Add 1 teaspoon each of the following, chopped: capers, gherkins, fresh parsley, fresh tarragon and fresh chervil, and a pinch of sugar. Combine and chill. I sometimes add a little finely chopped garlic. Good with grilled and poached fish, and almost a 'must' with deep-fried mussels, oysters or prawns.

Sauce Rémoulade: Add 1 tablespoon each of chopped fresh tarragon, chopped fresh basil or chervil and chopped fresh flat-leaf parsley, then 1 finely chopped clove garlic, 1 teaspoon dry mustard, 1 teaspoon capers and 2 small pickles, finely chopped. Combine and chill. Serve with grilled fish, prawns and lobster. Excellent with cold meats, too.

Green Sauce: Whirl the mayonnaise in a blender with

4 tablespoons of finely chopped watercress leaves and 2 tablespoons each of finely chopped fresh chervil, flat-leaf parsley and fresh tarragon leaves. Season to taste with lemon juice, salt and freshly ground pepper. Serve chilled with fish and shellfish. Especially good with poached or grilled salmon, fish pâtés or mousses, and with hard-boiled eggs.

Blender Mayonnaise: Combine 2 whole eggs, 150ml/5fl oz olive oil, 4 tablespoons lemon juice or vinegar, ½ level teaspoon each dry mustard and salt, and freshly ground pepper to taste, in a blender. Place the lid on and turn the motor to high. When blended, remove the cover and add 300ml/10fl oz olive oil in a thin steady trickle, blending continuously. Correct the seasoning and use as desired.

Béarnaise

3 sprigs of fresh tarragon, coarsely chopped
3 sprigs of fresh chervil, coarsely chopped
1 tablespoon chopped shallots
2 crushed peppercorns
2 tablespoons tarragon vinegar
150ml/5fl oz dry white wine
3 egg yolks
1 tablespoon water
225g/8oz soft butter, diced
salt
lemon juice
cayenne pepper

Combine the coarsely chopped herbs, chopped shallots, crushed peppercorns, tarragon vinegar and white wine in a heavy saucepan. Cook over a high heat until the liquid is reduced to two-thirds of its original quantity. Strain through a fine sieve, pressing the herbs well with a wooden spoon, into the top of a double boiler.

Beat the egg yolks with the water and add to the juices in the top of the double boiler. Stir briskly over hot water with a wire whisk until light and fluffy. Never let the water in the bottom pan begin to boil, or the sauce will not 'take'.

Gradually add the butter to the egg mixture, whisking briskly all the time as the sauce begins to thicken. Continue adding butter and stirring until the sauce is thick. Season to taste with salt, lemon juice and cayenne pepper. Strain through a fine sieve and serve. Excellent with grilled, poached or fried fish.

Choron Sauce: Make a Béarnaise as above, and flavour to taste with tomato paste.

Classic Madeira

50g/2oz butter
2 shallots, thinly sliced
2 tablespoons flour
700ml/25fl oz hot beef stock
1 small carrot, sliced
1 small turnip, sliced
1 stick celery, sliced
4 mushrooms, sliced
4 plum tomatoes, sliced, or
  1–2 tablespoons tomato paste
1 bouquet garni (3 sprigs of fresh
  parsley, 1 sprig of fresh thyme,
  1 bay leaf)
2 cloves
12 black peppercorns
salt
6 tablespoons Madeira
2 tablespoons finely diced butter

Heat the butter in a heavy saucepan until it browns. Do not let it burn or your sauce will be bitter. Add the thinly sliced shallots and simmer, stirring constantly, until golden. Stir in the flour and continue cooking, stirring constantly, for 1 to 2 minutes longer. The good colour of your sauce depends upon the thorough browning of these ingredients without allowing them to burn.

When this is done, remove the saucepan from the heat and pour in the hot stock. Return the pan to the heat and stir over a medium heat until the sauce comes to the boil. Allow it to boil for 5 minutes, skimming all the froth and impurities from the top.

Add the sliced carrot, turnip, celery, mushrooms and tomatoes or tomato purée to the sauce, with the bouquet garni, cloves, peppercorns, and salt to taste. Simmer the sauce gently for at least 30 minutes, stirring from time to time. Then strain the sauce through a fine sieve into a clean saucepan, pressing well down on the vegetables and aromatics with a wooden spoon to extract utmost flavour. Return to the heat and continue to simmer until the sauce is reduced by half.

When ready to serve, add the Madeira to the sauce and heat through, without allowing the sauce to come to the boil. Remove the pan from the heat and whisk in the diced butter to give thickness and gloss to the sauce.

Hollandaise

1 teaspoon lemon juice, plus extra
  to season
1 tablespoon cold water
salt and white pepper
100g/4oz soft butter
4 egg yolks

Combine the lemon juice with the cold water and a little salt and white pepper in the top of a double boiler. Divide the butter into 4 equal pieces. Add the egg yolks and a quarter of the butter to the liquid in the saucepan, and stir the mixture rapidly and constantly with a wire whisk over hot, but not boiling, water until the butter is melted and the mixture begins to thicken. Add the second piece of butter and continue whisking. As the mixture thickens and the second piece of butter melts, add the third piece of butter, stirring from the bottom of the pan until it is melted. Be careful not to allow the water over which the sauce is cooking to boil at any time. Add the rest of the butter, beating until it melts and is incorporated in the sauce.

Remove the top part of the saucepan from the heat and continue to beat for 2 to 3 minutes. Replace the saucepan over the hot, but not boiling, water for 2 minutes more, beating constantly. By this time the emulsion should have formed and your sauce will be rich and creamy. Finish the sauce with a few drops of lemon juice. Strain and serve.

If at any time in the operation the mixture should curdle, beat in 1 or 2 tablespoons of cold water to rebind the emulsion.

Mustard Hollandaise: Flavour to taste with Dijon mustard.

Mousseline Sauce: Add 4 to 6 tablespoons whipped cream before serving.

Sweet sauces

Apple Sauce

450g/1lb cooking apples
2–4 tablespoons water
1–2 slices lemon
1 tablespoon sugar
1 clove
¼–½ teaspoon pure vanilla essence
2 tablespoons heavy cream
  (optional)
pinch of ground cinnamon
  (optional)

Wipe, quarter and core the apples. Cut the quartered apples into thick slices and put them in a thick-bottomed saucepan together with the water, the lemon slices, sugar and clove. Bring to the boil, then cover the pan tightly and simmer gently for 10 minutes, or until the apples are fluffy.

Remove the lemon slices and clove and purée the sauce through a fine sieve.

Flavour with vanilla essence to taste. Stir in heavy cream for a richer sauce and add a pinch of ground cinnamon, if desired.

Serves 6

Zabaglione Sauce
3 egg yolks
25g/1oz sugar
3–4 tablespoons Marsala or
**   medium sherry**
1½ tablespoons Cognac

Combine the egg yolks with the sugar and 1 tablespoon of the Marsala or sherry in the top of a double saucepan. Whisk the mixture over hot, but not boiling, water until the sauce thickens enough to coat the back of a wooden spoon thickly.

Stir in the rest of the Marsala or sherry and the Cognac. Serve warm over cakes, puddings, sweet soufflés and ice-cream.

Makes about 300ml/1/2 pint

Pastry

Flaky Pastry
275g/10oz flour
generous pinch of salt
squeeze of lemon juice
200g/7oz butter
iced water

Sift the flour and salt into a clean, dry bowl and add the lemon juice. Divide the butter into 4 equal parts. Take one of these pieces and rub it into the flour with the tips of your fingers until the mixture is quite free from lumps. Then add just enough iced water to form the dough into one lump. Mix with your hands as lightly as possible and turn out on to a floured board.

Knead lightly until free from cracks, and then roll out into a long narrow strip, about 5mm/less than ¼in thick. Take one of the remaining portions of butter, and

with the point of a knife put it in even rows of small pieces all over the pastry, leaving a 2.5cm/1in margin without butter round the edges. (If the butter is too hard, work it on a plate with a knife.)

Fold the pastry strip exactly in three. Press the folds down sharply with the rolling pin so as to enclose some air, then re-flour the surface lightly and turn the pastry around 90°. Roll the pastry out again into a long narrow strip, and proceed as before until the two remaining portions of butter have been used.

If the butter becomes too soft during the rolling, refrigerate the pastry briefly then carry on.

The last time, roll the pastry out to the desired thickness, and if it requires widening, turn it across the board and roll across. Never roll in a slanting direction, or the lightness of the pastry will suffer. This pastry is not quite as rich as puff pastry. It may be kept for several days in the refrigerator if wrapped in wax paper, aluminium foil or a damp cloth.

Fingertip Pastry
225g/8oz flour
1 teaspoon confectioners'
**   sugar**
½ teaspoon salt
150g/5oz cold butter
1 medium-sized egg yolk
1 teaspoon lemon juice
2 tablespoons iced water

This is my favourite rich pastry.

Sift the flour, confectioners' sugar and salt into a large mixing bowl. Cut the cold butter directly from the refrigerator into 6mm/¼in dice. Add these to the bowl and toss lightly in the flour mixture.

Using a pastry blender (or two knives, held one in each hand and cutting across each other like scissor blades), cut the cold diced butter into the flour mixture until it resembles coarse breadcrumbs. Then scoop up some of the mixture

in each hand, and, holding your hands above the bowl, lightly rub your thumbs and fingertips together, letting the crumbs shower back into the bowl as you go. Repeat 6 or 7 times, or until the mixture is further reduced to the consistency of fine breadcrumbs.

Beat the egg yolk in a small bowl with a fork. Add the lemon juice and iced water and mix again.

Sprinkle the egg mixture over the contents of the bowl and, using a fork or spoon, stir it into the flour mix. When about three-quarters of the pastry is holding together, use your hand to form the pastry lightly and quickly into one piece.

Shape the pastry into a ball, pressing the ball lightly against the bottom and sides of the bowl to gather up any remaining 'crumbs' left behind. Wrap the pastry ball in a sheet of wax paper, or aluminium foil, and chill for at least 1 hour to allow the pastry to 'mature' before using.

To Roll Out the Pastry: Leave the pastry at room temperature for 15 to 20 minutes before rolling it out, otherwise it will be a little too firm to roll out successfully.

Lightly dust your working surface and rolling pin with flour (I use a small strainer). Flatten the ball of pastry with a few strokes of the rolling pin. Then start rolling it out to a circle about 30cm/12in in diameter and as thin as you can get it: about 3mm/⅛in is perfect. Turn the sheet of pastry over once or twice on the working surface while rolling (dusting the surface with a little more flour if necessary) and don't worry too much if the pastry cracks or separates while you are rolling it: just press it lightly back into place with your fingers (that is why I call it 'fingertip' pastry). When the pastry is rolled out, dust off any excess flour with a soft pastry brush. The pastry is now ready for use.

Index

Index